IMMAN

IMMANUEL KANT

LUCIEN GOLDMANN

VERSO

London • New York

This English-language edition first published by New Left Books 1971
© Verso 2011
Translated from the French and German by Robert Black
Translation © NLB 1971

First published as *Mensch, Gemeinschaft und Welt in der Philosophie Immanuel Kants*
© Europa-Verla 1945
Revised and enlarged edition published as *Introduction à la philosophie de Kant*
© Gallimard 1967

3 5 7 9 10 8 6 4 2

Verso
UK: 6 Meard Street, London W1F 0EG
US: 20 Jay Street, Suite 1010, Brooklyn, NY 11201
www.versobooks.com

Verso is the imprint of New Left Books

ISBN-13: 978-1-84467-782-5

British Library Cataloguing in Publication Data
A catalogue record for this book is available from the British Library

Library of Congress Cataloging-in-Publication Data
A catalog record for this book is available from the Library of Congress

Printed in the US by Maple Vail

TO MADELEINE DUCLOS AND THÉOPHILE SPOERRI

Contents

Acknowledgments : We would like to thank the following for permission to quote passages from works by Kant published by them: Macmillan & Co. Ltd for *Critique of Pure Reason*; Manchester University Press for *Selected Pre-critical Writings*; Cambridge University Press for *Kant's Political Writings*; The Clarendon Press for *Critique of Aesthetic Judgement*; Harper & Row for *Religion within the limits of reason alone*; Bobbs-Merrill Company Inc. for *Critique of Practical Reason*; and University of Chicago Press for *Kant : Philosophical Correspondence 1759–99.*

Translator's Note: This was Lucien Goldmann's first book. Originally his doctoral thesis for the University of Zürich, it was published there in 1945 under the title *Mensch, Gemeinschaft und Welt in der Philosophie Immanuel Kants*. A French translation, incorporating some changes,[1] was first published in 1948, under the title *La communauté humaine et l'univers chez Kant*. A second French edition with the new title *Introduction à la philosophie de Kant* appeared in 1967. The latter forms the basis of this translation, but I have not hesitated to refer to the original German where I have found it clearer than, and not materially different from, the French.

References to the works of Kant are made first to the standard Prussian Academy edition, by volume and page number, and then to the standard English translation, if one exists. The latter are encoded as follows:

Aesth. J   *Critique of Aesthetic Judgement*, trans. J. C. Meredith, The Clarendon Press, 1911.

Ethics   *Critique of Practical Reason and Other Writings in Moral Philosophy*, trans. L. W. Beck, Chicago, 1949.

Groundwork   *The Moral Law: Kant's 'Groundwork of the Metaphysic of Morals'*, trans. H. J. Paton, Hutchinson, 3rd edn., 1956.

Metaph. I   *The Metaphysical Elements of Justice*, trans. J. Ladd, Bobbs-Merrill, 1965.

Metaph. II   *The Doctrine of Virtue*, trans. M. J. Gregor, Harper Torchbooks, 1964.
(The above two books constitute the two parts of the *Metaphysic of Morals*.)

Phil. Corr   *Kant: Philosophical Correspondence 1759–99*, trans. A. Zweig, University of Chicago Press, 1967.

Polit   *Kant's Political Writings*, ed. Hans Reiss, trans. H. B. Nisbet, Cambridge University Press, 1970.

1. The principal alterations are the addition to the first chapter of material on the social foundations of the tragic vision of the world in seventeenth-century France and the suppression of an appendix on the relations between Heidegger and Lukács.

Prac. R	*Critique of Practical Reason*, trans. L. W. Beck, Bobbs-Merrill, 1956.
Pre-crit	*Selected Pre-critical Writings*, trans. G. B. Kerferd and D. E. Walford, Manchester University Press, 1968.
Proleg	*Prolegomena to any Future Metaphysics that will be able to present itself as a Science*, trans. P. G. Lucas, Manchester University Press, 1953.
Pure R	*Critique of Pure Reason*, trans. N. K. Smith, Macmillan, 2nd edn., 1933.
Religion	*Religion within the limits of reason alone*, trans. T. M. Greene and H. H. Hudson, Harper Torchbooks, 1960.
Tel. J	*Critique of Teleological Judgement*, trans. J. C. Meredith, Oxford University Press, 1928.

In addition, references to the *Critique of Pure Reason* are given with the page number of the original edition, in the usual manner. Thus, for example, 'III, 385; *Pure R*, 488; B 600' denotes volume III, page 385, of the Prussian Academy edition, or page 488 of Kemp Smith's translation of the *Critique of Pure Reason*, corresponding to page 600 of the 1787 edition.

No estate is so useless as that of the man of learning in his natural innocence, and none so necessary in conditions of oppression by superstition or by force.

(Kant, Posthumous works, *Gesammelte Schriften*, vol. xx, p. 10.)

Moral luxury. In sentiments which have no effects.

(Kant, Posthumous works, *Gesammelte Schriften*, vol. xx, p. 9.)

Preface to the
1967 French edition

This book was my first work. With it I began an inquiry
which I later pursued in several studies and which led to
the gradual development of a new method for the understanding and explanation of cultural creation. When, in this
work, I laid the foundations for this type of sociological
research, I was of course unaware of the future development
of my work. My principal intention at the time was to write
a history of dialectical thought which would itself form an
essential part of the development of that thought.

Hegel and Marx have taught us that the problem of history is the history of problems, and that it is impossible
validly to describe any human fact without bringing into
that description its genesis. This implies that one must take
into account the evolution both of ideas and of the way in
which men represent to themselves the facts studied, since
that evolution constitutes an important element in the genesis of the phenomenon. Of course, the converse is also valid.
The history of problems is the problem of history, and the
history of ideas can only be positive if it is closely bound to
the history of the economic, social and political life of men.
Finally Marx, in a famous passage referring to Darwin,
whom he profoundly admired (and to whom, moreover, he
had wished to dedicate *Capital*), formulated a further essential methodological principle of the human sciences in asserting that the anatomy of man is the key to the anatomy of the
ape.

These considerations explain why, in wishing to create
a system of dialectical philosophy, I began with its history,
and also why, in devoting the first study to the philosophy
of Kant, the main emphasis was upon those aspects of his
philosophy which pointed towards later developments, and
in particular towards the Hegelian dialectic.

This said, I nevertheless believe that I succeeded in picking out a number of essential aspects of Kant's thought, in particular the importance of the precritical period, the unity of the development of that thought, and the fundamental place of the idea of totality in the critical philosophy itself. In doing so, I formed quite a new picture of Kant's philosophy, which allowed me to bring to light the nature and origins of the neo-Kantian distortion.

But whilst the idea of totality is central to this study, another particularly important dialectical idea is unfortunately neglected: that of the identity of subject and object, in the elaboration of which Kant's philosophy constituted a not insignificant step. This is frequently termed, using Kant's own phrase, his *Copernican revolution*. But here too, I believe that the meaning and importance of that 'revolution' can only be properly understood in terms of the Hegelian and Marxist positions.

Kant's Copernican revolution involves three ideas whose later development in philosophical and scientific thought has been extremely fruitful, but which can only be judged and understood in the light of that development, viz.:

1. The opposition between universal form and particular content. This has played an important part in the elaboration of the Marxist analysis of man in liberal society and of the distinction (central to that analysis) between formal democracy and real stratification, between formal equality and real inequality, and so on, a development which culminates in the theory of reification. This aspect of Kantian analysis is to some extent studied in the present work.

2. The distinction between two kinds of knowledge: that based upon experience and that based upon synthetic *a priori* judgements (which do not, as the positivists claim, have an analytic and tautologous nature). For Kant, the distinction is rigid and universal, valid for all human knowledge. Certain later thinkers have tried to give it a basis in empirical reality and in the situation of man in relation to the universe: the sociological epistemology of Durkheim and the genetic epistemology of Jean Piaget, to mention but the two most important attempts. However much the positions of Durkheim and especially of Piaget may differ from

the rigidity of transcendental analysis, it is nonetheless possible to say that the most general framework in which these reflections are situated is Kantian in character.

3. The idea that man creates (for Kant, creates only in part) the world which he perceives and knows in experience. This is the famous transcendental subjectivity of space and time and of the categories. But since this creation clearly could not be attributed to the empirical individual, Kant was obliged to limit it to formal structures and to confer upon it an abstract and transcendental character. The fate of this conception in neo-Kantianism and, in our time, in the thought of Husserl and in phenomenology is well known.

The other branch of the development, which leads from Kant to Hegel, Marx and Lukács, has also extended this aspect of the Copernican revolution, but in this case by transcending transcendental analysis and integrating it with positive science through the replacement of the individual subject by the collective subject (or, to use a term which I prefer, the transindividual subject). Social groups and society, which are *empirical* realities, create the concrete character of the natural world *really* (by technical action), and, through the mediation of that action on nature, create all economic, social and political structures, psychological structures and mental categories (whose genetic character has been shown by anthropology, sociology, infant psychology and epistemology).

Here, too, Kant's thought formed a turning-point, opening the way to a scientific epistemology which has no further need for the transcendental ego and can remain wholly on a positive level. Although not completely ignored, this development is but little dealt with in the present volume. Here I can only refer the reader to the now classic chapters on reification in Georg Lukács's *History and Class-Consciousness* (1923).

For the dialectical thinker, philosophical reflection does not constitute an entirely autonomous reality, radically separated from the remainder of social life. Whilst recognizing its *relative* autonomy and its need for extreme internal rigour, dialectical thinkers have always been convinced that the elucidation of the meaning of a philosophical system experienced in practice is an important element for the understanding of its objective meaning and for any judgement wholly founded upon its validity and its limits.

In this context, I should like to acknowledge a debt to a school of thought with which I have never been in agreement – existentialism. The philosophy of a period of crisis in Western society, existentialism was principally centred on the limits of individual existence, on death, anguish and defeat. It is in the name of the classical tradition, of Kant, Hegel and Marx, that, with the majority of dialectical thinkers, I have set against this philosophy the existence of a collective, transindividual subject and the possibility of an immanent historical hope which transcends the bounds of the individual.

Nevertheless, it can be seen today, at a time when philosophical thought is returning either to an abstract and formalist rationalism or to irrationalism, that the powerful development of existentialism has had at least the merit of bringing the philosophical thought of its time – even of those thinkers who did not accept its position – closer to the real and concrete life of men. By its explicit influence, but also by diffusion, it has contributed to the fact that once again writers and philosophers are being questioned about what might be called the existential sense of their writings. From this point of view – and despite my distance from any form of existentialist thought – the present work contributes to an intellectual climate which I believe is still valid today and which should not be too readily abandoned.

At a time when so many brilliant minds and men of remarkable intelligence are neglecting and disowning the humanist tradition and turning towards a formalist structuralism or towards praise of the irrational, at a time when, to the crisis of the social and economic structures of our societies, there seems to be added a no less radical crisis of philosophical thought and the human sciences, I should like to express the hope that this book may help some of its readers to set themselves against the stream.

Paris, May 1967

From the Preface
to the
first French edition, 1948

... Were I to rewrite this work today, I should make certain changes in it.

Firstly, very often where I wrote 'Kant was the first to ...' I could have said Blaise Pascal. However, I do not think that this calls for any sweeping modification of the work. Kant's thought developed quite independently of Pascal; the analysis of its content, of the influences undergone by it, and of the social conditions which favoured it is thus in no way altered. ...

Further, my book was written in 1944–45 under the direct influence of the thought of Georg Lukács, whose early works – at that time completely unknown – I had chanced to discover. Today, the name of Lukács is beginning to be known. In 1946, at Geneva, he took part in the symposium on the European mind, where his exchanges with Jaspers overshadowed all other contributions. After an interruption of almost twenty years, he has now actively resumed his philosophical publications. ...

In these circumstances it is no longer necessary to draw the attention of the philosophical public to him, and, with the aid of distance, I believe that today I can see his work in a clearer light. As in 1945, I still consider Georg Lukács the most important philosophical thinker of the twentieth century; nevertheless, I believe I do him better justice in saying that he is a great essayist, and not a systematic thinker. Now *essayist*, by its very definition, means precursor, one who announces a system but who does not construct it. Whilst still fully recognizant of the importance of his work, and of the enormous intellectual debt of gratitude that I owe him, I should hesitate today to put him on the same level as Kant, Hegel and Marx, as is done throughout this book.

Finally, I must admit that so far as the immediate future is concerned my hopes have not been fulfilled. In place of a better world and a better community, new clouds are gathering. The possibility of another war has become part of the normal order of things. If one day it breaks out, it will come as a surprise to no one.

In the midst of this depression and disquiet, conditions are clearly unfavourable for a philosophy of optimism and hope. Nihilist philosophies and philosophies of despair become ever more widespread and – no less disturbing – on all sides representative voices are raised to disown the heritage of classical humanism in the name of the exigencies of the present and of the immediate future.

We can no longer close our eyes to the fact that humanism today is undergoing a crisis which threatens its very existence, and which demands a rigorous reassessment of the situation. What weight can the works of Kant or of Pascal, of Goethe or of Racine, carry today in the age of atomic weapons? What can they still offer us? What, above all, can they prevent?

We have no right to be satisfied with our 'good conscience'. When it loses contact with reality, it also loses any real value and becomes a weakness or an escape. Against the humanist tradition real forces are drawn up which also speak in the name of a certain future and of a certain culture. Some of these forces by their very reality imply values. Whatever is real is rational, said Hegel.

If I am nevertheless reissuing this work, it is because I believe that the crisis, despite its gravity, is a passing one; I am convinced that one day men will succeed in giving a rational meaning to life and a human meaning to the universe. Whatever is rational is real, said the same Hegel. Like him, I continue to believe in the final victory of man and of reason – a victory to which even those hostile forces which today seem to carry the field will have contributed. The road will no doubt be longer than we thought. But the path which leads to the goal is still the same: opened by Pascal, Kant, Hegel, Marx and so many others, it must now more than ever be continued. . . .

From the Preface
to the
original (German) edition, 1945

The present work is neither a wholly historical or literary study, nor is it wholly self-contained. It is intended only as the first stone towards the building of a system of dialectical philosophy to be gradually outlined in subsequent works. However, an essential preliminary to such a system is to examine the formulation of the dialectical problem in the history of philosophy.

I have begun with Kant because it is with Kant that philosophy first attains knowledge of one of the most important dialectical oppositions – between empiricism and totality, between form and content – and because Kant was the first to set out this opposition in all its starkness and to place it at the centre of his philosophical system.

Nevertheless, I believe that my work also contributes on the purely historical and scholarly level to the clarification of the neo-Kantian misunderstanding, to the overthrow of the 'Kant myth' which grew out of it, and to the restoration of the original meaning of Kant's philosophy. I hope also that projected future works on the history of the dialectic in Goethe, Fichte, Schelling, Hölderlin, Hegel and Marx will lead by stages to a re-establishment of the true history of German idealism.

Once again it is clear that a truly historical treatment of philosophy can never be purely 'scholarly' but is only made possible by the actual experience of philosophical problems, whilst being nonetheless indispensable to their solution. . . .

Introduction

I

In presenting to the reader today a study of man and human community in the thought of Kant, I feel that I must forestall a number of possible misunderstandings. From the title, the reader might expect a more or less erudite work on a secondary problem. Indeed, to this day, most of the 'experts' have seen Kant merely as a pure epistemologist, or at most as a systematic moral philosopher, who did occasionally, in a few brief works, express his opinions on the French Revolution, perpetual peace, the society of citizens of the world, and so forth, but for whom such questions were subordinate and peripheral to his philosophical activity. It is of course conceded that studies on Kant's attitude to 'social problems' or 'questions in the philosophy of history' may be of value, for it is always interesting to know what a great man thought about these things, but no more importance is attached to them than to the writings of a great physicist or of any other specialist, an Einstein or a Planck for example, on contemporary social and political problems. All this belongs to scholarship, possibly to political polemics, but certainly not to philosophy.

To mark the contrast between these viewpoints and my own, I would point out first of all that the theme of man and human community is central not only to Kant's thought but to the whole of modern philosophy. We are not here concerned with matters of scholarship – although precise knowledge of the texts and of the facts is a necessary condition for any serious study – but with the most important philosophical and human problems, with the central point from which alone the positions of the different philosophical systems *vis-à-vis* the problems of epistemology, morals and history become fully comprehensible and meaningful. *We are concerned with what in Kantian language would be called metaphysics.*

In support of this claim and before any further development, I call upon the most authoritative witness, Kant himself. At the beginning of the *Anthropology*, in the chapter entitled 'On Egoism', Kant distinguishes three types of egoism, which he will subsequently analyse: 'Egoism can imply three usurpations: of the understanding, of taste, and of practical interest; that is, it can be logical, aesthetic or practical.'[1] Having studied the three forms in turn, he concludes: 'Only *pluralism* can be set against egoism, that is, the following way of thinking: to consider oneself and to behave not as containing the whole universe in oneself, but rather as a mere citizen of the world. This much belongs to anthropology. For in so far as metaphysical concepts are concerned with this distinction, it lies wholly outside the field of the science with which we are here dealing. If the question were merely whether I, as a thinking being, had reason to accept, apart from my own existence, the existence of a corpus of other beings in community with me (called the universe), this would not be an anthropological question, but a purely metaphysical one.'[2]

Without wishing to read into the text more than is actually there, it nevertheless seems to me that two ideas emerge from this passage:

1. For Kant, egoism – the problem of man and the human community – has three aspects: logical, aesthetic and practical, three aspects which correspond precisely to the three *Critiques*.[3]

2. The study of the three forms of egoism, and especially of man's relation to 'a corpus of other beings in community with [him] (called the universe)', falls into two parts, one of which, according to Kant, belongs to *anthropology* (today we should say to sociology), the other to *metaphysics*. I shall attempt to show that the question of man's relation to the

---

1. VII, 128.   2. VII, 130.
3. 'Logical' here has the sense of 'theoretical'.

community is the essential problem of what Kant calls metaphysics, and which today we should prefer to denote by the less tainted name of philosophy.

In addition to the above two points, I should like here to introduce a third: that in Kant's thought the concepts of *universe* and *totality* are closely connected with the concept of the *human community*.

To demonstrate the pervasive importance of the idea of human community in Kant's thought, and since the *Anthropology* was only published in his old age, I should like further to quote a passage from the period of the formation of the critical philosophy. It concerns the *Dreams of a Visionary*. Indeed, I could quote here the entire second chapter from the first part of that work, where the idea of the *community of spirits*, a prefiguration of the later notion of the *intelligible world*, occurs on almost every line. I shall, however, be content to mention the following two passages from the letter which Kant sent with the work to Moses Mendelssohn:

'In my opinion, everything depends on our seeking out the *data* of the problem, how is the soul *present in the world, both in material and in non-material things*',[4] and a little further on: 'If, for the time being, we put aside arguments based on propriety or on the divine purposes, and ask whether it is ever possible to attain such knowledge of the nature of the soul from our experience – a knowledge sufficient to inform us of the manner in which the soul is present in the universe, in relation both to matter and to beings of its own sort – we shall then see whether *birth* (in the metaphysical sense), *life* and *death* are matters we can ever hope to understand by means of reason.'

An exhaustive work would naturally have to embrace the two aspects of the problem of the human community in Kant's thought, the sociological and anthropological aspect and the philosophical and metaphysical one. However, the first has already been studied in a considerable number of works, whilst the second, to my knowledge, has only been dealt with in two brilliant but today almost forgotten books,[5]

4. Letter to Moses Mendelssohn of 8 April 1766; *Phil. Corr*, 54–7.
5. E. Lask, *Fichtes Idealismus und die Geschichte, Werke*, vol. I, Tübingen,

and indeed, even there only in a partial and indirect manner.

Contrary, no doubt, to the expectations of most of my readers, and in order to confine myself to what is essential, I shall therefore neglect Kant's sociological and political writings and concentrate upon the strictly 'philosophical' texts, in particular, the three *Critiques* and the corresponding passages from the posthumous works. However, it is proper to add that it would be impossible to make a sharp distinction between the two groups of writings and that in any case there are among the sociological and political fragments some extremely interesting and sometimes prophetic passages; however, to quote them here would be to go beyond the limits of this work.[6]

II

Another misunderstanding with regard to my method of exposition may yet remain. I could have dealt with the questions which I have set myself while remaining exclusively within the fields of epistemology, ethics and

---

1923; and G. Lukács, *Geschichte und Klassenbewußtsein*, Berlin, 1923 (English translation, *History and Class Consciousness*, London, 1971).

6. I shall be content to quote as an example two passages which are little known, but which are particularly relevant today, where Kant speaks of the dangers of the German nationalism then emerging:

'It has not, at least up to the present, been in keeping with the German character that people should chatter about national pride. It is indeed an accomplishment of that character not to have such a pride and even rather to recognize the merits of other peoples than its own.' (xv, No. 1351.)

'On the German national spirit. Because it is the design of Providence that peoples should not be combined, but that by a force of repulsion they should enter into conflict with one another, national pride and hatred are necessary to separate the nations. That is why a people loves its own country before others, whether from religion, believing that all others such as the Jews and the Turks are accursed, or because it attributes to itself the monopoly of intelligence, all others being in its eyes incompetent or ignorant, or of courage, believing that all should fear it, or of liberty, believing that all others are slaves. Governments love this folly. This is the *mechanism* of world organization which instinctively binds us and separates us. Reason, however, prescribes to us this law: that the instincts, since they are blind, direct the animal part of us, but must be replaced by the maxims of reason. That is why this national folly must be rooted out and replaced by patriotism and cosmopolitanism' (xv, No. 1353).

aesthetics, avoiding any empirical and above all any sociological references. The work would then have been more
scholarly and more in keeping with usual academic practice, the more so since this was Kant's own method in the
three *Critiques*, and also, in our time, that of Lask in the work
referred to above, which is one of the most brilliant analyses
of German idealism.

If I have decided nevertheless to refer freely to sociology,
it is because I feel that I should neglect nothing which might
contribute to a better understanding of the problem, and
also in conscious reaction to certain examples of contemporary philosophy, where the 'metaphysical' style in which
the problems are dealt with seems to me largely to obscure
them and to disguise cross-influences and connections.

One example will suffice, one which is in any case of some
importance for our subject, and one of the most celebrated
works to appear in recent years: Martin Heidegger's *Being
and Time*. This book cannot be understood without the
realization that it constitutes largely, though perhaps implicitly, a debate with Lask, and above all with Lukács' work,
History and Class-Consciousness. In the latter, however,
philosophy, sociology and politics are almost inextricably
intermingled, whereas Heidegger has transported the whole
debate into the realm of 'metaphysics'.

A historian of contemporary thought would find it difficult to understand existentialism, and would in any case
form a false picture of its origins, if he were unaware of
these connections and if he neglected the influence of
political life between 1914 and 1919 on what I should like
to call the young Heidelberg circle.[7]

7. To distinguish it from the old Heidelberg circle (Windelband, Rickert).
Lask, who was obviously the centre of the circle, was killed in action in
1915. One may conclude from Rickert's obituary article that he had had himself sent to the front more or less voluntarily. It seems that a development
towards true consciousness, towards authentic life, impelled Lask and Lukács
towards 'action' and 'community', Lask towards the patriotic and national
community, Lukács towards the revolutionary community of class. Lask paid
with his life, Lukács with a long philosophical silence which was broken only
a few years ago. Heidegger, on the other hand, directed himself towards
'ontology' and has become the philosopher of anguish, of the 'will towards
death', and the most famous thinker of a decadent society. On Lask, see the

I have mentioned these facts because I shall refer frequently to Lask, Lukács and Heidegger; some knowledge of their mutual relations is therefore important for the reader.

III

The most important of the sociological terms that I shall use is that of *classical bourgeois thought* and the philosophy which corresponds to it. The word 'bourgeois' has here of course a *sociological* sense and implies no value judgement. An expression is needed to denote the essential features of Western civilization and thought of the seventeenth and eighteenth centuries whilst indicating the ties which bind such apparently diverse phenomena as the emergence of towns in Europe in the eleventh and twelfth centuries, the birth of the modern nation-state, the culture of the Renaissance, the development of classical philosophy and literature in England, France and Germany, and above all, the progressive and – until a few decades ago – uninterrupted growth in consciousness of the two fundamental values of modern thought: *freedom* and *man* as individual.

The most general historical and sociological investigation suffices to show that the single element common to all these phenomena is that they are creations of the Third Estate, of the bourgeoisie. To understand the thought of Kant, his relations to his predecessors, Descartes, Leibniz and Hume, what is essentially new in his contributions, the later development through Fichte, Schelling and Hegel to modern philosophy, with Bergson, Lukács, Heidegger and Sartre, we must start from this fact: both Kant himself and those thinkers who had a decisive influence upon him belonged to that classical bourgeois tradition of thought whose essential values were the *individual* and *freedom*.

We shall see in Kant the most profound and the most advanced thinker of this individualist culture of the classical

---

obituary articles by Rickert, reproduced as the preface to the *Gesammelte Werke*, Tübingen, 1923, and by Lukács in *Kant-Studien*, 1918.

bourgeoisie, a culture whose limits he clearly perceived without, however, being able completely to transcend them. Nevertheless, it was precisely that clarity which enabled him to take the first decisive steps towards a new philosophical category, that of the *universe*, of the *whole*, and thus to open the way for the later development of modern philosophy. We shall also see (this must continually be emphasized in order to avoid particularly dangerous misconceptions) that he saw what was *ahistorical* in bourgeois thought, that he was aware of the eternal human value of freedom, and that he defended this freedom with all his strength against the mystique of feeling and intuition, whose dangers he recognized and unmasked in magisterial fashion more than a hundred years before the arrival of Bergson or Scheler.[8]

Of course, I have neither the right nor the desire to subsume everything under the term 'classical bourgeois'. Depending on the country, the period and the individual, there are essential differences between the thinkers we shall be considering. These differences constitute what is specific to the work of each of them, and it is just these specific elements which must be picked out. But I believe it is only possible to understand them in terms of that which is common to them all and the foundation of their thought. That is why I feel that a 'purely metaphysical' treatment of the subject, unburdened with any sociological analysis, would have been much less clear and was therefore better avoided.

IV

One last point: the aim of this work is to provide an *introduction* to Kant's philosophy, not a detailed exposition of it.

I wish particularly to emphasize those points which seem to me to have been neglected or distorted by the neo-Kantian interpretation. I shall attempt to restore to them their true significance. I would add, however, that I have sometimes had to bestow upon certain elements of Kant's thought a value and an importance which differ from those

8. See 'What is orientation in thinking?', VIII, 131; *Ethics*, 293.

given them by Kant himself, having examined them in the
light of the whole of later philosophical development. In
doing so, I believe I have remained faithful to the spirit of
Kant, who more than once urged his followers not to confuse philosophical study with narrow and blinkered
scholarship.[9]

9. See III, 246; *Pure R*, 310; B 370 and also IV, 24.

Part I

Chapter 1

Classical Philosophy
and the
Western Bourgeoisie

I

To begin a philosophical work with a chapter which is for
the most part empirical and sociological may appear rash.
It thus seems appropriate to provide some preliminary
observations on what the Germans call the 'sociology of
knowledge', that is to say, on sociological interpretation of
the products of intellect.

This term was much in fashion during the years which
followed the First World War; for some readers it will
doubtless bring to mind the names of several writers who
were much talked of at that time, notably Max Scheler,
Georg Lukács and Karl Mannheim. Imbued to some degree,
overtly or implicitly, with historical materialism,[1] they were
the authors of several undoubtedly important works on
various specific problems in the history of ideas, but, with
the exception of Georg Lukács, they hardly ever tackled
the genuinely philosophical problems. To my knowledge,
Lukács is the only one to have attempted a sociological
analysis of the basic elements of philosophical thought.
That being also the aim of the present work, at least in some
of its aspects, we must consider to what extent such an
undertaking is justified or even possible.

All genuinely philosophical thought sets out from the
premiss that there is in human existence something eternal
and immutable, the search for which constitutes the principal task of philosophy; this point of departure thus assumes

---

1. Particularly Karl Mannheim who, despite his attempts to appear independent, remains heavily dependent upon Marx and Lukács. See especially
his best-known work: *Ideology and Utopia*.

the existence of *objective truth*. However, sociological interpretation, in so far as it relates all knowledge to historical and
social conditions, would seem to deny the existence of this
objective truth, resulting in a modern and scientific form
of an older relativism. Is there not a contradiction between
these two points of view? Is it possible to do philosophy, and
at the same time to recognize the credentials of a sociology
of knowledge? Is not such an attempt doomed from the
outset? At all events, these questions cannot be ignored.

Nevertheless, I believe that the idea of a sociology of
knowledge involves no contradiction, for although there
may always exist one single objective philosophical truth,
more or less independent of space and time, *possibility of
acquaintance with it* depends upon the social conditions in
which a thinker lives. And although an individual can perhaps change his own position and broaden his own horizons,
this becomes incomparably more difficult, and indeed is
usually impossible, for a whole social group, for a nation or
a class.

The objection will doubtless be made that in intellectual
matters it is individuals, and not social groups, which are in
question. But need we accept such a categorical assertion?
I think not. For the individual whose ideas, however correct,
are in conflict with the social interests and conditions of
existence of all the groups among which he lives remains a
lonely 'eccentric', a genius perhaps, but nonetheless a tragic
and unknown figure who will in all likelihood fall victim to
his lack of community and contact with his fellow men. Who
knows how many men of genius have lived and died without
any of their ideas having come down to us, simply because
they exerted no influence and left no trace?

A genuinely great thinker is one who achieves the maximum *possible*[2] truth starting from the interests and social
situation of some particular group, and who succeeds in
formulating it in such a way as to endow it with real scope
and effectiveness. For in philosophy, as in intellectual life

2. The phrase 'the maximum *possible*' itself indicates that the thinker must
be in the vanguard of the group, leading the way and making no compromise
with the actual given thought of its members. Compare Lukács' distinction
between 'actual' and 'possible' consciousness.

in general, only that which contributes to the transformation of human existence is important; and *human existence*
is not that of the isolated individual, but that of the *community* and, within this, of the human *person*, for the two
can never be separated.

That is why any endeavour to study a philosophical
system of the past must from the beginning take into account
the relations between the basic elements of the system and
the social conditions of the men among whom it originated
and developed, even if sometimes – and such is the case in
the present study – this sociological analysis can only be
carried out in a very general and schematic way.

II

Kant's world-view constituted even in his lifetime the philosophical system most representative of the German bourgeoisie, and, with the single exception of the Hegelian
period, remains so to this day.[3] Almost every important
German thinker, even if he has not remained a Kantian, has
at least started out from Kant and from the need clearly to
define his position with respect to Kant's ideas. One need
only think of Fichte and Hegel, or in our time, of Lask,
Lukács and Heidegger.

Thus, if we are to begin with an analysis of the social
conditions in which the Kantian system was formed, we
must first of all study the birth and development of the
European bourgeoisie in general and of the German bourgeoisie in particular.

The world-view which characterized the European bourgeoisie from the twelfth to the eighteenth centuries began
with one fundamental concept, *freedom*, from which all the
others developed. *Stadtluft macht frei*: such was the principle adopted by the very first small towns which developed
with difficulty in the midst of feudal society; and *freedom*

---

3. The thought of Kant himself must of course be distinguished from that
of the neo-Kantians, for the two world-views are essentially different, both
in content and historically.

was still the first word of the fiery declamation with which the French bourgeoisie announced to the world its 'Declaration of the Rights of Man'. Naturally, in the course of its history the European bourgeoisie has often come to act in a way directly opposed to freedom. It was this bourgeoisie which created absolutism: absolute monarchy would have been inconceivable without the support of the Third Estate. But these were merely passing historical necessities in the struggle against feudalism. That is why most of the ideologists of the bourgeoisie have never seen them as contradictory.

The second element of the bourgeois world-view was *individualism*. This is merely the other side of extreme freedom: the individual is the man freed from all bonds, limited solely by the obligation to respect the freedom of his fellows.

Finally, as a consequence of freedom and individualism, we must add *equality before the law*, for where privilege exists, there the individual is not completely free.

Freedom, individualism, equality before the law: these are the three fundamental elements of the world-view developed with and by the European bourgeoisie. In the different spheres of intellectual life they found various forms of expression; those in the field of philosophy are our primary concern in this work. Here the three elements found a privileged form of expression in *rationalism*, and another, less important and above all less radical, in *empiricism* and *sensualism* as developed particularly in England.

Rationalism means above all freedom – more precisely, freedom in two respects:

(a) freedom with regard to all external authority and constraint, and

(b) freedom with regard to our own passions, which link us to the external world.

It would lead us too far out of our way to illustrate the return of bourgeois thought to rationalism with the countless examples afforded by the history of philosophy. Suffice it to mention such well-known cases as the revival of Platonism during the Renaissance, the revival of Stoicism, the close ties between modern philosophy and mathematics in Descartes, Leibniz and Spinoza, Descartes' 'method of doubt', his *Treatise on the Passions*, and so on. And since the present work deals with the philosophy of Kant, I quote the following passage from the *Critique of Pure Reason*: 'Our age is, in especial degree, the age of criticism, and to criticism everything must submit. Religion through its sanctity, and law-giving through its majesty, may seek to exempt themselves from it. But they then awaken just suspicion, and cannot claim the sincere respect which reason accords only to that which has been able to sustain the test of free and open examination.'[4]

But rationalism also means the breaking of the bonds which existed between the individual and the universe or the human community. For where each individual, autonomously, independently and without any relation to other men, decides what is true, good or beautiful, there is no longer any room for a whole which transcends him, for the *universe*. The universe and the human community then

4. I V, 9; *Pure R*, 9; A xii. On the subject of freedom, I should like to quote another passage from the *Critique of Pure Reason*:

'A constitution allowing the *greatest possible human freedom* in accordance with laws by which *the freedom of each is made to be consistent with that of all others* – I do not speak of the greatest happiness, for this will follow of itself – is at any rate a necessary idea, which must be taken as fundamental not only in first projecting a constitution but in all its laws. For at the start we are required to abstract from the actually existing hindrances, which, it may be, do not arise unavoidably out of human nature, but rather are due to a quite remediable cause, the neglect of the pure ideas in the making of the laws. Nothing, indeed, can be more injurious, or more unworthy of a philosopher, than the vulgar appeal to so-called adverse experience. Such experience would never have existed at all, if at the proper time those institutions had been established in accordance with ideas, and if ideas had not been displaced by crude conceptions which, just because they have been derived from experience, have nullified all good intentions. The more legislation and government are brought into harmony with the above idea, the rarer would punishments become, and it is therefore quite rational to maintain, as Plato does, that in a perfect state no punishments whatsoever would be required. This perfect state may never, indeed, come into being; none the less this does not affect the rightfulness of the idea, which, in order to bring the legal organization of mankind ever nearer to its greatest possible perfection, advances this maximum as an archetype. For what the highest degree may be at which mankind may have to come to a stand, and how great a gulf may still have to be left between the idea and its realization, are questions which no one can, or ought to, answer. For the issue depends on freedom; and it is in the power of freedom to pass beyond any and every specified limit' (III, 247–8; *Pure R*, 312; B 373–4).

become external things, atomized and divided. They may be contemplated or observed; their 'laws' can at best be established 'scientifically'; but they no longer have any human and living relation to the subject, to man. This atomistic view is most clearly expressed in the monadology of Leibniz, but it is present no less strongly in Descartes or Malebranche, and even Kant begins his *Anthropology* with the words: 'That man can represent the "I" to himself raises him infinitely above all other living beings on earth.'[5]

Finally, rationalism implies the *equality before the law* of all individuals, since before Reason the rights of all men are equal. There is no privilege in the knowledge of geometrical theorems or moral obligations. *'Le bon sens est la chose du monde la mieux partagée ... la raison est naturellement égale en tous les hommes'*, wrote Descartes, and Kant too was always hostile to privileges of birth or social standing.

These few brief and superficial remarks bring us at once to the heart of Kant's philosophy. We can now understand why of the two fundamental categories of human existence – *freedom* or *autonomy of the individual* on the one hand, and on the other the *human community*, the *universe*, the *totality* as the meaning and product of this freedom in the actions of free men – the most important predecessors of Kant (with the sole exception of Spinoza) could recognize only the first.

Kant seems to me to be the first modern thinker to recognize anew the importance of the *totality* as a fundamental category of existence, or at least to recognize its problematic character. Kant's importance lies in the fact that he not only expressed with the utmost clarity his predecessors' individualist and atomist conceptions of the world taken to their logical conclusions, and thereby encountered their ultimate limits (which become for Kant the limits of human existence as such, of human thought and action in general): he did not stop, as did most of the neo-Kantians, at the recognition of these limits, but took the first steps, faltering no doubt but nevertheless decisive, towards the integration into philosophy of the second category, that of the *whole*, the *universe*, thus opening the way for the later development which leads

5. VII, 127.

from Fichte, Hegel and Marx, through Lask, Sartre, Heidegger, Lukács, and modern French personalism, to contemporary Marxism, and which is still far from completion.

III

Having considered the general features common to the whole of classical Western thought, we must now examine its specific characteristics in the various countries of the West – in England, in France, and particularly in Germany.[6] The economic and social development of the bourgeoisie has been very different in each of those three countries, and the differences were bound to be felt throughout their national cultures as well as in the particular field of philosophy.

The most economically and politically advanced country was without doubt England. There the bourgeoisie had very rapidly acquired economic ascendancy, and, after 1648 and 1688, also political power. As a result of this early and rapid development, English thought took much more pragmatic and, more importantly, much less radical forms than that of the continent. The young and powerful English bourgeoisie came up against a nobility which was still strong, capable of resisting it and, above all, economically active. There could be no question of completely eliminating the nobility from economic and political life as was later to happen in France; on the contrary, the bourgeoisie often needed the support of the nobility in its struggle against royal absolutism. That is why, despite the two revolutions of 1648 and 1688, the conflict between the two opposed classes ended with a compromise from which the England of today is descended.

A compromise is a limitation of one's original desires and hopes accepted under pressure of external reality. Where the economic and social structure of a country is born essentially of a compromise between two opposed classes, the

---

6. A complete study would naturally have to take into account the other Western countries, particularly Holland, which has played a major role not only in economic history and in the history of painting but also in the history of philosophy: both Descartes and Spinoza lived there.

world-view of its philosophers and poets will also be much more pragmatic and less radical than in countries where a long struggle has kept the rising class in radical opposition. This would seem to be one of the principal reasons for the fact that the philosophical thought of the English bourgeoisie has been empiricist and sensualist rather than rationalist as in France. Once the individual had been freed from political and ecclesiastical bonds, his dependence upon external perceptions and upon his own sensations, feelings and instincts seemed much less dangerous to English thinkers than to the continental rationalists.

This attitude was further reinforced by two other factors which are really only consequences of the first, namely:

(a) the absence of strong rationalist traditions, a natural consequence of the moderate nature and short duration of the struggle between the bourgeoisie and the nobility, and

(b) the decisive fact that the most important English thinkers, Locke, Berkeley and Hume, wrote at a time when the bourgeoisie had already seized political power, and were no longer in opposition as they were in France at the time of Descartes, or in Germany at the time of Kant.

Only a class already in power could permit itself to answer the fundamental question of the connections between the elements which constitute the universe with the assertion that those connections are not *necessary a priori* but that they are nonetheless established *in fact* by habit, association of ideas, and so on. One can only have recourse to a fact if that fact is already actual and universally acknowledged. This was impossible in countries where those connections were only to be awaited, or even merely wished for, in the future.

On the continent, and particularly in Germany, where the birth of the bourgeois social order and of the democratic state was still problematic and in any case projected for a distant future, to assert that the freedom of the individual could not guarantee the realization of a harmonious and *necessary* connection, that there exist no *a priori* laws of thought and action which would *necessarily* assure harmony between reasonable and free individuals, must have appeared a heresy, or at any rate a dangerous scepticism, casting doubt upon the most sacred values. It was only much later – in France a little before the Revolution, and in western Europe generally in the second half of the nineteenth century – when the bourgeoisie had *already* achieved political ascendancy, that despite all the contrary traditions continental thought could feel a growing sympathy for empiricism and this could become the dominant current of thought, until the grave crisis of the twentieth century once again transformed the situation, allowing mystical and irrationalist tendencies to become the dominant trends of contemporary European thought.

IV

If we now direct our attention towards the continent, to France and Germany, we find a quite different situation. Without being oversubjective, I think one may describe the development of France as 'healthy' and that of Germany as 'sick'. (I use these terms in the sense they had for Goethe when he said that the classical is the healthy and the romantic the sick.)

The French state is the product of a normal organic development of the Third Estate which until very recently had never been shaken by a crisis sufficiently profound to put in question the foundations of social and economic life. Even the years 1789–1815 were but a powerful and magnificent episode in an organic development which it neither arrested nor diverted. French absolute monarchy arose out of a struggle against the feudal overlords, and with the aid of a permanent and durable alliance with the Third Estate. The bourgeoisie gave the king the financial means to meet his expenses, particularly those of the permanent army of mercenaries; in exchange, the monarchy protected it from the exactions of the nobles and favoured its economic interests.

As economic development and the increasing power of the monarchy hastened the decline of the nobility, so the Third Estate, by the buying of offices and the creation of the *noblesse de robe*, took over the political and administrative apparatus of the state. When finally the nobility lost all real economic and military power, the Third Estate no longer needed its alliance with the monarchy, which it increasingly regarded as an irksome, unjust and above all costly burden. Its growing opposition culminated in the Revolution and, after the two Napoleonic periods, the birth of purely bourgeois French democracy, in which the nobility as such no longer has any part.

In Germany, on the other hand, since the Thirty Years War economic and political development had been extremely slow and was almost at a standstill. A unitary national state could not be created until 1871, or even, strictly speaking, until the twentieth century. Moreover, this national state was created from above, even partially against the bourgeoisie, and in no way against the nobility. The peace of Westphalia in 1648 had divided the country into a large number of sovereign principalities, the smallness of which naturally inhibited any national intellectual life. The discovery of America and the associated shift of the great trading routes away from the Mediterranean and towards the Atlantic arrested and stifled the beginnings of economic take-off which had appeared in Germany in the fifteenth and sixteenth centuries, for example in the Hanse. The Thirty Years War had devastated and impoverished the country. With a few rare exceptions (e.g. Hamburg and Leipzig), economic life in Germany was completely stagnant and even in decline. From the political, social and economic point of view, Germany was 'sick' and abnormal.

All these circumstances were clearly an enormous obstacle to the birth of a national culture. It must be borne in mind that even under Frederick the Great French was the principal language at the Court and at the Academy of Berlin, and that Leibniz, the first great German philosopher, who spoke and wrote his mother tongue perfectly, was obliged to write in French to assure a cultivated public for his works. Who could imagine Descartes or Locke writing the *Discourse on Method* or the *Essay* in German?

For all these reasons, the words 'normal' and 'sick' seem best to characterize the difference between the political, economic and social development of France and that of Germany, at least during the period 1648–1871. This difference, of course, had repercussions on intellectual life and in particular on philosophical thought in the two countries.

It is characteristic of the gravely sick that they think above all of their malady and of the means of curing it, whilst the healthy rarely if ever consider their own health, their attention being principally directed towards the external world. This is also the essential difference which for more than two centuries separated the two great European cultures, German culture and French culture. It also explains why, in recent years, as the malady has spread to the whole of western Europe, French thought too has approached that of Germany from two different directions. On the one hand, philosophers of feeling, such as Bergson, have returned to the German mystics, to Schelling and in part to Schopenhauer (or Sartre to Heidegger); personalism, on the other hand, and Marxism, which is beginning to have an effect in France, are currents of thought which, although not always clearly conscious of it, come close to the problems of German humanism, even though – we are in the twentieth century – they seek to go further than it did.

Having developed in a 'healthy' society, French thought is principally directed towards the external world, seeking to know and to understand it. *Theoretical* truth, epistemology, mathematics, psychology and sociology have provided the main problems and preoccupations of French philosophy. In contrast, German thought, that of a 'sick' society, was mainly directed inwards, towards its own malady and the means of curing it. All the great German philosophical systems start out from the problem of *morals*, from the 'practical', a problem virtually unknown to French philosophers before Bergson.

It is sufficient to mention some famous and characteristic examples. Montaigne writes: '*Les autres forment l'homme, je le récite.*' Descartes, the first and foremost modern French philosopher, was primarily interested in physics, mathematics and epistemology. What he sought was the *True*; the Good was for him in the last instance secondary. Does he not declare that he will make do with a provisional code of conduct whose first rule is to accept the most moderate opinions of those about him, without, however, ever trying to replace it with a definitive system of ethics? In the same

way, all the original contributions of French philosophy –
the 'occasional causes' of Malebranche, the 'effort' of Maine
de Biran, the 'identity' of Meyerson and, on the whole,
even Bergson's 'intuition' – are physical, psychological and
above all epistemological categories, not ethical ones.

In Germany, on the other hand, it would be difficult even
with Leibniz to assimilate a monad, which is conscious,
reflects the world and aspires to a maximum of clarity, to a
physical atom. It seems clear that one must see in it a reflection of the human person, and that even in Leibniz the
problem of morals already occupies a preponderant place.
Thereafter, however, there is no longer room for doubt. In
the primacy of practical reason for Kant, the famous scene
in Goethe's *Faust* where Faust translates *logos* by 'act', the
Tathandlung of Fichte, the 'will' of Schopenhauer, in
Nietzsche's Zarathustra, everywhere it is the 'practical',
the will, action, which form the central problem and the
point of departure of all the great German philosophical
systems.

This difference is no less perceptible in the field of literature. The French novel and French literature in general
(with some exceptions, the most important being Pascal)
are in first place realist, psychological, sometimes historical
and sociological. When man is discussed, it is to analyse and
to understand him. The author seeks to know what man
thinks, feels or does, not what he *ought* to do. It is enough to
call to mind the principal works of Goethe, Schiller, Hölderlin or Kleist to feel the difference immediately. Here it is
almost always a question of the ideal, of what *should* be – in
philosophical language, of moral problems. French rationalism is primarily epistemological, scientifically and onto-
logically orientated; it is a contemplative world-view,
whereas in its highest forms, German rationalism, albeit
a general philosophical rationalism, is in first place a practical and moral rationalism.

Another consequence of the difference in social and economic development has been the *quite different positions of
humanist writers and philosophers* in the two countries. In
the whole of Europe – in France and in Germany, as in
Italy, in England or in Holland – the development of

humanist (rationalist or empiricist) thought has been closely linked with the economic development of the country concerned, that is, with the development of a commercial and industrial bourgeoisie. The existence or, by contrast, the absence of this Third Estate has also determined the position of humanist or mystical writers in the society.

In France, humanist and rationalist writers were organically bound to their public and to the nation as a whole. They were a part of it and expressed its thoughts and feelings; to be a writer was just one profession among many others. A Montaigne, a Racine, a Descartes, a Molière or a Voltaire is the most perfect expression of his country and his age. Behind his writings is the whole cultivated part of the nation; that is why his attacks are so dangerous, his satire so lethal for all those at whom it strikes. The old proverb, *Le ridicule tue en France*, best characterizes the situation.

In Germany, however, the position is just the reverse. Social and economic stagnation and the almost complete absence of a powerful commercial and industrial bourgeoisie having for more than two centuries prevented the blossoming of powerful humanist and rationalist currents of thought, Germany was open to mysticism and to the outpourings of intuitionism and the philosophy of feeling. That is why in Germany humanist and rationalist writers and thinkers lacked any real contact with the public and the society around them.

Solitude is the basic and perpetually recurrent theme of the biographies of the great German humanists. Leibniz in his old age, Lessing, Hölderlin, Kleist, Kant, Schopenhauer, Marx, Heine, Nietzsche and so many others – they stand alone in the midst of a German society which does not understand them and with which they can find no point of contact. That is why there are so many broken lives among them. Hölderlin, Nietzsche and Lenau became mad; Kleist committed suicide; Klopstock, Winckelmann, Heine, Marx and Nietzsche lived abroad in more or less voluntary exile; Kant and Schopenhauer led the lives of isolated eccentrics; Lessing died in godforsaken Wolfenbüttel, where his poverty had bound him to a miserly and capricious local despot. Goethe seems to be the only real exception here, but when one thinks of his flight to Italy and his description in *Tasso* of the life of the poet of genius at Court, even this exception becomes doubtful. In his *Religion and Philosophy in Germany*, Heine once compared the German humanists to shellfish kept in a room far from their true natural surroundings: they still feel the distant movements of the sea, the ebb and flow of the tides; they still open and close, but in the midst of an alien world their movements are misplaced and meaningless.

In contrast to this, mystical and sentimental writers in Germany have always been in very close contact with their society and their age. From Jakob Böhme, through Hamann, Schelling and the romantics, to the more recent Rilke, George, Heidegger, and so on, there is scarcely a broken life among them. More often than not the romantics follow good bourgeois professions: very often they are civil servants and, paradoxical though this may seem, in Germany it is precisely the mystics, the ecstatics and the dreamers of the 'absolute' who best endure the most wretched and stifling surrounding reality.

The entire history of German philosophy and literature could be written in terms of the struggle between the two currents, the humanist and the mystical,[7] a struggle which

---

7. Edmond Vermeil has made a start in this direction in his excellent work, *L'Allemagne, essai d'explication.*

Obviously, one cannot place every German philosopher or poet in one or other of these two currents, as is possible with Kant, Goethe and Schiller, or Schelling and Novalis. Many have been influenced by both currents at the same time and in very different ways. To name but a few of the most famous, Kleist was broken by the struggle within him between the two world-views; Schopenhauer, whose pessimism expresses the despair of the German humanistic and democratic bourgeoisie at the fall of Napoleon, which seemed the definitive end of the French Revolution, was open, precisely because of his despair, to those mystical and reactionary tendencies which are of such great importance in his system, which is why contemporary mystics such as Bergson and Thomas Mann have been able to return to him. Others, like Fichte and above all Wilhelm von Humboldt, began in their youth as thoroughgoing humanists, but were later, particularly under the influence of the defeat of Jena, won over by the mystique of the Prussian state and of German nationalism. Finally, with others, such as Hegel, the two world-views are intermixed, but scarcely synthetically united. They can very often be distinguished and separated on one and the same page.

Moreover, the sequence of broken lives continues to this day: consider,

is not yet ended (consider, for example, Rilke, George, Thomas Mann and Heidegger for the mystics, Karl Kraus, Bertolt Brecht, Erich Mühsam and Georg Lukács for the humanists), but which, following the general extension of the crisis and the social malady, has become in our time one of the fundamental problems of European culture.

One last remark concerning this analysis: it also explains why Germany has so few satirists and comic writers. Laughter, said Bergson, is a purely intellectual attitude. But one can only laugh at that which is already virtually overcome and brought down; one laughs when the future is open, when one has the whole people behind one. That is why laughing has become almost a national virtue in France. It is for the same reason that the German rationalists and humanists have never been able to laugh. Their combat was too tragic, their position too isolated and exposed. Engaged alone in a struggle against a whole society and a whole people, increasingly aware of their own weakness and the strength of the adversary, laughter for them would have been misplaced. If a German humanist may sometimes chance to laugh, his humour has a tragic ring, as in the case of Heine or, in modern literature, of Karl Kraus.

All these considerations may appear to have led us far from Kant and his philosophy. But we were never so close, for only now can we understand why his philosophy could be born in Germany and only in Germany.

Kant had in common with Descartes, Locke, Hume and the other French and English thinkers the defence of individual freedom and the equality of all reasonable men. What separated him from them was the answer to the second question: how, once this freedom and equality have been achieved, will connection between the elements of the universe and harmony and concord between individuals be established? Two answers presented themselves to him: the *dogmatic* answer of Descartes in France and of Leibniz/Wolff in Germany, and in England the *sceptical* answer of Hume.

---

for example, the complete isolation of a Karl Kraus or the suicide of admittedly less important writers such as Stefan Zweig, Kurt Tucholsky, or Ernst Toller.

For the radical French bourgeoisie, who neither doubted the future nor had any reason to do so, the harmony of the universe was not a problem. Freedom of the individual would in any case render it necessary. Universal mathematics was to establish theoretical harmony whilst the Stoic morality of duty established practical harmony; and, as I have said, much less importance was attached to the latter since it appeared to follow of itself.

The English bourgeoisie was much less radical. It believed as little in universal mathematics as in the Stoic morality of duty. That is what Kant called scepticism. However, in England this sceptical attitude was also much less dangerous than on the continent. For the bourgeoisie *already had* power. It could thus point to the fact that even if the harmony was not *necessary*, it was nonetheless *real*. If its *a priori* character was problematic, there was no doubt about its reality. That is why it was possible to renounce innate ideas and be content with associationism, with the *actual* connection of ideas. And if it was necessary in ethical matters to renounce the requirements of the Stoic morality of duty, realizing that it surpassed the powers of man, it could nevertheless be objected that Epicurean and sensualist utilitarianism guaranteed a harmony which, if not necessary, was no less real and effective.

In backward Germany neither of these two points of view was tenable in the long run; liberal society and the democratic state were still too far away and the forces opposing their realization too powerful not to keep a clear head and to recognize their faults and limitations. On the other hand, simple recognition of a factual state of affairs could not satisfy the German humanists, who were as yet unacquainted with this 'fact'. Such a position appeared to them as a dangerous scepticism; precisely because they did not share the illusions of dogmatic rationalism, the possibility of transcending *empiricist* scepticism became for them an urgent and vital task. Thus it was precisely in backward Germany that there arose the Kantian system, which clearly perceived the essence of bourgeois man, describing him as an 'unsocial sociable' being, and reduced the harmony and concord to purely formal elements, relegating to the level of content all the possible conflicts which the future held.

Because this clearer and more profound insight was the result of a 'sick' situation, Kant could assert the primacy of practical reason, recognize the bounds within which free and independent man was still restricted and thus understand the need to transcend them. It is for all those reasons that today, when the limitations of bourgeois society have become more palpable than ever, when the sickness and the crisis are everywhere acute, the Kantian system appears as one of the most profound and relevant expressions of classical philosophy, and one which we may still take as our point of departure today, provided, of course, that we overtake it on the road it has opened for us.

Before closing this chapter, I must deal with a possible objection. Kant is not the only representative of classical thought who was clearly conscious of the limitations of the individual. Apart from the work of Goethe, this vision of man and of his existence also dominates the work of the two great French classical writers – Racine and Pascal. Considering only their world-views, one might indeed group Descartes and Corneille on one side, Kant, Goethe, Racine and Pascal on the other. But how can this be reconciled with the analysis I have just outlined? If the philosophy of Kant was only possible in Germany, how could a French poet and a French thinker arrive at the same world-view?

The general outline which I have sketched must not be conceived as a rigid and definitive system. If the analysis is pushed further, a whole series of distinctions soon arise. Thus, the French bourgeoisie is not one solid lump; there is, within the bourgeoisie, a multiplicity of groups whose different economic and social positions correspond naturally to different ideological shadings. The principal distinction is that between the Third Estate proper and the *noblesse de robe*. The latter, bourgeois in origin, had been ennobled by the offices of state which it occupied; thus, by its economic existence and by its traditions it found itself intimately linked with the absolute monarchy. Its bourgeois origin, its

antagonism towards the court nobility, the mixture of suspicion and envy with which this industrious group, fulfilling a real social function and perfectly conscious of that
fact, viewed the court nobility's life of enjoyment and liber-
tinage, all this made it aspire to a better world, to a reformed
society. On the other hand, it was too intimately linked with
the absolute monarchy to take up a really revolutionary
attitude or to contribute to the transformation of society.
The tragic vision of the world which sees the grandeur of
man in his aspirations and his pettiness in the impossibility
of realizing them, and which in Germany formed the ideology of the most advanced strata of the bourgeoisie, could
develop in France only in one very specific part of the bourgeoisie, that of the *noblesse de robe*. The institution which
most clearly expressed that ideology was Port-Royal, and it
is no accident that the two great French tragic writers, Pascal
and Racine, both came from there.

Between Racine on one side and Kant and Goethe on the
other, there are nonetheless considerable differences. Racine
feels and lives the limits of the individual in all their tragedy.
In the whole of world literature there is perhaps no other
poet who has expressed them so menacingly and inexorably.
And in spite of this, he feels neither the hope nor the need
to transcend them. His heroes are broken at those limits and
they die; they do not surmount them. No God, no eternity
helps them to go beyond themselves. Consciously and relent-
lessly, they march onwards to their doom. As Lukács once
said, 'God is a mere spectator: he never intervenes in the
action.' And the limits themselves appear in their most
basic – one might almost say their simplest – form, not as
barriers between man and the human community or between
man and the universe, but as barriers between one man and
another, sometimes even within a single family.[8]

8. This is no longer true in the two last tragedies, *Esther* and *Athalie*, written
by Racine after a silence of twelve years, and perhaps under the influence of
events in England. Here, not only does God intervene in the action, but the
people itself is represented by the chorus. It is certainly no mere coincidence
that God and the people appear simultaneously in Racine's tragedies.

But it is precisely in these two tragedies that the limits of man are presented .
only in their mythical and transcendent form and no longer in all their concrete depth and fatefulness. That is why I believe that Racine's art reached

With Kant, or in Goethe's *Faust*, the problem is posed in a quite different way, in a way which, whilst certainly not artistically more perfect, is philosophically broader and more profound. The question is posed immediately in its widest form, that of the relations between the individual, the human community and the universe in general.

Further, if consciousness of limitations is here the most important and pervasive element, enormous efforts are made to find some way of overcoming them. In the Transcendental Dialectic, in the thing in itself, in the archetypal intellect, in God, in history, in the beautiful for Kant, in the illusion of the ageing Faust for Goethe, everywhere we feel this effort towards something higher which transcends the individual, to grasp it, or at least to find reasons to hope for it, even if it does not yet seem possible to attain it in concrete and real existence.

And, once at least, in Faust's famous translation of the word *logos*, there arises an *immanent* and *concrete* possibility of transcending the individual: 'In the beginning was the act.' Truly, even the greatest modern philosophers realize all too little to what degree they are the heirs and continuers of the heights of classical thought.

---

its zenith in the earlier tragedies, in *Andromaque, Bérénice* and *Phèdre*, and not in *Esther* and *Athalie*.

The people, the human community, God, as ways of overcoming the limitations and the isolation of the individual, were categories which in seventeenth-century France could not yet be grasped and realized philosophically or artistically in all their human richness and depth (Pascal being, I repeat, the only exception).

Chapter 2

The Category of Totality in
the Thought of Kant
and in Philosophy in General

I

The clearest result of the long methodological controversies
of recent years has without doubt been to demonstrate the
existence in every scientific or philosophical work of premis-
ses for which the author makes no attempt to provide a
logical foundation. This admitted, the thinker's first duty
is to try to make his premises explicit instead of leaving
them, as most frequently happens, implicit.

The reader who has followed thus far will no doubt have
realized that *totality* in its two principal forms, the *universe*
and the *human community*, constitutes for me the most important philosophical category, as much in the field of epistemology as in ethics or aesthetics. Further, following
Georg Lukács, I do not see this totality as something existent
and given, but rather as a goal to be attained by *action*,
which alone can create the human community, the *we*, and
the totality of the universe, the *cosmos*. To the contemplative
philosophies of the 'I' from Descartes to Kant, to the active
philosophy of the *ego* of the young Fichte, to the modern
philosophies of anguish and despair, I think it is possible to
oppose a philosophy of the community, of the *we*, which can
resolve the contradiction between contemplation and action,
between the individual and the community.

Moreover, I believe that three fundamental types of
philosophical attitude may be established to which (or to
an eclectic mixture of which) the majority of modern philosophical systems belong, viz.:

1. The *individualist* and *atomist* philosophies, whose principal ethical categories are the *individual* and *freedom*, their

cosmological ones the *atom* or the *monad*, and their psychological ones the *sensation* and the *image*. Their principal
expression is *rationalism* and, in a less radical form, *empiricism* (Lask has revealed the close kinship between the two).

In these world-views, the possibility of the whole is based,
to use an expression of Kant's, on 'the composition of the
parts, which can nevertheless also be conceived apart from
any composition'.[1] 'Society', therefore, here means at most
the interaction of autonomous individuals; 'universe', an
assembly of atoms or monads. To the extent to which, in
spite of individualism, it is nevertheless necessary to maintain a minimum of connection between individuals, this
minimum takes the form of *divine intervention* (occasional-
ism for Malebranche, pre-established harmony for Leibniz),
of *universal validity* or, for the empiricists, of a simple
matter of fact (habit, association, etc.).

As the principal representatives of this world-view, we
could list Descartes, Leibniz, Locke, Hume, in part Fichte,
and in modern times the neo-Kantians (including Lask and
socialists such as Max Adler) or for the empiricist stream
the Vienna circle. A penetrating analysis of these philosophies from the logical point of view is found in Lask and
from the sociological point of view in Georg Lukács.

One must, however, mention separately the forms this
world-view takes among those philosophers and poets who,
starting out from individualist atomism and remaining still
within its limits, have felt and recognized all their tragic
insufficiency.[2] With these writers, classical philosophy and
art reached the summit of their achievement. The names of
Goethe, Racine, Pascal and Kant will doubtless already have
occurred to the reader. For these thinkers and poets, the
meaning of human life lies in aspiration towards the absolute, towards totality. But all four still think of man as an

1. XVII, No. 3789.
2. Unfortunately, I must here remain schematic. However, I would draw
attention to an article by Georg Lukács, 'Metaphysik der Tragödie', published in *Logos*, XVII, p. 190 (reproduced also in G. von Lukács, *Die Seele und
die Formen*, Berlin, 1910). Although this essay does not refer directly or explicitly to Kant, to my knowledge it is the best introduction to the essential
content of Kant's philosophy.

isolated individual and clearly recognize that such an individual cannot attain the absolute: man must pit his strength against this barrier, but he can never surmount it. That is why tragedy became the supreme form of classical art: the tragedy of Racine, where there is no means of escape and where man finds himself only in destroying himself; the tragedy of Kant and of Goethe, in the *Critique of Judgement* and in *Faust*, where man attains totality only in subjective appearance and not in concrete and authentic reality.

2. The *holistic world-views*, whose basic categories are the whole, the *universe*, and on the social level the *collective*, are opposed term for term to the individualist philosophies. Their principal ethical category is, most often, *feeling* under its multiple aspects, revelation, intuition, enthusiasm, etc., and their principal physical category the 'life principle' in its most diverse forms, *Weltseele, élan vital*, and so on.

The principal forms of the holistic view are the mystical philosophies of feeling and of intuition, from Jakob Böhme, through Jacobi, Schelling and the romantics, to Bergson, Scheler and Heidegger (its less important forms being organicism, vitalism, and so on). According to these world-views, the part exists only as a necessary means to the existence of the whole. Man must renounce all autonomy and lose himself entirely in God, in death, in the State, in the nation, in the class, and so forth. His autonomous self and his freedom can only be admitted through an inconsistency in the system, and most frequently they are not. (Scheler's ideal is *sich in eins fühlen*.) In so far as it is impossible completely to avoid recognizing the reality of the individual, he becomes the exception, the hero, the leader, the paragon, the adventurer.

Since this world-view has dominated European thought for the last twenty or thirty years, it has not yet been satisfactorily analysed and understood. To my knowledge, the best analysis is still Kant's clear and prophetic reply to Jacobi, 'What is orientation in thinking?',[3] in which he

---

3. VIII, 131; *Ethics*, 293. The antihumanist character of the philosophy of anguish is revealed in Heidegger's avoidance of the word 'man' and his substitution of the much more abstract term 'existence'. Stylistic criticism, even in philosophy, may at times reveal or clarify certain hidden problems.

points out the dangers which the philosophy of feeling implies for freedom of thought, and indeed for freedom *simpliciter*. Further criticism of these world-views can be found in the greater part of the work of all the German humanists, from Kant, Goethe and Schiller to Nietzsche and, in our own time, Karl Kraus.

3. Finally, the world-view for which, to use Kant's phrase, the universe and the human community form a whole 'whose parts presuppose for their possibility their union in the whole', where the *autonomy* of the parts and the *reality* of the whole are not only reconciled but constitute reciprocal conditions, where in place of the partial and one-sided solutions of the individual *or* the collective there appears the only total solution: that of the *person and the human community*. It would be difficult to name a major representative of this philosophy today, since it is still in the process of formation; however, much ground has been covered in the works of Kant, Hegel, Marx, and, in our time, Georg Lukács. The development of this philosophy seems to me to be the principal task of modern thought.

II

Before passing to my own analysis of Kant's thought, I should like first to clarify my position with respect to those of the two writers cited above: Emil Lask and Georg Lukács.

Lukács, in fact, says much more about classical philosophy in general than about Kant in particular, and, of course, he also discusses the neo-Kantians. His critique of neo-Kantianism is no doubt well-founded, for the neo-Kantians failed to grasp the importance in Kant's thought of the ideas of totality, of the human community and of the universe. However, Lukács seems not to realize (or at least does not sufficiently emphasize) the degree to which, in criticizing

---

The analysis of the social causes and effects of the modern philosophies of feeling, intuition and anguish presents an important task for the sociology of knowledge.

the neo-Kantians, he is merely defending against the trivial interpretation of the *epigoni* thoughts which at least in embryo were already to be found in Kant himself. On the other hand, in his critique of the neo-Kantians, even when referring to Kant himself, he often stresses what separates him from Kant – namely, Kant's belief that man cannot realize the totality, a fact easily explained by the social situation of eighteenth-century Germany – whilst neglecting the equally important fact that the absolute necessity of attaining and realizing the totality forms the point of departure and the centre of Kant's thought.

With Lask the problem is more complicated. To my knowledge, no neo-Kantian has grasped Kant's theory of knowledge so precisely as this today almost forgotten thinker. Not only is his knowledge of the texts exemplary, but the spirit of a whole part of the critical philosophy (the Logic, and the Transcendental Aesthetic and Analytic of the *Critique of Pure Reason*) could hardly be better expressed than it is in the few pages he devotes to Kant in his book on Fichte.

However, in order to discuss Lask's analyses, I must first clarify the meaning of two important concepts which he introduces, and which I shall also be using, namely *emanatist logic* and *analytic logic*.

1. *Emanatist* logic, according to Lask, is that which includes all that is limited and partial, starting from the necessarily prior knowledge of the *whole*, of the universe and of the human community. Lask has shown in exemplary fashion why, since the whole embraces everything, any significant emanatist logic must be a logic of *content* and can admit no separation between content and form.

However, Lask is convinced (and here Lukács follows him entirely) that in the natural sciences *any* emanatist logic must necessarily lead to speculative metaphysics, whilst in the social and historical sciences it could eventually (Lukács, with reason, says necessarily) lead to a truly dialectical method. I do not believe that the proposition concerning the natural sciences has yet been definitively established, but that is a matter outside the scope of the present work.

2. For *analytic* logic, which might also be called atomistic logic, individual elements constitute the only authentic reality. General concepts are formed by abstraction and simply denote classes of individuals with certain properties in common. It is used in science to establish more or less general scientific laws which ever more closely approach, but never actually reach, the individual. The individual remains the eternally irrational element against which thought must always struggle without ever being able to conquer it. Philosophy becomes *a priori* knowledge, an empty, formal logic which acquires content only from the individual and concrete 'given'. (Lask seems convinced that *any* analytic logic must lead to a deliberate separation of form from content. Whilst this is correct in general, and particularly with regard to Kant, it is nevertheless not an absolute necessity: consider, for example, Descartes.)

In the epistemological debates between the neo-Kantian schools of Heidelberg and Marburg,[4] the former laid most stress upon analytic logic with its atomistic and individualistic conception of substance, whilst the latter, starting from mathematics, emphasized functional concepts and tended towards emanatist logic, albeit in a purely 'scientific' and contemplative sense. Lask recognized that the two camps could lay equal claim to Kant,[5] for the simple reason that in Kant's thought the logic of mathematics (space and time) is diametrically opposed to that of the sciences of matter. The first is emanatist, the second analytic. From the historical and philosophical point of view, Lask is doubtless right when he stresses that in the critical philosophy the analytic logic of the physical sciences is much the more important, mathematics representing only a subsidiary concern.[6] However, I cannot follow him in upholding that hierarchy today. Emanatist logic could be of only secondary importance for Kant, but with it he opened the way for so

4. See particularly H. Rickert, *Die Grenzen der naturwissenschaftlichen Begriffsbildung*, and E. Cassirer, *Substanzbegriff und Funktionsbegriff in der Philosophie*.

5. Rickert had already noted Kant's acceptance of emanatist logic for mathematics and geometry, but he had not given sufficient weight to this fact.

6. As we shall see later, this is less true of the precritical period.

much later philosophical development that I believe it is of prime philosophical importance today.

My principal reproach to Lask, however, is that, like all the neo-Kantians, he sees the critical philosophy as primarily the Logic and the Transcendental Aesthetic and Analytic, whilst completely underestimating the importance of the Dialectic. This leads him to an entirely false picture of Kant's thought.[7] However, I shall return to this point later.

Lask's analysis of Kant's philosophy of history also seems very questionable. He sees this as an entirely rationalist and atomistic philosophy, the category of totality appearing only with Hegel. This is certainly to underestimate the outline of a conception of history as totality which, at least *qua* project, dominates the *Idea for a universal history with a cosmopolitan purpose*. In fact, Kant's philosophy of history, too, is an attempt to reconcile the two categories: rationalist and atomistic *universality* and concrete *totality*.[8] With Kant, as with Hegel, one and the same logic dominates both the philosophy of nature and the philosophy of history. That is why Lask's attempt to unite Kant's analytic logic of physics with Hegel's emanatist philosophy of history seems to me the least philosophical aspect of his otherwise remarkable book.

Admittedly, Lask returns to this question in the third section of his book, where he admits that in the sociological field Kant provides a clear elaboration of the category of totality. However, comparing this with the later works of Fichte, he makes two criticisms of Kant which seem to me, on the contrary, to indicate the superiority of Kant and a step backwards on the part of Fichte, viz.:

1. That for Kant the individual is equal in dignity to the community and constitutes its *essential goal*. Any association of men 'is in the last instance no more for him than a means towards the morality of individuals, and not for the working

---

7. See the introduction and the final section of his book.
8. The opposition between these two conceptions is most clearly evident in his oscillation between two diametrically opposite attitudes to concrete historical problems, for example, that of the revolution: see page 213 of the present work.

out of cultural tasks which devolve exclusively upon a collective which stands over and above the individual',[9] and

2. That Kant's idea of community, which embraces *the whole of humanity* and not, as with Fichte, simply the nation, is an 'abstract' notion.

On the other hand, Lask's remarks on the relations between the concepts of space and time and the idea of the human community in Kant's thought, which are all three but expressions of the category of totality, seem to me extremely pertinent.

Finally, I believe that the greatest difference between the world of Heidegger and that of Kant is that for Heidegger the world is *given*, whilst for Kant it is *to be created*. In the language of Heidegger, we might say that for him a fundamental category of existence is *being in the world*; for Kant, on the contrary, it is *the task of creating a world*.

And now, after this long introduction, it is time to begin our study of the works of Kant himself.

9. Lask, op. cit., 248.

Chapter 3

The Precritical Period

I

If, after this preamble which has already introduced us, up to a certain point, into Kant's thought, we pass to the analysis of that thought itself, we know now that we shall have two different directions to follow, corresponding roughly to Lask's distinction between analytic and emanatist logic. In the problem which principally interests us here, to these two points of view – that of the relations between the parts in the entirety of the universe and between the individuals in the association of the human community – there correspond two distinct categories and two replies.

According to the emanatist point of view, the *whole*, the *totality*, is a necessary condition for the existence of the parts and the individuals. For the analytic point of view, on the contrary, individuals are the only authentic reality; since their existence is independent of the whole, their connection is based only upon the generality of their attributes or upon the universality of moral or logical laws. Universe, whole and totality, on the one hand, generality and universality on the other: we must now examine the significance of these categories in Kant's thought.

It must be noted at the outset that from the precritical period onwards the category of totality occupies a most important place. Indeed, it provides the key to the development of Kant's thought, a point which most of the neo-Kantians failed to grasp. Therefore, although the critical philosophy is my main concern, I shall begin by examining the category of totality in the precritical period.

Kant's preoccupation with the problem of the whole during this period is clear if only from the large number of reflections upon it to be found in the posthumous writings. Obviously I cannot quote all of them here. I shall be content to cite a few especially characteristic examples.[1] Thus, Kant writes: 'The *respectus* of a part and its *complementum ad totum* must be mutual and homogeneous; thus an effect cannot be a part of its cause and belong with its cause to one and the same whole. Thought is not a part of man, but his effect.'[2] Thus every whole is homogeneous. It follows implicitly that the universe, which is not homogeneous, does not constitute a whole. Kant draws the ultimate conclusions from this point of view: 'Thought is not a part of man, but his effect.'

Elsewhere he returns to the same problem: 'The question is whether in a *compositum substantiale* there is no substance, but only substances, and whether here only the plural is possible. A *totum syntheticum* is one whose composition is grounded in its possibility upon the parts, which can also be conceived apart from any composition. A *totum analyticum* is one whose parts presuppose in their possibility their composition in the whole. *Spatium* and *tempus* are *tota analytica*; bodies, *synthetica*. *Compositum ex substantiis est totum syntheticum. Totum analyticum nec est compositum ex substantiis nec ex accidentibus, sed totum possibilium relationum.*'[3] This time there is perhaps a whole. Moreover, the distinction – so important for the critical theory of knowledge – between emanatist logic in mathematics (space and time) and analytic logic in physics (bodies) is already definitively set out. On another occasion, he writes: 'Either space contains the ground of the possibility of the copresence of many substances and their relations, or the latter contain the ground of the possibility of space.'[4]

At times he becomes quite concrete, allowing us to see the perhaps unconscious background to the problem: 'In a kettle of boiling water there is more heat than in a spoonful thereof, but not greater. Two donkeys draw a cart with more speed, but not with greater. If many units cannot be

---

1. According to Adickes, they are all roughly of the same period (*circa* 1764 to 1766).

2. XVII, No. 3787.   3. XVII, No. 3789.   4. XVII, No. 3790.

combined in such a way as to give a higher level . . . More virtue, greater virtue; more welfare, greater welfare.'[5] Finally, as if concluding a long reflection, he writes: 'If the concept of universe signified the whole of all possible things, namely those which are possible in relation to sufficient reason, it would be more fruitful.'[6]

To show the importance of the category of totality for Kant in ethics as well, I shall quote two further reflections from a later period (about 1772), where indeed both totality and universality appear. 'The value of an action or a person is always determined by the relation to the whole. But this is only possible through conformity to the conditions of a general rule.' Or further: 'The whole determines absolute value; everything else is merely relative and conditioned. A thing must have a value in relation to feeling, but the generality of this value determines it absolutely.'[7]

A detailed study of the development of the idea of totality in Kant up to the birth of the critical philosophy would be valuable, but it would go beyond the limits of this work. Here I must be content briefly to enumerate the principal steps, knowledge of which seems to me indispensable for the understanding of that philosophy. First, however, I should like to stress two facts noted by Lask concerning the importance of the category of totality in German idealism:

1. In the thought of all the great philosophers and of Kant in particular, the categories of mathematics and the natural sciences on the one hand, and historical and sociological categories on the other, have a reciprocal influence on one another. However, this is not, as Lask appears to believe, a

---

5. XVII, No. 3793. Here, Kant contrasts qualitative change ('greater') with quantitative increase ('more'). The latter is merely simple addition of independent parts; the former creates a higher unity. This formulation of the problem was later to be of the utmost importance in the work of Hegel, Marx and Lukács. Lukács' main thesis is that on the human and spiritual level *communal action* alone can produce qualitative change and create the 'higher level'. In the two reflections quoted above (Nos. 3787 and 3793), Kant draws the ultimate conclusions from an atomistic world-view pushed to the extreme, no doubt the better to understand and judge it.

6. XVII, No. 3799.   7. XIX, Nos. 6711–12.

fortuitous matter. It is not simply that the same man tends to employ the same mode of thought in different fields; we are dealing here with an utterly conscious phenomenon. For philosophical thought consists precisely in the search for a central vision in terms of which the different regions of reality and of intellectual life can be grasped and understood.

2. In the work of Kant, the category of totality finds several forms of expression, the most important being time, space, the universe, the human community, and God, ideas whose connections must always be kept in mind.

Passing now to the enumeration of the principal stages of Kant's precritical thought, it seems to me that the earliest element (which, moreover, remains unaltered in the critical philosophy) is the assertion that to physics and to bodies on the one hand, and to mathematics and to space and time on the other, correspond two entirely different kinds of knowledge. Physics starts out from the individual, from simple and limited elements, attaining in due course knowledge of their combination. In geometry, on the other hand, the individual and the limited can only be understood as a part of a greater whole. Space is infinitely divisible precisely because it forms a whole which is not made up of individual monads.

The recognition of this fact was soon to be joined, however, by the realization that the wholes of space and time are not given, and that one can only advance towards knowledge of them through the infinite division and infinite composition of their parts. The dialectical contradiction inherent in knowledge where the parts can only be understood through the whole which envelops them whilst the whole can only be understood through factual knowledge of the parts, was to be one of the most fruitful problems of Kant's thought, influencing its development right up to the birth of the critical philosophy. (Another idea, which I here mention only in passing, but which also exerted an influence over a long period, is that in mathematical thought, where knowledge of the whole is a necessary condition for knowledge of the parts, changes must be continuous.)

The earliest clear expression of this view is in the *Monado-logia physica*[8] of 1756, although the problem of the universe had already been posed a year earlier, in the *Principiorum primorum cognitionis metaphysicae nova dilucidatio*. Kant announced in the preface to the latter that he would 'lay down two new principles of no little importance for metaphysical knowledge' and that he would thus 'open an untrodden path', which indeed he does in the third and last part of the work. These two principles are:

1. The principle of *succession*. 'No change can affect substances, except in so far as they are connected one with another; their mutual dependence thus determines their reciprocal change of state.'[9] Kant is aware that this assertion runs counter to Wolffian atomism as well as to the theories of Leibniz: 'Although this truth depends upon a chain of reasons which is certain and easy to grasp, it has been so little noticed by those who give the Wolffian philosophy its name that they assert rather that the simple substance, by virtue of an inner principle of activity, is subject to perpetual change. I know their proofs well enough, but I am just as persuaded how false they are.' 'If anyone wishes to know how changes then occur . . . he should direct his attention to the consequences of the interconnection of things, that is, of their interdependence in their determinations.'[10] 'The pre-established harmony of Leibniz is wholly overthrown, not, as is usually the case, from final causes which are often of little assistance, being, as is thought, unworthy of God, but because of their own inner impossibility. For from what has been shown it follows immediately that the human soul, once freed from its connections with external things, would be completely unable to change its internal state.'[11]

2. The principle of *coexistence*. 'Finite substances stand in no relations through their existence alone, being in community only in so far as they are maintained in their mutual relations by a common principle of their existence, namely

8. The full title is *Metaphysicae cum geometria iunctae usus in philosophia naturali, cuius specimen I continet monadologiam physicam* (*Werke*, 1).

9. I, 410.   10. I, 411.   11. I, 412.

the divine understanding.'[12] Here too, Kant stresses his disagreement with Leibniz and Malebranche: ' . . . there is a general *harmony* of things. But from it there does not follow the *pre-established* harmony of *Leibniz*, which in truth introduces only *concordance* and not *mutual dependence* between substances . . . nor do we here admit the action of substances by the *occasional causes* of *Malebranche*.'[13]

The two new fundamental principles by means of which Kant wishes to 'open an untrodden path' and to give new and more solid foundations to metaphysics may thus be formulated as follows:

(a) Changes are only possible through mutual relations and dependence between monads. Since the changes exist and are real, the mutual relations and dependence exist and are real also. There is a universe.

(b) This universe cannot result from the mutual influences of limited and independent beings, but must have its basis in a common principle, in the divine understanding.

Obviously we cannot go into the details of this text (whether several universes can coexist, and so on). It suffices to have established that as early as 1755, in seeking to rebuild metaphysics on new and more solid foundations, starting from the idea of the entirety, the whole, the universe, Kant was in conscious opposition to the monadology of Leibniz, to Wolff and to Malebranche.

However, in the following year the *Monadologia physica* appeared, marking a clear beginning of the development which was to lead to the elaboration of the critical philosophy. As indicated by the title, *Metaphysicae cum geometria iunctae usus in philosophia naturali*, the principal theme of the work was the distinction between two different modes of knowledge, 'metaphysics' and 'geometry', and their union in natural philosophy. To avoid any misunderstanding, it must be borne in mind that 'metaphysics' here denotes the knowledge of bodies, in contrast to geometrical knowledge of space, and that 'natural philosophy' denotes the union of the two in what Kant was later to call experience.

12. I, 412–13.   13. I, 415.

Let us examine these two modes of knowledge a little more closely. With regard to knowledge of bodies, the results of the *Nova dilucidatio*, which had appeared a year earlier, seem entirely forgotten. There is no further reference to a universe or to the mutual dependence of monads. In all essential points, Kant now follows Leibniz. His main argument against Leibniz, the mutual dependence of monads, which had carried so much weight in the earlier text, here loses almost all its importance. This is clear from the beginning of the first theorem:[14] 'Bodies consist of parts which have a durable existence even when separated. But since the composition of the parts is only a relation, and consequently a contingent determination which may be taken away without taking away their existence, it follows that it is possible to abrogate all composition of a body, whilst all the parts which were before in composition nevertheless remain.'

Does this indicate that the problem of the universe, of the unity and mutual dependence of the parts, has become something subordinate or perhaps even disappeared? Not at all: its place and meaning within the system have merely evolved. The emanatist point of view is no longer held valid for all reality and all knowledge in general, but only for space and geometry. Here Kant's position is exactly the reverse:[15] 'The space which bodies occupy is infinitely divisible and therefore does not consist of primitive and simple parts.'

The aim of the theory of monads developed in this text is to show how these two modes of knowledge, which correspond in very large measure to the analytic and emanatist logics of Lask, can be united in a single natural philosophy – we might almost already employ the critical term: *experience*. The problem is set out in the preface:[16] 'But how in the matter at hand can metaphysics be joined with geometry, since it is easier to couple a horse with a gryphon than transcendental philosophy with geometry? For the former denies obstinately that space is infinitely divisible, whilst the latter affirms this with its usual certitude. . . . Although to resolve this conflict appears no small task, I have put some effort into its accomplishment.'

These passages demonstrate how misguided are those theories which see the starting-point of the critical philosophy in the psychological distinction between the faculties of the mind or the epistemological distinction between sensibility and understanding. The true starting-point seems to me to be the epistemological question of the whole and the parts, of geometrical and analytic knowledge. It is this which leads Kant to the separation of knowledge of space and time from knowledge of bodies. From this separation, with enormous mental effort, Kant derived the other distinctions: between sensibility and understanding; between understanding – the faculty of judgement – and reason.

But how did Kant arrive at this formulation of the problem? The influence of the debates between Newtonians and Leibnizians on the question of space has often been remarked upon in this connection: the writings of Kant are thus seen merely as an attempt to find an intermediate position reconciling the two opposing theories. For Leibniz, who started from individuals, monads, as the only authentic reality, space was relative, a relation between monads. Newton, the physicist, affirmed the existence of absolute space, without which there could be no bodies, let alone relations between them. Kant is seen as taking up an intermediate position in an attempt to reconcile monadology with absolute space.

I think it extremely likely that Kant's formulation of the problem was influenced by the debates between the followers of Leibniz and Newton. Indeed, it would be scarcely conceivable that a philosopher should find his problems anywhere but in the preoccupations of his age. His greatness, however, lies in his recognizing and sifting out the universal elements contained in those problems and giving to them a philosophical character by developing from them essential premises for all future knowledge. It is possible and even probable that Kant took the idea of absolute space from Newton. Kant's genius lay in his transformation of this idea into the category of totality, to be applied in turn to physical, theological and anthropological problems. This transformation first appears in 1755, rather than in the Inaugural Dissertation of 1770 as has often been supposed.

One further distinction must be mentioned because of its importance for Kant's later thought; the *Dilucidatio* speaks of the *changes* of the parts in and by the whole, whilst the *Monadologia* speaks of the *existence* of monads. Kant may indeed have seen in this distinction a possible means of reconciling the positions of the two works. However that may be, he was to grapple with this problem for some time to come.

Finally, I must single out an important element of Kant's precritical thought which is neglected in most treatments of the subject, namely the close relation between the already completely elaborated concepts of space and time, and the idea of God. This relation can be traced to the very threshold of the critical period. In the published writings it appears explicitly only once, and then with many reservations, in a scholium to the Inaugural Dissertation[17] where Kant mentions the possibility that space and time might be the sensible manifestations of God. With much reticence, however: 'If it were permitted to take even a small step beyond the boundaries of the apodictic certitude which is appropriate to metaphysics . . . But it seems more advisable to keep close to the shore of the cognitions granted to us by the mediocrity of our intellect rather than to put out into the deep sea of mystical investigations.'

In the posthumous works, this idea returns much more frequently. I quote three characteristic passages. 'Effects are symbols of causes, thus space . . . a *symbolum* of the divine omnipresence or the *phaenomenon* of divine causality.'[18] 'Infinite reality is the *substratum* of all possibility. The universal foundation. If all negations are limitations, no thing is possible except through another which it presupposes, save for the *ens realissimum*. All-embracing time, all-containing space, the sufficient thing.'[19] 'The necessary unity of space and time is transformed into the necessary unity of an original being, the incommensurability of the first into the universality of the second.'[20] I believe that these quotations suffice to show the relationship between the ideas of space, time and God in Kant's precritical thought. I also believe that that relationship is to be explained above all by the fact that all three are expressions of the category of totality.

Returning to the *Monadologia*, it is clear that there geometrical knowledge (space) already to some extent fulfilled the function of creating and maintaining the universe, a function which in the *Nova dilucidatio* was fulfilled by the divine understanding. Space is 'the appearance of the external connection of monads bound into a unity'.

We can now understand the train of thought leading up to the appearance in 1763 of *The only possible ground for a proof of the existence of God*.

II

We come now to the three principal works of the precritical period: *The only possible ground for a proof of the existence of God* (1763), forming one stage in the application of the category of totality to the theological field; *Dreams of a visionary explained by the dreams of metaphysics* (1766), where Kant for the first time applies the category of totality to anthropological problems, and where the concept of community appears; and finally, the Inaugural Dissertation of 1770.

However, it must not be thought that Kant had at this stage found a firm and stable position on the basis of which he had only to apply his conclusions to various particular fields. Far from it: although he recognized the importance of his new outlook, in its three principal applications he encountered immense and even insuperable difficulties. Questions and problems arose which necessitated a prolonged intellectual struggle, driving him onwards towards the critical philosophy. The works I am about to analyse are but three important steps on the road, three points at which

20. XVII, No. 4758.

Kant thought he had found a more or less definitive solution – a solution at which, however, he was unable to stop. Only by thus regarding them as stages of an intellectual development beset with difficulties can one grasp the significance of these works and of a whole series of details which would otherwise appear abstruse, scholastic and divorced from reality. I shall try to reconstruct the general features of this development in Kant's thought. Part of my reconstruction will of course be hypothetical, but this seems unavoidable if we really wish to understand the development as a whole.

Let us recall once more the conclusions of the *Monadologia physica*. Space is an infinitely divisible totality which is not composed of simple parts. Bodies, on the contrary, are composed of monads, centres of force acting in space. From the union of the two, of space and monads, of the whole and the autonomous parts, nature is born. From the *Nova dilucidatio* we know also that autonomous monads cannot of themselves enter into any mutual relations and that such relations could only originate in 'a common principle of their existence, namely the divine understanding', and, from the *Monadologia*, that space is 'the appearance of the external relations of united monads'.[21] If we suppose Kant still holding to *both* works, it follows logically that space is the phenomenal appearance of the divine understanding, which, as we have already seen, is expressly asserted in several passages of the posthumous works and also in a scholium to the Dissertation.

However, one question remains open: what is the relation between the monads and the divine understanding? Two consistent replies are possible, but each presents grave difficulties. The *transcendent* conception, according to which the harmony of the monads is introduced from outside by the divine understanding, leads to *atomistic rationalism* or to *empiricism*. The *immanent* conception, which identifies the divine understanding with the totality of monads, the universe, when developed to its ultimate consequences leads through Spinozist pantheism to the *Hegelian dialectic*.

We have already seen Kant's categorical refusal to accept the transcendent conception, Leibniz's pre-established harmony or Malebranche's occasional causes, which seemed to him to imply a radical atomism and the renunciation of the category of totality.

The most natural solution would have been the immanent conception, which was no doubt much closer to Kant's own way of thinking. This, however, raised an old problem, with which the Eleatics had struggled and to which nobody (with the exception of Heraclitus) had yet provided a satisfactory answer: *the problem of change*. It still seemed obvious to philosophers that categories were absolute, eternal and immutable. But a consistently immanent point of view was bound to encounter the contradiction between eternal and immutable categories and changing empirical reality. This contradiction could only be resolved in two ways: either by reducing empirical reality to pure appearance, as all Platonists had done since the Eleatics, or by admitting that the categories themselves can vary, which no one since Heraclitus had dared to do. Hegel was the first to revive this viewpoint, thereby taking a decisive step towards the dialectical method. Kant, however, shrank from such a step. He saw that a consistent philosophy of totality implied immanence and that this must lead him through Spinozistic pantheism to the idea of a changing God and to the dialectic, and for that very reason he rejected it.

Kant never made an explicit analysis of Spinozism. However, a very characteristic passage at the beginning of *The only possible ground* seems to me to be of considerable importance, even though Spinoza is only mentioned there as an example. Developing his critique of the ontological proof for the existence of God, Kant wishes to show that the word 'is' very often signifies only a logical connection between subject and predicate, and not real existence.[22] 'Thus this "is" is legitimately employed even with the relations impossible entities bear one another. For example, the God of Spinoza is subject to perpetual change.'

22. II, 74.

Even though during this period Kant seldom refers explicitly to Spinoza, there are numerous passages in which he asserts the incompatibility of change with the divine dignity.[23] 'From the proof which I believe I have provided, anyone may very easily draw such obvious conclusions as: I who think am not an absolutely necessary being, for I am not the foundation of all reality, I am changing; no other being whose non-existence is possible, that is, whose removal does not do away with all possibility, no changing or limited thing, not even the world is absolutely necessary; the world is not an *accidens* of the divinity, since conflict, imperfection and change, all contradictories to the determinations of a divinity, are to be found in it.'

However, in taking this view, Kant rejected the only two consistent replies to the question of the mutual relations of the parts in the whole, that is, the transcendental reply of Leibniz or Malebranche, and the immanent pantheism of Spinoza which, as he clearly recognized, led logically to a dialectical philosophy. He had thus to seek a third position.

I interrupt my analysis to pause briefly on the question of the relations between Kant's precritical thought and the Hegelian dialectic. The category of totality stands at the centre of Hegel's dialectical method. I cannot here embark upon a detailed analysis of that method, but this fact seems to me apparent from any of Hegel's works. What sets Hegel apart from all other philosophers since Heraclitus – I am tempted to say what sets him above them – is the fact that for him the fundamental categories themselves are not eternal, rigid and given once and for all, but realize themselves in and through their development. The principal characteristics of the idea of totality in Hegel may be enumerated as follows. The totality is:

1. *concrete and content-full*, in contrast to formal logic and abstract scientific laws;

2. *changing*, in perpetual evolution, in contrast to the 'eternal truths' of abstract atomism;

3. developing by *contradictions*, according to the famous triadic schema: thesis, antithesis and synthesis.

Concrete, content-full, changing, developing by *contradictions*, such are the principal characteristics of the Hegelian totality.

The young Kant, who, as I have shown, had also started from the idea of totality, inevitably encountered the same problems. We have already seen that he shrank from the idea of a changing totality, although he saw clearly that any immanent conception would necessarily lead to this. That is why he adopted an intermediate position, recognizing only the formal and immutable aspects of totality – space, God (and later time) – whilst with regard to content, the empirical given, he resorted to the atomistic monadology of Leibniz.

Thus the question might have been closed: one could imagine Kant never again encountering the problems of *contradictions* and of the *concrete*, the more so since with respect to the purely formal totalities of space and time all change appeared continuous. (To go from one point in space to another, it is necessary to cross all the intermediate points.) That is why it seems to me remarkable that, preoccupied with the problem of totality, he should have encountered these two questions again and that this encounter should have occasioned two short works.

The first is a prize essay for the Academy of Berlin, published in 1764 but written in 1762, entitled: *Enquiry concerning the clarity of the principles of natural theology and ethics.* Although in the title there is no mention of the philosophy of nature, the work begins with a chapter on the distinction, so important for Kant, between 'the manner of achieving certainty in mathematical and in philosophical knowledge'. We already know that in the former emanatist thought is predominant, and in the latter, analytic thought. What seems to me important, however, is that the second section of this first chapter should be entitled: 'Mathematics in its reductions, proofs and conclusions examines the universal under symbols *in concreto*; philosophy examines the universal by means of symbols *in abstracto*.'[24] Even if in the text perhaps a little too much importance is accorded

24. II, 278; *Pre-crit*, 8.

to the 'symbols', it seems nonetheless clear to me that what we have here is the distinction between concrete totality and the abstract empirical given which was to be of such great importance in the thought of Hegel.

In the other work, *An attempt to introduce the concept of negative quantities into philosophy*, which appeared in 1763, Kant attempts to clarify the distinction between logical negation on the one hand and mathematical and real negation on the other, and shows that although logical negation is merely the opposite of assertion, mathematical and real negativities have as much reality as positive elements. Logical contradictions are inconceivable: mathematical oppositions and real contradictions are actual. Deborin, in his studies on the history of the dialectic, has noted that this is one of the earliest expressions of what was to become with Hegel the theory of dialectical contradictions and the critique of formal reason.

Now in spite of this, Kant did not become a dialectical thinker, but the creator of the critical philosophy. What closed the road of the dialectic to him was that he was unable to break with the Platonic and rationalist tradition and to admit a totality subject to development, a 'God subject to perpetual change'. Having thus rejected, for different reasons, the only two logically consistent positions – the transcendent conception of Leibniz and Malebranche and the immanent conception of Spinoza – he had to seek a third and intermediate formula. It is on this basis that we shall be able to understand *The only possible ground for a proof of the existence of God*.

III

I must admit, however, that this text seems to me rather less clear and more hesitant than any other of Kant's works. Moreover, Kant himself seems to realize this. In the preface he is at pains to stress that it is not a definitive opus, but only a preparatory work. He does not provide a proof, but only a 'ground for a proof' of the existence of God.[25] Such lack of precision and elaboration is so rare with Kant that one must ask whether there is not a deeper and more objective reason than those 'other concerns' which left him 'insufficient time'.

I believe that this lack of clarity derives from the fact that in the establishment of his 'ground for a proof' Kant starts from the concept of *whole*, of *universe*, and that this leads him in spite of himself to a position so close to pantheist Spinozism that the distinction becomes merely verbal. It is the continual effort to avoid immanent pantheism which leads him to employ expressions which do not correspond to clearly defined concepts and which, as a result, seem at first sight confused, hesitant and at times even scholastic.

In the analysis of this work, two different elements must be distinguished:

(a) consideration of the views of other philosophers;

(b) Kant's own 'only possible ground for a proof of the existence of God'.

In the preceding pages we have already encountered Kant's criticisms of Leibniz, Malebranche, Wolff and Spinoza. The first part of the work contains in its fully elaborated form the critique of Descartes' ontological proof for the existence of God which, taken up again later in the *Critique of Pure Reason*, has become famous in philosophical literature. 'Existence is not a predicate or a determination of any thing', but 'the absolute positing' of it; that is why one can never prove existence by the analysis of a concept.

The physico-theological proof is then discussed at much greater length in the second part. This penetrating methodological analysis, apart from the obviously dated examples, seems to me even today to retain all its validity. In the dependence of all things upon God, Kant distinguishes two

---

25. 'What I offer here is only the basis of a demonstration, building materials laboriously brought together and submitted to the examination of experts, who may employ those pieces which are useful to construct an edifice according to the rules of durability and adequacy' (II, 66).

'The considerations which I advance are the result of much thought, but the manner of exposition bears the character of an incomplete working out, as various other concerns left insufficient time for it' (ibid.).

dichotomous classifications which, if consistently followed
through, lead to two opposing conceptions of God: the
immanent conception and the *transcendent* conception.

1. The *non-moral* or *moral* dependence of things upon
God.

2. Their dependence upon God *mediated by the natural
order* or *not so mediated*.

Moral dependence *extraneous to the natural order* presupposes *transcendence* and a *conscious will* of God by which
things exist and events occur, things and events which must
therefore be *contingent*. Here two kinds of supernatural
must be distinguished: the *material* supernatural, where the
order of nature is not respected at all; and the *formal* supernatural, where God makes use of this order to attain a particular and contingent goal.

In *non-moral* dependence of things upon God *mediated
by the natural order*, the intention and the conscious will of
God have no part. God is no longer the being who creates
the universe by his will, but only the 'ground of the inner
possibility of things and events which are all *necessary*'. The
latter thus no longer depend upon his *will*, but only find in
his *existence* the ground of their possibility. It seems clear
to me that this considerably reduces the transcendence of
God and, even if Kant does not seem clearly to realize it,
ultimately leads to an immanent conception. A system in
which things do not depend at all upon the will of God, but
only upon his existence becomes hard to distinguish from
pantheism.

What, then, is Kant's attitude towards the *moral* and
supernatural dependence of *contingent* things with respect
to the divine *will*? In principle, a negative one. 'It is a well-
known rule of philosophy, nay rather of sound reason in
general, that nothing should be held to be a miracle or a
supernatural event without the most cogent of reasons.'[26]
Conventional physico-theology has three faults, viz.:[27]

1. 'It considers all perfection, harmony and beauty in
nature as contingent and arranged by wisdom, although

26. II, 108.   27. II, 117–23.

these features frequently result necessarily from the most essential rules of nature.'

2. 'This method is not sufficiently philosophical, and has often greatly hindered the development of philosophical knowledge. A natural circumstance need only be useful to be immediately commonly explained by an intention of the divine will or by a particular and deliberate ordering of nature. . . . Hence, in such cases, bounds are set to the investigation of nature.'

3. 'This method can only serve to demonstrate an author of the connections and artificial combinations of the universe, but not of matter itself or the origin of the constituents of the universe.'[28]

Nevertheless, Kant did not entirely reject this kind of dependence: there were two questions to which he believed that no scientific answer was possible and where he felt obliged to admit the supernatural intervention of divine providence, of the transcendent will of God. These were:

1. The existence of things at all. The investigation of nature can show that the universe as it exists is subject to immutable and necessary laws, but how and why it exists at all is a question outside the province of science. The *connections*, the *laws* which rule the universe may appear necessary to reason; the actual existence of things will always have to be considered *contingent*, a product of the divine will. 'Thus when I assert that God contains the ground of the existence of things, I admit that this dependence is always moral.'[29] 'All things in nature are contingent in their existence.'[30]

---

28. At first sight, this passage seems unclear and in contradiction with what comes after. From the whole, however, two ideas emerge:

(a) The *goal-directedness* of a thing necessitates only a creator of its *form* and not of its matter, which might be uncreated. 'Thus Aristotle and many other philosophers of antiquity explained only form and not matter by divine creation.'

(b) God *by his will* created things, but not *the possibility of things*, upon which their unity and harmony are based and which must exist prior to them.

The two ideas are clear and in no way contradict the argument set out above, but their combination may sometimes lead to confused and unclear formulations.

29. II, 100.   30. II, 106.

2. The existence of *organic* beings. 'Nevertheless, nature is rich in phenomena of another type, for which any philosophy which reflects upon their coming to be finds that it must abandon this way [that of explanation by the natural order]. ... The construction of plants and animals exhibits an arrangement for which the general and necessary laws of nature are inadequate.'[31]

Even here, however, Kant immediately adds two qualifications 'to show the necessity of according to the things of nature a greater power to produce their consequences according to general natural laws than is usually admitted.'[32] These qualifications are:

(a) We must not unconditionally accept a particular intention of the divinity for each organic being. It suffices 'that we recognize in the plants and animals of the original divine creation the ability not only to develop, but actually to procreate others after their kind'.[33]

(b) Even in the production of the freest human actions 'natural rules' play a major part. 'Experience confirms this dependence of even the freest actions upon a great natural rule. For however free the decision to marry may be, we find nevertheless that in any given country the proportion of the married to the living remains approximately constant if one takes large numbers.'[34] Similarly, 'Everyone knows how human freedom can contribute to the lengthening or shortening of life. Nevertheless, this free action must be subject to a greater order, since on average, taking large numbers, the number of the dying stands in a constant ratio to that of the living'(!)[35]

Let us now examine this methodological discussion from the scientific and philosophical point of view.

1. As a scientist, not only was Kant equal to the best of his age, but even in our time a conscientious investigator, not wishing to establish hypotheses without real empirical foundations, would find little to object to in Kant's point of view. Science today still proceeds from the axiom that every change is necessary and must be explained by laws of nature without the intervention of a transcendent God. But it also

---

31. II, 114. 32. II, 115. 33. ibid. 34. II, 111. 35. ibid.

still remains out of place and helpless when faced with Kant's two exceptions, the origin of the universe and the origin of organic life. Out of place in the first, which any serious scientist regards as outside the province of science; helpless in the second, where, in spite of much research and countless experiments, the claim that organic life can be explained on the basis of inorganic matter today seems hardly better founded experimentally than in the time of Kant. This problem still forms the principal argument of vitalism and all teleological philosophies. To avoid any misunderstanding, let me say at once that I do not wish to enter into the debate between mechanistic and vitalistic biology nor to assert or deny the possibility of a future explanation of life in terms of inorganic matter. My claim is merely that even today, for the positive scientist who abides by the results of his experiments, the problem remains open; there is thus no reason to find fault with Kant for being unable or unwilling 180 years ago to affirm the possibility of such explanation. And it must be emphasized that both Kant's qualifications tend to diminish the transcendent intervention of God in our universe by relegating it to the origin of things. Another curious and noteworthy coincidence is that the examples chosen by Kant – marriage and suicide – were later to form the theme of Durkheim's *Suicide*, one of the fundamental works of French scientific sociology.

2. But remarkable though Kant seems to me as a *scientist* here, the *philosophical* conclusions which he draws appear very doubtful. The two problems quoted above, which he finds insoluble for positive science, seem to me to provide no justification whatever for the hypothesis of a transcendent God. From a strictly logical point of view, there is no difference between the hypothesis of a universe which is not created and exists from all eternity (with or without organic life) and the hypothesis that the universe is the creation of a God, similarly not created and existing from all eternity. The first hypothesis seems as incomprehensible as the second, for the question 'Who created the universe and living beings?' is in no way more justified from the logical or epistemological point of view than the question 'Who created God?' It is merely more familiar to us at first sight

because time-honoured religious tradition permeates our thought and our language. As a matter of fact, the hypothesis of an omnipotent God who created the universe by his will, but who since then has had no further influence on its development, seems to me even less comprehensible than that of a universe existing from all eternity and subject to more or less immutable laws.[36]

If, after this analysis, such a profound and rigorous thinker nevertheless accepted the hypothesis of a transcendent God, there must have been other more solid reasons. We shall have occasion to examine these in the following section.[37]

IV

We come now to the 'Only possible ground for a proof' itself. Kant distinguishes four kinds of proof for the existence of God. Two of them, the cosmological proof and the physico-theological proof, proceed from the *existent*; the third, the *ontological* proof, proceeds from the concept of the possible, which, however, is seen as a *principle* from which follows the assertion of the existence of God. Kant's new ground for a proof proceeds from the concept of the *possible as a consequence* to the existence of God as the *foundation* and necessary *principle* of this consequence.

If something is possible, a necessary being must exist, for all possibility 'presupposes some existence'. 'It is easy to see . . . that possibility disappears not only in the case of inner contradiction, of logical impossibility, but also in the case where there is no matter, no datum to be thought. For then there is nothing thinkable, and anything which is

36. Kant makes this point several times: see the third 'fault' of physico-theology cited above.

37. The text also contains a summary of the *Natural history and theory of the heavens*, published much earlier and later to become famous as the 'Kant-Laplace theory'. This theory is relevant to the question of the universe in Kant's philosophy, but I shall leave it aside here, since I am analysing only the philosophical aspects of the category of totality and not its scientific applications.

possible is something which can be thought.'[38] There must be something actual '*in which and through which*[39] everything which may be thought is given'.[40] Its non-existence would remove not only all reality, but further, all possibility. 'If all existence is taken away, nothing whatever is laid down, absolutely nothing is given, there is no matter for anything thinkable, and all possibility wholly disappears.'[41] But this being whose existence is necessary cannot be an individual and limited thing, for the non-existence of such a thing takes away 'not that which is laid down in the thing, but something else, and in this there is therefore never any contradiction'.[42] Only 'that whose suppression or negation removes all possibility is absolutely necessary'.[43]

It seems clear to me that the proof of the existence of God is here developed on the basis of the totality, the *universitas*, which contains not only everything actual but also everything possible. The question remains: how is it that Kant does not end up with the immanent God of pantheism, but on the contrary seems firmly convinced that he has found the ground for a proof of the existence of a transcendent God, the God of the Christian religion? For it is no less clear that Kant does not in the least wish his God to be identified with the universe. 'Though such a being is the most real of all possible beings, in that all others are only possible through it, it is not to be understood by this that all possible reality belongs to its determinations. This is a confusion of ideas which has been remarkably prevalent.'[44] For the God of pantheism would not only be subject to perpetual change: he would even possess negative or contradictory attributes.

This seems to me to be the weakest point of the work. For between that 'in which and through which everything which may be thought is given' and 'whose suppression or negation removes all possibility' and the God of whom it is stressed that 'not . . . all possible reality belongs to its determinations' there seems to be a contradiction which it will not be easy to resolve. Kant believes he can do this by

38. II, 78.   39. My italics. – L. G.   40. II, 83.   41. II, 78.
42. II, 82.   43. II, 83.   44. II, 85.

describing God not as a *concept embracing* all things, but as the *foundation of the inner possibility* of things. As I have said, this seems to me to be a purely verbal distinction, corresponding to no clear and precise content, and I cannot see how this conception even partially dissolves or overcomes the difficulties confronting Kant. The question will still remain: how can a God who is immutable, purely positive and devoid of contradictions constitute the foundation of the inner possibility of a world of changing things with negative and contradictory attributes?

Here, however, I must refer again to a consideration which was to acquire its full significance only later, in the critical period, but which no doubt even at this stage played some part in Kant's thought. What separates Kant from pantheism and immanence is not only the problems of change and of negative and contradictory attributes; it is also, and perhaps above all, the conviction that an immanent conception would mean the obligation to choose between the *totality* and the *individuals*, without ever being able to unite them. If the immanent given is a whole, a universe, then individuals, monads, no longer have any true reality; if, on the contrary, they are indeed real, then the whole is no longer a universe but only an aggregate of monads. Now Kant wished at all costs to retain the two elements in a synthetic unity.

Whilst I cannot here embark upon a discussion of this problem, it seems to me that the hypothesis of a transcendent God can no more provide a solution to this than to the earlier problems. For the same question then arises in a scarcely changed form: how can a unique, eternal and immutable God give rise to countless autonomous and changing individuals? However this may be, Kant doubtless retained for some time the illusion that he had found a new synthetic view, intermediate between absolute transcendence and pure immanence. But he was bound sooner or later to recognize his mistake and to abandon this conception. As we know, this occurred not long afterwards.

However, it is essential for us to see the considerable importance of the idea of totality, of the whole, in this, the first of Kant's theological writings, and how, precisely by means of this idea, his thought may be distinguished from the conceptions of God of most earlier philosophers (Descartes, Leibniz, Aristotle).

Although all this seems clear enough, especially in the light of the passages quoted above where Kant relates God to the whole, I should nevertheless like to mention one more argument, drawn from one of the later works of Kant himself, namely, from the *Critique of Pure Reason*.

In the Transcendental Dialectic, Chapter III of Book II speaks of 'the transcendental ideal', that is, the idea of God. Sections 4, 5 and 6 deal with 'the impossibility of an ontological, cosmological and physico-theological proof of the existence of God' and are probably known to most readers, if not in the original text at least through some of the innumerable studies which have been devoted to them. The majority of the neo-Kantians, however, barely paused upon the rather curious fact that whereas the text of 1763 spoke of four proofs of the existence of God, Kant here recognizes and discusses only three. Nor did they pause on the fact that Sections 2 and 3, entitled 'The transcendental ideal' and 'The arguments of speculative reason in proof of the existence of a supreme being', deal with a further proof which corresponds in large measure to the fourth proof of 1763, except that Kant now speaks much more clearly on almost every line of the *whole* and of the *totality*.

Would it be over-bold to claim that Kant is here unmasking and analysing his own 'illusions' of the precritical period, and that he can now describe his earlier arguments with far greater precision if only because, having passed them, he is no longer afraid of coming too close to pantheism? At any rate, purely external arguments speak in favour of this hypothesis: for example, the appearance of the expression 'ground for a proof (*Beweisgrund*)' in the title of the work of 1763 just as in that of Section 3, or the position of this analysis *before* the other three proofs.

But these are merely external considerations. Let us now examine the content of the two sections a little more closely. Section 2, especially, could be quoted here in its entirety, so frequently does Kant there speak explicitly of the whole and of totality. He first distinguishes the *logical determination of* (*abstract*) *concepts* from the *complete determination of* (*concrete*) *individual things*. The latter 'does not rest merely on the law of contradiction, for, besides considering each thing in its relation to the two contradictory predicates, it also considers it in its relation to *the sum-total of all possibilities*, that is, to the sum-total of all predicates of things'.[45] 'In accordance with this principle, each and every thing is therefore related to a common correlate, the sum of all possibilities. If this correlate (that is, the material for all possible predicates) should be found in the idea of some one thing, it would prove an affinity of all possible things, through the identity of the ground of their complete determination. Whereas the *determinability* of every *concept* is subordinate to the *universality* (*universalitas*) . . . the *determination* of a *thing* is subordinate to the *totality* (*universitas*) or sum of all possible predicates.'[46] Kant expresses himself much more clearly here than in 1763. The key to the argument is in the relation of everything to the totality, the *universitas*. This is repeated and stressed several times in different forms. 'All manifoldness of things is only a correspondingly varied mode of limiting the concept of the highest reality which forms their common substratum, just as all figures are only possible as so many different modes of limiting absolute space.'[47]

If Kant can now express himself so distinctly, it is because, as I have said, he no longer accepts this argument. Again he demonstrates how one passes from the 'whole' to the 'ground of the possible'. 'The derivation of all other possibility from this primordial being cannot, strictly speaking, be regarded as a *limitation* of its supreme reality, and, as it were, a *division* of it. For in that case the primordial being would be treated as a mere aggregate of derivative beings; and this, as we have just shown, is impossible, although in our first rough statements we have used such language. On the contrary, the supreme reality must condition the possibility of all things as their *ground*, not as their *sum*.'[48]

But all this is mere dialectical illusion. For 'It is obvious that reason . . . does not presuppose the existence of a being

45. III, 385; *Pure R*, 488; B 600.   46. III, 386; *Pure R*, 488; B 600.
47. III, 389; *Pure R*, 492; B 606.   48. III, 390; *Pure R*, 492–3; B 607.

that corresponds to this ideal, but only the idea of such a being.'[49] 'If . . . we proceed to hypostatize it . . . In any such use of the transcendental idea we should . . . be overstepping the limits of its purpose and validity.'[50]

This second section finishes with a reflection which is extremely important for an understanding of the critical philosophy. After having thus analysed the former argument and laid bare the dialectical illusion which engenders it, Kant asks whether this reasoning might not be natural, and, implicitly, whether the empirical use of the category of totality could not, apart from this dialectical illusion, have an epistemologically legitimate foundation. He comes to the conclusion that such is indeed the case in *empirical knowledge of phenomena*, where 'nothing is an object *for us*, unless it presupposes the sum of all empirical reality as the condition of its possibility'.[51]

The third section begins by summarizing once more the argument of *The only possible ground*. 'If we admit something as existing, no matter what this something may be, we must also admit that there is something which exists *necessarily*.'[52] 'Such, then, is the natural procedure of human reason. It begins by persuading itself of the existence of *some* necessary being. This being it apprehends as having an existence that is unconditioned. It then looks around for the concept of that which is independent of any condition, and finds it in that which is itself the sufficient condition of all else, that is, in that which contains all reality. But that which is all-containing and without limits is absolute unity, and involves the concept of a single being that is likewise the supreme being. Accordingly, we conclude that the supreme being, as primordial ground of all things, must exist by absolute necessity.'[53]

There follows a much fuller discussion and refutation of this argument than that of the preceding section. 'If what we have in view is the *coming to a decision* . . . then the foregoing way of thinking must be allowed to have a certain

49. III, 389; *Pure R*, 491; B 605-6. 50. III, 390; *Pure R*, 493; B 608.
51. III, 391; *Pure R*, 494; B 610. 52. III, 393; *Pure R*, 496; B 612.
53. III, 394; *Pure R*, 497; B 614-15.

cogency. . . . If, however, we are not required to come to any decision, and prefer to leave the issue open . . . then the foregoing argument is far from appearing in so advantageous a light.'[54] Further, even if we accept '*first*, that from any given existence (it may be merely my own existence) we can correctly infer the existence of an unconditionally necessary being; *secondly*, that we must regard a being which contains all reality, and therefore every condition, as being absolutely unconditioned . . . it by no means follows that the concept of a limited being . . . is for that reason incompatible with absolute necessity.'[55]

Having shown that the argument from the idea of totality to a unique God is not logically impeccable, Kant concludes the section with a foretaste of a *practical* and *moral* proof of the existence of God.

I hope that I have adequately shown in what large measure the theological work of 1763 has its point of departure in the idea of totality, and what exceptional importance must be attributed to that idea even at this stage in the development of Kant's thought. This is what distinguishes him from the majority of his predecessors – from Descartes, from Leibniz and from Aristotle – and what makes him a truly independent and original thinker. What nonetheless held him back from a thoroughgoing philosophy of totality was the dangerous relation of such a philosophy to Spinozan pantheism and an immanent conception of God.[56]

54. III, 394; *Pure R*, 497–8; B 615.

55. III, 395; *Pure R*, 498; B 615–16.

56. One final point still requires clarification. How can the two sections just analysed be reconciled with the title which follows them: '*There are only three possible ways of proving the existence of God by means of speculative reason*'? These are, of course, the ontological, cosmological and physico-theological proofs which are examined in Sections 4, 5 and 6. Are the arguments developed in Sections 2 and 3 also part of these three proofs? Or do they constitute a fourth? Was Kant guilty of unnecessary repetition or did he contradict himself? And why, when there were *four* proofs in 1763, are there now only *three*?

It seems to me that the answer to these questions is to be found in the expressions employed by Kant: *ground* for a proof of *the existence of a supreme being*, and *way* of proving *the existence of God*. Kant himself expresses here what I pointed out at the beginning of this section. The 'ground for a proof' does not allow us to conclude more than the existence of a supreme being, which can be the immanent totality of pantheism just as easily as, if not more

V

Three years after *The only possible ground* a work appeared
which represents an extremely important step in the history
not only of Kant's thought but of German idealism in
general: *Dreams of a visionary explained by the dreams of
metaphysics*. The idea of totality is there for the first time
applied directly to the knowledge of man, leading to the
admittedly still rudimentary elaboration of the principal
categories of the later critical philosophy, viz.:

  (a) the *community*, which is divided into:
  i. *the community of spirits*, already referred to as *the
  intelligible world*, and
  ii. *the imperfect community of men*.
These are the first forms of what will later become not
only the intelligible world and the sensible world in Kant,
but also the 'in itself' and the 'in and for itself' of spirit in
Hegel, true and false consciousness in Lukács, and authentic
and inauthentic existence in Heidegger.

  (b) The contradictory nature not only of human society
but of the human character in general, which Kant will later
call the 'unsocial sociability' of man. It must be stressed,
however, that Kant is speaking of *man in general* and not
merely of a certain *historical* type of man.

  (c) *Hope for the future*, which is here put forward only as
Kant's own point of view, but which later, in the Kant of the
critical philosophy and in Hegel, Marx and Lukács, will
increasingly become the foundation of all real philosophy.

  The work begins with a preliminary note indicating the
reasons which induced such a sober, rational thinker to
publish a work on the dreams of a visionary.[57] There are
two:

---

easily than, the transcendent God of the Christian religion. It is as valid for
the God of Spinoza as for the God of Leibniz, Descartes or Aquinas. Transcendence comes only in the three proofs which follow, but for them the
existence of a supreme being is a necessary presupposition. That is why the
'ground for a proof' is dealt with first. It must however be admitted that in
the development of these five sections this separation is not carried through
in a strict and rigorous manner.

57. The visionary was Swedenborg, against whom the work is directed.

1. The attack upon the fantasies of Swedenborg is at the same time an attack on the Roman Catholic church and those governments which, for reasons of State, give it their support.[58] 'The kingdom of shadows is the paradise of dreamers . . . hypochondriac vapours, nursery-tales and miracle stories provide no shortage of materials. The philosophers trace out the plan, changing or rejecting it as is their custom. Only Holy *Rome* there has lucrative provinces; the two crowns of the invisible realm support the third as the corruptible diadem of its earthly majesty, and the keys which open both gates to the other world open also the coffers of the present one.'[59] Unfortunately, it is usually impossible to attack the arguments of the church, for 'The pretensions of the kingdom of spirits, in that it is established for reasons of state, are raised high above the impotent objections of schoolmen, and their use or misuse is already too respectable for them to have to submit to such ignominious examination.' That is why one must be content with 'vulgar tales' which 'are not supported by the argument from advantage (*argumentum ab utili*), which is the most convincing of all'.[60]

2. Kant deals with Swedenborg seriously and without prejudice, for 'to believe *nothing* without a reason . . . is as stupid a prejudice . . . as to believe *everything* without examination'.[61] But his efforts led to no positive results. 'He found – as is usual where there is nothing to look for – he found nothing.' However, 'a large book had been bought, and what was worse, read, and this labour was not to be lost'. To that was added 'the insistence of friends known and unknown'. Thus the work was born.

---

58. It would be quite wrong, however, to take this attack upon the Catholic church too literally, and to see Kant as a faithful Protestant wishing only to attack that particular church. It is obvious that the attack is aimed at *all* the churches. But in Protestant Prussia, of course, despite the 'freedom of religion' under Frederick the Great, only the Roman Catholic church and those governments which supported it could be publicly attacked. In the letter cited above which Kant sent with the work to Moses Mendelssohn, he wrote: 'Although I am absolutely convinced of many things that I shall never have the courage to say, I shall never say anything I do not believe' (*Phil. Corr*, 54). It seems to me that there is no room for misunderstanding here.

59. II, 317.   60. ibid.   61. II, 318.

However, these were merely external reasons. Did the work not have its origins in a deeper philosophical necessity? I believe that it did. This seems to be indicated in the very title: 'Dreams of a visionary explained by the dreams of metaphysics.' The visionary is Swedenborg, but who is the metaphysician? On reading the work, it is clear that it is Kant himself. He had cherished all the hopes which he describes in the second part; it was in seeking positive empirical confirmation for his own hopes that he had become interested in the strange tales of Swedenborg. And if he produced an entire work on the subject, it was not only because Swedenborg turned out to be no more than an extravagant dreamer, but also because Kant himself now doubted the justification and the grounds for his own hopes, and, with heavy heart, had to admit that perhaps, or even probably, these too were only 'dreams'. But that Kant had not yet completely renounced those dreams is evident from the detailed manner in which he describes them, from the undefinitive nature of his conclusions, and above all from the retention, though admittedly with modifications, of these ideas (community, intelligible world) in the critical philosophy.

I could quote here the entire second section of the work; lack of space, however, obliges me to be content with a few examples. In the first subsection, Kant explains what is denoted by the word 'spirit', and asserts that, by the existence of living beings, we are persuaded 'if not with the conviction of a demonstration, at least with the presentiment of a not unexercised understanding, of the existence of immaterial beings, whose special laws of action will be called *pneumatic*, and, inasmuch as corporeal beings are the intermediate causes of their actions in the material world, *organic*'.[62] 'Since these immaterial beings are self-acting principles . . . the conclusion to which we first come is this, that they are directly united together, making perhaps one great whole, which can be called the immaterial world (*mundus intelligibilis*).'[63] 'This *immaterial world* may thus be regarded as a whole subsisting for itself, whose parts are in mutual

62. II, 329. 63. ibid.

connection and community . . . with the result that their relations mediated by matter are merely contingent and rest upon particular divine arrangements, whilst their community is natural and indissoluble.'[64]

It could thus be imagined that 'even in this life the human soul is in indissoluble community with all the immaterial natures of the spirit world . . . but of which as man it is unconscious, so long as all is going well'.[65] There would be a strict separation: *qua* human soul bound to the body, it would have no knowledge and no memory of the intelligible world of spirits; conversely, *qua* integral part of the intelligible world, it would have no access to the material world. It would thus have a sort of 'dual personality', an illustration which indeed Kant himself uses.

But how does the metaphysician arrive at such dreams and hopes? It is knowledge of the real human community, of what Kant will later call the 'unsocial sociability' of man, which impels him. 'Among the forces which move the human heart, some of the most powerful would seem to lie outside it, forces which consequently do not merely relate as means to self-interest and personal need as to an end which lies *inside* the man himself, but which act so that the tendencies of our emotions have the focus of their union *outside us*, in other rational beings. There thus arises a conflict of two forces, namely of egoism, which relates everything to self, and of the general utility, by which the mind is impelled or drawn towards beings other than itself.'[66] 'A mysterious power impels us to direct our attention towards the good of another, or according to the choice of another, although this often goes against the grain and is in violent opposition to our selfish inclinations; the point at which the directions of our impulses converge is therefore not simply within us: there are other forces which move us in the wills of others outside us.'[67] 'In this we see ourselves dependent in our most secret motives upon the *rule of the general will*, and there results in the world of all thinking natures a *moral unity* and a systematic constitution according to purely spiritual laws.'[68]

64. II, 330.   65. II, 333.   66. II, 334.   67. ibid.   68. II, 335.

Kant believes it possible that man's moral sentiments may be merely a consequence of this natural and perfect community of spirits to which the soul belongs. 'Would it not be possible to imagine the appearance of moral impulses in thinking natures, as they are mutually related one to another, as the result of a truly active force by which spiritual natures flow into one another, so that moral feelings . . . could be a consequence of the natural and general interaction by which the immaterial world attains its moral unity?'[69] The imperfection and the insufficiency of the community and of the morality of men in the sensible world would thus be explicable, and after death the soul would continue its existence in a natural and indissoluble community of spirits and would achieve perfect morality. Moreover – a point of great importance – all this would occur 'according to the order of nature'. 'This last circumstance is of particular importance. For in a conjecture based wholly upon reason, it is a great difficulty if, to avoid the inconvenience which arises from the imperfect harmony between morality and its consequences in this world, it is necessary to take refuge in an extraordinary and divine will.'[70] Here Kant gives overt expression to what I believe is an essential element for the understanding of the critical philosophy of religion, namely that the postulation of the existence of God is only a philosophical substitute for the *immanent totality* which seemed impossible to attain in its two principal forms: the *universe* and above all the *human community*.

Such were the dreams of the metaphysician. And Kant explains that if they were well-founded, there could be exceptional men having certain relations with and a certain knowledge of the spirit world. Such men would appear to others, to normal men, as dreamers and visionaries, but would in fact be the most valuable confirmation of metaphysical hopes. That is why Kant undertook such a thorough examination of Swedenborg's works.

The third section, however, shows us the other side of the coin. It is also quite possible that the fantastic claims of the visionary are not founded upon real knowledge of the spirit

69. ibid.   70. II, 337.

world, but are the much more banal effect of simple organic disturbances, just as the metaphysical developments might be the expression not of well-founded hopes, but merely of the subjective desires of the thinker. For 'the balance of the understanding is not wholly impartial, and one of its arms, which bears the inscription *hope for the future*, has a mechanical advantage such that even slight reasons falling into its pan will raise the other, loaded with speculations far weightier in themselves. This is the sole error which I cannot and indeed would not wish to remove.'[71] Experience will never be able to decide definitively between the two possibilities. For here there is no *knowledge*, but only *opinion*. Kant clearly holds that the second alternative is the more probable and believes that these hopes are only dreams.

Nevertheless, he cannot bring himself entirely to renounce 'hope for the future' and to eliminate it completely. 'The reader is free to judge; but for my part, the reasons of the second section are sufficient to turn the scales at least so that I remain gravely undecided on hearing the many strange tales of this kind' – this, however, with 'the usual but curious reservation that I doubt each individual one, yet give some credit to them all, taken together'.[72] However this may be, the value of the work lies in having established a clear distinction between *knowledge* and *opinion*.

Part II contains an analysis of Swedenborg's work and shows him to be merely a magniloquent dreamer, possessing no real knowledge of the spirit world and consequently unable to communicate it to others.

As I have said, *Dreams of a visionary* seems to me to constitute a decisive point in the development not only of Kant's thought but of German idealism in general. The idea of totality is here directly applied to the knowledge of man and of human life, thus establishing the basic concepts of German idealism in moral philosophy, the philosophy of religion, and the philosophy of history, namely:

1. Inadequate empirical human existence is contrasted with another, ideal existence, hoped for in the future and *qualitatively* different from the first. This contrast is central

not only for the mature Kant, but also for Hegel (the 'in itself' and 'for itself' of spirit), Marx, Lukács and Heidegger.

2. The means of transcending this inadequate existence are no longer sought in the individual but in the totality, in the perfect *community*; that is why this work seems to me infinitely superior to those of so many later philosophers.

3. Kant sees and expresses clearly how the possibility of an *immanent* overcoming of the limits of individual existence by means of the community renders superfluous the 'great difficulty' of the intervention of a transcendent God. God becomes no more than the theological expression of man's aspiration towards a perfect community. Kant thus indicates the possibility of a future replacement of the philosophy of religion by a philosophy of history, a substitution later accomplished in part by Hegel and completed by Marx and Lukács.

4. The basis of all German humanism and perhaps of all true philosophy – 'hope for the future' – is thus established, although for the moment it is subjective, valid only for the author himself ('the reader is free to judge').

Kant thus opened the path which humanist thought was to follow thereafter, and which indeed it still follows today.

VI

Ten years had passed between the *Monadologia physica* and *Dreams of a visionary*, ten years during which a number of important conclusions had accumulated in Kant's mind. In conscious opposition to his rationalist and dogmatic predecessors, Kant had adopted the idea of totality as the point of departure and centre of his philosophical thought. Thus he had arrived at the 'new ground for a proof', that is to say, at a new if somewhat confused conception of God. Above all, he had restored to the concepts of *universe* and *community* their true significance for philosophical thought. These remarkable results, which have retained their decisive influence on the European mind to the present day, would be sufficient in themselves to make Kant one of the most important of modern thinkers.

Furthermore, in considering the universe and the community from the point of view of totality, Kant had arrived
at a distinction which embodied the very essence of developing bourgeois society and thus of European man for 150
years to come: the distinction between *form* and *content*.[73]
In the knowledge of the *universe*, he had distinguished the
content, the autonomous and independent monads, from
the *formal whole* constituted by infinitely divisible space,
which is not composed of simple parts; the *concrete content-
full totality* had to be relegated to his new and rather
problematic conception of God, to the 'ground of all inner
possibility'. In the knowledge of *human society*, he had distinguished moral forces from the forces of self-interest, and
again the *perfect content-full totality* had to be located in the
no less problematic 'community of spirits', the 'intelligible
world'. Thus, a number of decisive elements in the later
critical philosophy had already been established. And in
Dreams of a visionary we even find certain basic ideas of the
critical aesthetics, although as yet in a negative form.[74]

However, all these elements remained isolated. They did
not yet form a system, but indeed appeared totally independent of one another. Moreover, their systematic combination was to present insuperable difficulties so long as
Kant hesitated to carry through a radical and general separation between the formal totality and the concrete content-
full totality (assuming that he would not and could not

73. This distinction in Kant's philosophy must not be confused with a similar distinction in Aristotle and Aquinas. To show the difference, it is sufficient
to mention that for the latter the central problem was how a given *content*
acquired its form, whilst for Kant the question is how an empty *form* acquires
the content which fills it.

74. According to Kant, there may exceptionally be men who can acquire
a certain knowledge of the intelligible world, of the perfect community of
spirits. However, this could not occur through logical and theoretical knowledge, but solely because spiritual representations 'pass into personal human
consciousness, not immediately but in such a way that in conformity with
the law of association of ideas they awake in us pictures and analogous sensible
representations which, though not themselves spiritual concepts, are nonetheless their symbols. In this way, ideas imparted by spiritual influences are
clothed in the signs of everyday *speech*, the felt presence of a spirit takes on a
human form, the order and beauty of the immaterial world appear as fancies
which delight our senses in everyday life, and so on' (11, 338–9).

accept an immanent and dialectical conception). In a post-humous fragment, Kant himself indicates how difficult and complicated all these problems then appeared to him. 'At the beginning I saw this system as it were in twilight. I sought earnestly to prove certain propositions along with their contradictories, not to erect a sceptical doctrine, but, because I suspected an illusion of the understanding, to discover where it lay hidden. The year '69 brought great enlightenment.'[75]

From these labours and from the 'enlightenment' of 1769 was born the Inaugural Dissertation of 1770, *On the form and principles of the sensible and intelligible world*. We are accustomed to regard this as the first critical work in that the distinction between sensibility and understanding is completely developed, or, as it is often put, the Transcendental Aesthetic is wholly worked out.

In that form, the assertion is not quite correct, for the following reasons:

First, the distinction between understanding and reason ('real' and 'logical' employment of the intellect) is not yet fully elaborated.

Secondly, we are not yet primarily concerned, as in the *Critique of Pure Reason*, with the distinction between two faculties of the mind, but rather with the distinction between the two worlds to which they correspond. The distinction between the two faculties is, of course, developed *implicitly*.

Thirdly, it would also be incorrect to say that the distinction between the sensible world and the intelligible world is made here *for the first time*. As we have seen, it already formed the central point of *Dreams of a visionary*.

Nevertheless, those who see this work as a decisive step in the development of the critical philosophy are not mistaken, for in the extension of the distinction between the sensible world and the intelligible world from the human and moral totality, the *community*, to the natural totality, the *universe*, the different and seemingly independent achievements of Kant's thought over the preceding ten years are at last combined in a general system. Moreover, the parallel between the theoretical and the practical employment of reason, that cornerstone of the critical philosophy, at last appears.

What, then, are the general features of Kant's system in the Dissertation?

The work begins with the definition of the concept of a world. 'In a substantial composite, just as analysis does not come to an end until a part is reached which is not a whole, that is to say a *simple*, so likewise synthesis does not come to an end until we reach a whole which is not a part, that is to say a *world*.'[76] A world is thus 'a whole which is not a part'. In this exposition Kant also pays some attention to its 'twofold genesis'. 'Thus it is one thing, given the parts, to conceive for oneself the *composition* of the whole, by means of an abstract notion of the intellect; and it is another thing to *follow up* this general *notion* . . . through the sensible faculty of knowledge, that is to represent the same notion to oneself in the concrete by a distinct intuition.'[77] Kant thus recognizes that knowledge of the perfect content-full totality cannot be attained through the senses, although *reason* requires it absolutely. This is one of the starting-points of his system.[78]

In what follows we learn that in the definition of a world three moments require attention:

'1. *Matter* (in the transcendental sense), that is the *parts*. These are here taken to be *substances*.'[79] On this point, it must be added that 'Given several substances *the principle of the interaction* possible between them does not consist in their existence alone.'[80] Atomized matter, monads, sensations *alone* do not constitute a world.

'2. *Form*, which consists in the *co-ordination* of substances, not in their subordination. . . . This co-ordination is con-

76. 11, 387; *Pre-crit*, 47.

77. ibid.

78. See the letter to Garve of 21 September 1798. 'It was not the investigation of the existence of God, immortality, and so on, but rather the antinomy of pure reason . . . that is what first aroused me from my dogmatic slumber' (*Phil. Corr*, 252).

79. 11, 389; *Pre-crit*, 50.

80. 11, 407; *Pre-crit*, 75.

ceived of as *real* and objective, not as ideal and depending on the mere whim of a subject. . . . For by taking several things together you achieve without difficulty a *whole* of *representation*, but not thereby the *representation of a whole*.'[81]

'3. *Totality*, which is the *absolute* allness of its component parts.'[82] The latter 'thorny question' constitutes 'a crux for the philosopher'. One can only extricate oneself by starting out from the fact that *sensible intuition* is not implied in the *intellectual* concept of a whole. 'It is sufficient for this concept that co-ordinates should be given, no matter how, and that they should be all thought of as pertaining to one thing.'[83]

We thus have:

1. (a) *atomized matter*, and

(b) the *form* which confers upon it a purely formal unity, both given by the senses.

2. The rational concept of *absolute totality*, whose validity for Kant is still based upon the validity of the two sensible elements. To denote these, the terms *phenomena* and *noumena*, things 'as they appear' and 'as they are', are already employed.

In the field of sensibility, a distinction is made between pure intuition, whose principles are *space* and *time* and upon which pure mathematics (pure geometry, mechanics, arithmetic, etc.) is based, and empirical intuition, containing sensations, which is the basis of the natural sciences, of physics and of psychology. In the field of the intellect, a distinction is made between its *logical* use (in the critical philosophy, the understanding) which, united with sensibility, gives rise to experience, and its *real* use (in the critical philosophy, reason) whose aim is knowledge of the totality. The highest intellectual concepts are, in the theoretical field, *God*, and in the practical field, *moral perfection*.

At first sight, Kant seems with this work to have come very close to the critical philosophy. There is, however, still a considerable difference, in that Kant here argues *from the sensible, from phenomena, to the intelligible, to noumena.*

81. II, 390; *Pre-crit*, 51.
82. II, 391; *Pre-crit*, 53 (translation slightly amended).
83. II, 392; *Pre-crit*, 54.

As is well known, most of the neo-Kantians reproached Kant with having contradicted himself in asserting that causation is a category of the understanding valid only within the realm of sensible experience, whilst employing it himself beyond that experience when he admits the thing in itself as the necessary *cause* of phenomena. Here in the Dissertation he probably comes closest to such a conception, but even here the difference between Kant's thought and the neo-Kantian interpretation is still very great, for:

1. Kant does not argue from phenomena to the intelligible world as their necessary cause, but only from their *a priori form*, from space and time. Because there is a formal *totality*, because there are 'principles of the form of the sensible world' by which 'all substances and their states belong to the same whole which is called *a world*',[84] he can argue for the totality as the sole cause of that whole.[85]

2. Here in the Dissertation such reasoning is however *in no way contradictory*, for the categories of the understanding have not been set out and recognized as such and thus the employment of the concept of cause is not yet limited to experience.

From the *Critique of Pure Reason* onwards, this argument will be not only abandoned, but even reversed. The critical system argues *not from phenomena to the thing in itself*, but conversely *from the thing in itself, from the intelligible, to the phenomenal character of all empirical reality*. But this did not prevent Bruno Bauch even in 1923 from reproaching Kant with a logical contradiction which existed only in his own imagination, thus demonstrating the extent to which he had misunderstood Kant's thought.

It is significant that even here Kant notes the possibility of reversing his argument: 'If, as the inference is valid from a given world to the unique cause of its parts, so also conversely the argument proceeded similarly from a given cause common to them all to the bond between them and so to the

84. 11, 398; *Pre-crit*, 62.
85. This also explains the remark mentioned above, in which Kant indicates the possibility that space might be *phenomenal omnipresence*, which is not far from Malebranche's view, 'namely that we intuit all things in God' (11, 409–10; *Pre-crit*, 79).

form of the world (although I confess that this conclusion does not seem equally clear to me). . . .'[86] In this form, it was not only less clear, but quite simply impossible. How it was developed in the critical philosophy we shall have occasion to see in the second part of this work.

86. II, 409; *Pre-crit*, 77.

Part II

Chapter 1
The Critical Philosophy
and its Problems

In presenting the critical philosophy, I shall be able to use a quite different method from that employed so far. The Kant of the precritical period was almost unknown to most readers and even to those with a more specialized interest in philosophy. I was thus obliged to quote the actual texts as much as possible, the more so since most of the neo-Kantians who studied them had overlooked the essential points – hence the numerous quotations and chronological order.

With the critical philosophy, the situation is reversed. There are numerous critical works on the subject, and anyone interested in philosophy will have read the principal texts or at least some exposition of their content. I have no intention of adding to the many detailed works on Kant's philosophy with a work of the same nature. Whilst such a work is certainly necessary and would be extremely useful, it would demand considerable labour and would grossly overstep the limits I have set myself. For the moment, I shall be content to study the essential points at which the neo-Kantian interpretation and that of the nineteenth century in general have distorted Kant's thought and which I believe need to be put into their true perspective. Since we are not concerned with questions of detail but with the most important general features of Kant's system, I shall assume some knowledge of the texts and shall thus be able to adopt a form of exposition less burdened with quotations.

I

I must begin, however, with a biographical question, that of the almost complete silence from Kant which followed the Inaugural Dissertation. For between 1770 and the appearance of the *Critique of Pure Reason* in 1781 Kant published only four philosophically insignificant little essays.

In the first place, there is doubtless a purely external reason for this. Kant had finally become a professor, thus escaping his most pressing material worries. From even a superficial acquaintance with his works, one can appreciate how hard it must have been for Kant before the Dissertation to bring himself to publish in an unfinished state all those painful attempts to achieve clarity. Kant who, with Spinoza and Marx, was one of the most rigorous and honest thinkers of modern philosophy and who henceforth would publish nothing which he did not believe to be definitive and solidly established could certainly have done this only reluctantly. But publication was a pressing external necessity, for he was poor[1] and without personal fortune. Up to the age of 46 he lived from the proceeds of his lessons, to which from 1766 he added a miserable stipend from the badly paid and time-consuming job of assistant librarian. His only hope of material security lay in the prospect of a university chair, and this he could only hope to obtain by publication. He thus had no choice. After 1770, however, his material situation was sufficiently assured for him to defer publication to a time when, having worked out his system, he could offer to the reader a work which he regarded as definitive.

All this, however, is secondary and does not suffice to explain Kant's silence; for we have seen that in the Dissertation he had already found a more or less general system. There must thus have been a more important reason for the eleven years of silence. That reason was his encounter with the ideas of David Hume.

Attempts have been made (by Alois Riehl in particular) to place Hume's influence on Kant much earlier, in the pre-critical period. But such attempts seem to me to fail completely, even though all the facts cited by Riehl appear correct or at any rate plausible. Even if Kant was indeed acquainted with the writings of Hume before 1770 and

---

1. Although he later contested this in order to prevent an indiscreet publication.

spoke of them in his lectures, as Herder testifies, and even if, consciously or not, he used expressions borrowed from Hume in his own writings, I do not regard this as sufficient proof of any decisive and profound influence. For the influence of one thinker upon another does not date from the first reading, nor even from the first borrowing of a few expressions, but only from the time when the ideas of the first become obstacles or essential contributions to the thought of the second. This was certainly not the case with Kant and Hume during the precritical period. As we have seen, that period was dominated by the arguments with dogmatic rationalism, with Leibniz, Wolff, Descartes, Malebranche and Spinoza. Kant nowhere states his position with regard to empiricism.

In the critical period, however, the situation is very different. There are countless passages in both the theoretical and the practical writings which refer overtly or implicitly to Hume and appear primarily directed against him. What had happened? Why had Hume's philosophy, empiricism, acquired such importance at this point?

The question is not difficult to answer when one recalls that Hume had directed his attacks against the concept of *cause*, and that even in the earliest of Kant's works, but above all in the Dissertation, the whole edifice of the intelligible world rested upon this concept. It is because the form of the sensible world (space and time) must have a cause that there necessarily exists an intelligible world, a God, said Kant. 'Cause' merely denotes an empirical association of ideas; we thus have no right, on the basis of this concept, to deduce the existence of something which cannot be empirically given, asserted Hume.

Nor could Hume's philosophy admit the second possibility mentioned by Kant, that of arguing from the intelligible world to the sensible world. Hume, with his atomistic conception of the world, denied the existence and the possibility of any totality (except in mathematics, a point to which I shall return).

Kant naturally recognized the importance of empiricism and of the fundamental objections to his own doctrine which could be drawn from it. That is why he had to clarify his position with regard to Hume. To judge from the eleven years of silence, the internal debate was long and arduous. We know absolutely nothing of the manner in which it was carried out, for the letters to Marcus Herz of that period tell us little. We can only judge from the results, that is, from the *Critique of Pure Reason.*

From the outset, it must be noted that, under the weight of the empiricist arguments, Kant had been forced to make essential modifications to his system. Henceforward he will eschew any transcendent employment of the concept of causality. The latter becomes a category of the understanding and its use is no longer legitimate outside the field of experience. If Kant now so frequently protests at any transgression of these limits, this constitutes an attack not only upon Descartes, Leibniz and Wolff, but also and above all upon his own position in the Dissertation.

But what of the other form of argument, that which starts with the totality, the *universitas,* and concludes with phenomena? During the critical period, in the arguments with the dogmatic rationalists, it was generally agreed that there was a real and necessary bond between the elements of the universe, that the totality actually existed. This was a tacit assumption common to all and doubted by none. Kant could therefore object to Leibniz and to Malebranche that this bond could not be established merely externally by a pre-established harmony or by continuous divine action, and that consequently, to be indeed real, it must be situated in the elements themselves. He could object to Descartes that it was illegitimate to argue from concept to existence, and to Spinoza that the totality could not contain the individual and limited elements since it was immutable and they subject to change. We have seen what difficulties he then encountered in defining this totality which was neither wholly transcendent nor wholly immanent.

Faced with Hume, however, Kant realized that empiricism would, or at any rate could, accept all these arguments, but that it would draw from them an extremely dangerous conclusion: that there exists *no totality.* There is no *theoretical* totality, because human knowledge is restricted to *factual* connections resulting from habit and the association of ideas. There is no *practical* totality, because we have no right to argue from what is to the possibility of a better or higher existence, the empirical given being the only true and legitimate source of knowledge.

Now, the very possibility of a transcendental system depended upon the refutation of this thesis. But here, too, Kant had to concede a great deal. He had never maintained that the *universitas*, the content-full totality, was immediately accessible to our knowledge. In the Dissertation he had said that an argument based upon this assumption did 'not seem . . . clear' to him. Henceforth, he was to renounce any totality which is *given* and *existing outside us*, which man has not to create but only to know. Here is the decisive influence of Hume upon Kant.

But for all this, empiricism had not carried the day. For the totality retained all its reality and all its importance. Kant had merely been seeking it in the wrong direction. It is not external to man, but *in him*; it is not *given* and existing, but an ultimate *goal* which gives man his human dignity. It is a transcendental idea, a practical postulate. This is the meaning of the famous passage on the 'Copernican revolution'. The transcendental subjectivity of experience had already been clearly recognized in the Dissertation. What is new is the idea expressed in the following passage: 'As regards objects which are thought solely through reason, and indeed as necessary, but which can never – at least not in the manner in which reason thinks them – be given in experience, the attempts at thinking them (for they must admit of being thought) will furnish an excellent touchstone of what we are adopting as our new method of thought, namely, that we can know *a priori* of things only what we ourselves put into them.'[2] That the authentic destiny of man is to strive towards the absolute is the fundamental premiss of the critical philosophy, and Kant frequently repeats that it neither needs to be nor can be proved.

Of course, Kant knew perfectly well that there are men who do not accomplish their destiny, who make no use of transcendental freedom, and who accept reality as given

2. III, 12–13; *Pure R*, 23; B xviii.

without even *wishing* to transcend it. He did not need his critics to bring this fact to his attention, for he had already incorporated it in the practical part of his system under the name of the 'evil principle' or the 'radical evil in human nature'. But for all his perspicacity, he probably did not foresee that one day the 'true consequences' of his philosophy would be called upon to defend this 'radical evil', if only in the theoretical field.

In the refutation of empiricism, however, one thing remained to be done. It had to be shown that the totality, the suprasensible in its different forms, the absolute, the intelligible world, is neither impossible nor inaccessible. For Kant was too profound a thinker to be content with the easy solution of a *radical separation* between theory and practice, between thought and action. He well knew that man cannot *seriously* strive towards the realization of an idea which he knows to be unrealizable. In so far as it implied this, empiricism had to be refuted, and to that end a critique of the human faculty of knowledge was necessary.

Empiricism embodied two assertions which threatened the critical system in its present form:

(a) that that which is suprasensible and qualitatively different from given experience is absolutely inaccessible;

(b) that in experience there are no necessary connections *a priori*. Experience is atomistic. (We must recall the insistence with which Kant repeated that independent and autonomous monads can never constitute a world.)

With regard to the first assertion, the whole of the *Critique of Pure Reason* and particularly the Dialectic is an attempt to prove that nothing theoretical or speculative can be said about the suprasensible; neither its possibility nor its impossibility can be asserted. But the second assertion remains within the limits of given experience; it had therefore to be accepted or refuted in the *Critique of Pure Reason*. It was on this point that the real battle against empiricism and against Hume's critique of the concept of causality had to be fought. Here I shall be content to stress two points:

1. Kant does not debate with the real Hume. He does not try to refute his actual writings. That would not be philo-

sophical discussion but scholarly polemics. For Kant, Hume represents a philosophy, scepticism (today we should say empiricism). It is thus appropriate to reply to all the objections which *could* be made from that standpoint, even if Hume did not express them, and equally, to perceive all the *possible* consequences of empiricism, even if Hume did not draw them.

This is particularly true in the case of mathematics, as Kant constantly insists. Hume had concentrated his attacks against causality, whilst maintaining the apodictic validity of mathematical judgements, which he considered analytic. Of course Kant cannot agree with this. Mathematical judgements are as synthetic as causal explanations: the objections raised by Hume against causality could equally well be raised by a thoroughgoing empiricism against the apodictic validity of mathematics. Only an argument of this kind could show the totally atomistic character of experience, and thus the impossibility of a transcendental system. But it would be in contradiction with science and with universal experience, which demonstrate the apodictic certitude of mathematics.[3] Reality, the given, is thus not atomistic: it constitutes at least a formal totality, if not a material and perfect one. Sensations are given in the whole constituted by space and time: there is pure intuition. Once this is accepted, the *a priori* character of the categories in general and of causality in particular remains to be deduced from the necessity of an experience now recognized as possible. Kant had had to prune the old system of the Dissertation in many ways and he was conscious of this. On the *essential* points, however, Hume and empiricism had been refuted.

It will now be easy to grasp the sense of that famous paragraph from the *Prolegomena*, the only one I shall quote of the countless passages relating to Hume. 'I freely admit: it was *David Hume*'s remark that first, many years ago, interrupted my dogmatic slumber and gave a completely different direction to my inquiries in the field of speculative philosophy. I was very far from listening to him in respect of his

---

3. For Kant, who was still subject to the illusion of reification. See also Section IV of the present chapter.

conclusions, which were merely the result of his not representing his problem to himself as a whole, and instead only
lighting on part of it, which can give no information without taking the whole into account. When we begin a thought
well-grounded but not worked out which another has be-
queathed to us, we may well hope through continued reflection to advance beyond the point reached by the sagacious
man whom we have to thank for the first spark of this light.'[4]

2. Secondly, I wish to stress that the debate with Hume
had a profound influence upon the tone and the external
structure of the *Critique of Pure Reason*. This is much less
true of the *Critique of Practical Reason*, which appeared seven
years later. The second *Critique* is thus constructed in a
more unified and systematic way. Kant has often been
accused of allowing himself to be dominated in the construction of the three *Critiques* by a concern for external
symmetry. I hope to show, on the contrary, that the internal
symmetry of their content is much deeper than its external
expression in the layout of the works. This is certainly clear
in the case of the *Critique of Pure Reason*, written under the
immediate influence of the writings of Hume and of the
need to answer the objections raised by empiricism.

II

In proposing to set out even the most general features of the
critical philosophy, it is essential first to discuss what can
only be called the neo-Kantian misunderstanding.

During the fifty years from 1870 to 1920, German university teaching – one could hardly call it philosophy – was
conducted under the banner of what is usually called neo-
Kantianism. A whole series of professors of philosophy,
grouped in various schools, had adopted the slogan 'back
to Kant' and claimed to be the true representatives and
legitimate continuers of Kant's thought. The most important of these schools were centred on Marburg and
Heidelberg, and had as their organs the two most important

philosophical journals in the country, *Kantstudien* and *Logos*.[5] Not being very orthodox Kantians at heart, however, they tried to achieve a 'synthesis' between the thought of Kant and that of some other philosopher, or rather their own version of it. At Marburg, Plato was preferred for this; at Heidelberg, Hegel; and at Vienna, Karl Marx.[6]

The most unfortunate result of this movement was that its adherents managed to get their thought accepted as *the* philosophy of Kant. Consequently, when later, after 1920, a real need for philosophy arose, Kant's thought had been compromised in the eyes of the finest thinkers in Europe. This is not to deny that the most important neo-Kantians, such as Windelband, Cohen, Lask and Cassirer, achieved a considerable output of historical scholarship and even made certain contributions to the theory of knowledge. But this was not philosophy, still less Kantian philosophy.

Of course, it is impossible completely to ignore the neo-Kantians, for their interpretation is still predominant in the minds of many readers. On the other hand, it would be monotonous to return to them in the exposition of each part of the critical philosophy, since almost all their errors spring from one basic misconception which lends itself very well to sociological explanation. I shall thus devote one section of this introductory chapter to the neo-Kantians, which will spare us the need to return to them again.

In my first chapter I discussed the social conditions which fostered the development of Kant's philosophy. At a time when the English bourgeoisie had held economic and political power for almost a century and a half and had created a democratic state, when in France intellectual and social criticism reigned triumphant and the bourgeoisie was on the point of overthrowing absolutism, the economic development of Germany had remained extremely backward, resulting in the development of a highly abnormal social and political organism. But the very sickness of German society allowed the progressive elements of the bourgeoisie to

5. The latter, like the whole Heidelberg school, was also neo-Hegelian.
6. In fact, among the neo-Kantian Marxists of Vienna only Max Adler was principally concerned with philosophy. The other thinkers of this group, assembled around *Marxstudien*, were mainly sociologists and economists.

attain a much clearer and more profound philosophical awareness than was possible in the rest of Europe.

(a) Since any serious struggle for the achievement of democracy was so far away, it was possible to maintain the critical spirit and not to fall into that exaggerated optimism which such a struggle necessarily engenders. In contrast to the optimistic rationalism of the French, Germany could offer a clear vision of the real inadequacies of the bourgeois individualist social order emerging in Europe.

(b) On the other hand, the surrounding reality was all too wretched to be tolerated with equanimity after the example of the English empiricists. It was essential to hope for a better future and to strive towards it, the more so since it was projected as more beautiful and more perfect than the existing order in England or that emerging in France. Dreams and hopes are always extreme, so long as the struggle for their realization is not an immediate possibility.

(c) But the most difficult and even apparently insoluble problem was how to pass from the present wretched state to the dreamed-of ideal. (In philosophical terms, the problem of the unity of theory and practice.)

All these elements find their philosophical expression in the Kantian system. The principal elements of that system will be dealt with more fully at a later stage. Here a schematic enumeration will suffice.

1. The idea that man's authentic destiny is to strive towards the absolute, that is, towards something completely different from the empirical given, in the theoretical sphere towards knowledge of the *universitas*, of things in themselves, of noumena, or in the practical sphere towards the highest good, the kingdom of God, etc.

2. The idea that man as he is empirically given (for Kant, man in general) is dependent upon something external (sensibility) and that he is consequently limited and can never attain the absolute. In the analysis of this limitation, Kant lays the philosophical foundations for a most penetrating critique of bourgeois individualist society. His successors could only develop this analysis and apply it to different fields. This critique of the thought and action of individualist man is to be found in the Aesthetic of the *Critique of Pure*

Reason and in the two Analytics of the *Critique of Pure Reason* and the *Critique of Practical Reason*.

3. Since man can only progress towards the absolute by means of given sensations and in spite of his sensuous inclinations, he must create the maximum he is able to achieve, that is to say, *theoretically, coherent experience*, and *practically, a life in conformity with the categorical imperative*. But this double goal is for Kant only a *pis-aller*, a tragic limitation. The knowledge of an archetypal understanding would not be ruled by general laws, and for a holy will there would be no categorical imperative.

Towards the end of the nineteenth century, the economic and social structure of Germany had become quite different from that described above. Bismarck had created a politically unified state, the *Reich*; German industry was on the point of catching up with and even overtaking that of the other Western countries; Germany had become the most industrialized country in Europe. But in spite of the dizzy speed of this development, one thing had not been acquired: a liberal spirit, analogous to that of the French or English bourgeoisie. There were two reasons for this. First, spiritual values are not created in ten or twenty years. They need a centuries-old tradition, such as existed in England or in France. In Germany, tradition was directly opposed to these values; the new spirit needed to overcome it (and which has yet to overcome it today) is a task requiring decades and perhaps centuries of uninterrupted struggle.

Secondly, the German bourgeoisie had not inherited the modern industrial state from their fathers, neither had they acquired it by their own efforts; they had quite simply received it as a gift from the ruling class, from the nobility, the Junkers. As the history books so aptly describe it, the German *Reich* was not created 'from beneath', that is, by the bourgeoisie, but 'from above', by Bismarck and the Junkers, and it was created in their likeness. The Junkers had reserved for themselves all the important positions, in particular the officer corps and the diplomatic service. The bourgeoisie had merely to follow and obey, which it did with enthusiasm so long as business was good and profits rose. Of course, the principal industrialists became powerful figures in the State, people with a say in both domestic and foreign affairs. But even in its most radical period, under the more or less socialist administrations after 1918, the German bourgeoisie never managed to gain control over the apparatus of State and really to democratize it: the important posts of State, the army and the diplomatic corps remained in the hands of the Junkers right up to 1932. During this period, being through its very youth less encumbered with the past, German industry could adopt the most advanced techniques, leaving French and even English industry far behind. Thus was born the typical German specialist we know so well today, outstandingly proficient in his field, a perfect organizer, disciplined in the extreme, obedient to his superiors, dictatorial to his subordinates, but lacking breadth of vision, personal thought, humour, and above all a desire for independence or freedom, things which can almost be taken for granted in England or in France.

All this, of course, was bound to have a decisive influence upon intellectual life in Germany, on art, science and philosophy. By about 1870, Germany had the most erudite professors of philosophy in the world, but the philosophical spirit had been almost entirely lost. Nietzsche and Marx, the last great German philosophers, lived abroad.

Neo-Kantianism is the 'philosophy' of this period. A whole series of professors of philosophy had discovered that an accurate analysis of modern man was to be found in the works of Kant. Thus the appeal 'back to Kant' rang out. This meant, quite overtly, a return not to the whole of Kant's philosophy but only to the Aesthetic[7] and the Analytic. Even these they completely distorted. What for Kant was a tragic limitation of man became for the neo-Kantians a normal, self-evident fact and, implicitly, an apology. These parts of the Kantian system were dissected and analysed down to the last detail in hundreds of books with an extraordinary expenditure of labour and erudition. But the spirit of Kant's thought had fled.

From this limited and apologetic point of view, the Dialectic could only appear totally incomprehensible. For most

---

7. Meaning, of course, the Aesthetic of the *Critique of Pure Reason*.

of the neo-Kantians, everything relating to the things in itself, the archetypal intellect, the highest good, or the intelligible world was a closed book. The only snag was that in the works of Kant, who had been hailed as philosophy's greatest genius, these problems were to be met with on every page. It was thus necessary to find some means of escape. According to its temperament, each school chose a different path. For example, the Dialectic could be ignored, the more easily since most readers would not read the original texts or at any rate not read them critically. But for a large number of neo-Kantian professors this was impossible, given the professional ethic which reigned in German universities. Another solution was thus found. At Marburg the Dialectic was usually disposed of by proving that it concerned only 'limiting concepts'. The Heidelberg school was more radical, presenting it either as a survival of the dogmatic period or quite simply as nonsense.

In view of the above remarks, it would be pointless to analyse the various neo-Kantian writings in detail. In any case, such a study would fill a library. I shall be content to take two examples and consider the treatment of the 'thing in itself' by two professors representing the schools of Marburg and Heidelberg. To this end I choose Hermann Cohen and Bruno Bauch. The contrast with the writings of Kant is evident at first sight. The Transcendental Aesthetic and Analytic of the *Critique of Pure Reason* in the Berlin Academy edition comprise a little less than 200 pages, the Dialectic alone 230. In Hermann Cohen's book, which bears the significant title *Kant's Theory of Experience*[8] (and not of knowledge), the analysis of the first two occupies 420 pages, that of the Dialectic 54. In Bauch's *Immanuel Kant,*[9] the critical theory of knowledge is spread out over 181 pages, whilst the section on rational knowledge (*Vernunftserkenntnis*) contains only 29.

The situation becomes quite clear when we consider the content of those pages. Hermann Cohen is at pains to explain in every possible or imaginable way that the thing in

8. H. Cohen, *Kants Theorie der Erfahrung*, 2nd edn, Berlin, 1885.
9. B. Bauch, *Immanuel Kant*, Berlin, 1923.

itself is not in fact qualitatively different from given scientific experience. He clings to the concept 'regulative', which he interprets in his own way. 'Rules are principles, and these principles, in contrast to synthetic principles which hold as constitutive, are regulative. . . . They give rules and indications, open out "points of view", provide "maxims" and draw "lines of direction" for investigation where mechanical principles, by their very nature, leave us in the lurch.'[10] He is thinking here of descriptive natural science; Kant should have 'asked whether the description of nature' might have served as a *'factum'* for the transcendental value of ideas.[11] 'The thing in itself is consequently the expression of the whole scientific range and coherence of our knowledge.'[12] 'From the outset, all doubt as to whether the unconditioned transcends experience must be laid aside.'[13] In another work he writes quite simply that 'the law is the thing in itself'.[14]

In the light of even a slight acquaintance with Kant's works, such claims are disconcerting. Kant stresses hundreds of times, quite unambiguously, that the laws of the mechanical sciences and the principles of the descriptive sciences result from the subsumption of sensible impressions under the concepts of the understanding by our faculty of judgement. The thing in itself is precisely what remains inaccessible to all these powers of knowledge and which could only be known by an archetypal intellect; it is the goal towards which our reason must ceaselessly strive without ever being able to attain it. But Hermann Cohen was quite simply unable to understand this, far less to attribute it to such a great thinker as Kant. He therefore tries to 'rescue' him. We have seen the result of this attempt.

Bruno Bauch takes the opposite course. It is clear to him that reason and understanding, law and experience, on the one hand, and the thing in itself on the other, are essentially and qualitatively different concepts. He concludes from this that the thing in itself is an absurdity. Let him speak for himself: 'I have . . . already remarked that I regard Kant's

10. Cohen, op. cit., p. 514.   11. ibid., p. 417.
12. ibid., p. 518.   13. ibid., p. 521.
14. H. Cohen, *Kants Begründung der Ethik*, Berlin, 1877, p. 27.

"thing in itself" as the most serious mistake in his critique of reason. In all events the "thing in itself" of the Transcendental Aesthetic is quite the most unfortunate piece of dogmatism introduced by Kant into the critical philosophy.'[15] 'Kant nevertheless willingly retains "things in themselves" and thus burdens his doctrine with a veritable *crux*.' 'Behind Kant's doctrine of the thing in itself hides the most fatal psychologism.'[16] Kant has been tricked by a word: 'And secondly, it is just the word, and not, as he thinks, the concept of appearance which leads him to the thing in itself.'[17]

One gets the impression that Immanuel Kant had the misfortune to live too early. If only he had heard a few of Bruno Bauch's lectures he might have become a real philosopher. That Bauch speaks in the same vein of the highest good goes without saying. 'Indeed it is clear that Kant does not completely master the difficulties here.'[18] 'Here and there [he] relapses quite deeply into the sensual mode of thinking.'[19] The highest good 'darkens the infinity of the tasks of reason in its *a priori* purity'.[20]

Here Bruno Bauch and Hermann Cohen meet. I spare the reader several pages of Cohen's long development and quote only his conclusions:[21] 'It is thus only from persistence in the upholding of Kant's basic ideas that I advocate the rejection of the whole idea of the highest good as a consequence of Kantian ethics.' 'Kant thought to strengthen the reality of the moral law by means of the highest good. . . . But we have no need of this "best of worlds",' and so forth.

The above examples should suffice. In reading these books one cannot help thinking of the words of Faust in the scene with Wagner:

> *Das ist im Grund der Herren eigner Geist,*
> *in dem die Zeiten sich bespiegeln.*

The most important features of the neo-Kantian misunderstanding may be set out as follows:

---

15. Bauch, op. cit., p. 163.   16. ibid., p. 164.   17. ibid., p. 165.
18. ibid., p. 333.   19. ibid.   20. ibid., pp. 334-5.
21. H. Cohen, *Kants Begründung der Ethik*, pp. 312-13.

(a) In the theoretical field, empirical experience is, according to the neo-Kantians, the supreme goal that man can hope and strive for. *The aspiration towards totality is only quantitative*: it is nothing but the need forever to experiment and to establish new scientific laws, supposing that this aspiration is not simply dogmatic and metaphysical nonsense. On the contrary, according to Kant (and equally according to Hegel, Marx and Lukács), there exists a kind of knowledge which is essentially and *qualitatively* different from that of man (according to Kant, of man in general; according to Marx and Lukács, of present-day man living in an atomized and individualist society). Man must always strive towards this knowledge although it is for ever inaccessible to him. The quantitative range of our experience at any point is in a way the precipitate, the result of this effort towards a higher and qualitatively different kind of knowledge. (From this it is easy to understand the importance for Hegel and Marx of the idea that quantitative differences are transformed into qualitative ones.)

In a word, just when anthropological research was showing the enormous difference between the thought of primitive peoples and our own, the neo-Kantians confused man's thought in present-day society with thought in general, an epistemological regression even from the positions of Kant and Hegel.

(b) In the ethical and practical field, the neo-Kantians saw in the fulfilment of the categorical imperative the highest goal that man must strive to attain – thus bringing Kant quite close to Stoicism. But since the absolute fulfilment of ethical norms is impossible for man, they in fact ended up with the 'ideal type' of the citizen who, conscious of his moral duties, seeks to fulfil them so far as is possible, but, when his effort is vain, can confidently blame his weakness on human insufficiency. That the moral law should always remain a mixture of pleasure and displeasure, an irksome duty to be carried out with greater or lesser repugnance, seemed to go without saying for the neo-Kantians. Any other conception would 'darken the infinity of the tasks of reason in its *a priori* purity' for 'we have no need of this "best of worlds"'.

The highest good, the intelligible world, the kingdom of ends, the kingdom of God on earth – of all these essential concepts of Kant's ethics nothing remained. The apologetic spirit had precluded any understanding of them.

(c) Kant's philosophy of history became, in the fat books of Rickert and his pupils (with the partial exception of Lask), the 'construction' of the concepts of the historical and human sciences. With Kant, all the categories were directed towards the future; with Rickert, they are directed towards the past or at most towards the present. The fundamental ideas of Kant's philosophy, 'the society of citizens of the world', 'perpetual peace', have disappeared, to be replaced by an abstract 'philosophy of values' into which an apologia for present-day society or at the very least some 'scientific' content can be inserted at will.

All this should suffice to show how important it is today, as interest in philosophy quickens once again, to sift out the true meaning of Kant's thought by freeing it from this misunderstanding. In the further development of the present work, I shall not return again to the neo-Kantians. The foregoing remarks will enable the reader to take up this critique and apply it himself to those of the neo-Kantians who particularly interest him.

III

A very important question for us today, in the light of the developments of the last thirty years, is that of the relations between Kant's thought and the mystical doctrine of intuitionism. (I am consciously and deliberately avoiding the use of the word 'philosophy'.) In his philosophical works Kant does not investigate this problem in any depth, beyond a few incidental remarks on *Schwärmerei*. And rightly so, since it never occurred to him to consider intuitionism as a philosophy. The views to which he was opposed (empiricism, scepticism, rationalist dogmatism, Stoicism and Epicureanism) had in common with his own at least that minimum which he considered necessary for a system of thought to qualify as a philosophy. They all recognized reason as the supreme authority, and implicitly defended the freedom of the individual. In the modern age, intuition had yet to find its philosopher.[22] Schelling was to be the first, and, in due course, the founder of a school. We must thus attach all the more importance to a little article published by Kant on the intuitionist doctrine, an article which I believe remains unsurpassed to this day.[23]

Friedrich Jacobi had invoked Kant in his debate with Moses Mendelssohn on the subject of Lessing's Spinozism. It was well known that Kant had considerable personal regard for Jacobi, and that he had even advised his friends in Berlin 'to refrain from any provocative attack on Jacobi'. To avoid any possible misunderstanding, he published in the *Berliner Monatsschrift*[24] an article which not only furnished a reply to Jacobi but which remains valid for the systems of Schelling, Bergson or Scheler.

Kant begins by establishing that with respect to knowledge of God (Kant says of 'supersensuous objects': today we should say 'the absolute' or better, to use an expression of Lukács', the achievement of 'true consciousness'), the question is whether we should be guided by 'sound reason', as Mendelssohn wished, or by *Schwärmerei*, 'the complete overthrow of reason'. He leaves Jacobi a way out, not wishing to attribute to him 'the intention of establishing such a ruinous way of thought'.[25] He continues: 'On the other hand, I shall show that in fact reason alone is required for orientation and not some alleged secret truth-sense [for which we might well substitute Schelling's 'intellectual intuition' or Bergson's 'intuition' – L.G.], nor a transcendent

22. Unless we include Jacob Böhme among the philosophers, as has been customary since Schelling.

23. 'What is orientation in thinking?', VIII, 131; *Ethics*, 293.

24. Here is what he wrote at the same time in a letter to Jacobi (30 August 1789): 'I have always thought it my duty to show respect for men of talent, science and justice, no matter how far our opinions may differ. You will, I hope, appraise my essay on orientation, in the *Berliner Monatsschrift*, from this perspective. I was requested by various people to cleanse myself of the suspicion of Spinozism, and therefore, contrary to my inclination, I wrote this essay. I hope you will find in it no trace of deviation from the principle I have just affirmed' (*Phil. Corr*, 158–9).

25. VIII, 134; *Ethics*, 294.

intuition dubbed faith. . . . I shall show, as Mendelssohn asserted with firmness and justified zeal, that it is only pure human reason by which he found it necessary and commendable to obtain orientation.'[26]

There follows a detailed account of Kant's own point of view where he establishes with clarity and precision what separates him from the dogmatism of Mendelssohn, stressing nevertheless that the latter 'had the merit of consistently seeking the ultimate touchstone of admissibility of a judgement solely in reason alone'.[27] For 'The concept of God and the conviction of His existence can be met with only in reason; they can come from reason alone, not from either inspiration or any tidings, however great their authority.'[28] The reply to Jacobi then follows.

After what I have just said, it is only to be expected that this reply should not have a philosophical character, but that it should be sociological, political and even prophetic. Kant simply says that sentimental romanticism protesting in the name of the freedom of the individual against the limits of reason actually endangers that true liberty which is one of the supreme values of man. The one thing that Kant could not foresee in 1786 was that a hundred and fifty years later there would be circles and even governments who would consciously cultivate this picture of the world in order to destroy freedom. This reply appears to me important enough to quote it *in extenso*:[29]

'Men of intellectual power and broad minds! I honour your talents and love your feeling for humanity. But have you considered what you do, and where you will end with your attacks on reason? Without doubt you will that freedom to think should be preserved inviolate, for without this your own free flights of genius would soon be at an end. Let us see what must naturally come out of this freedom of thought if such a procedure as you begin comes to prevail.

'Freedom to think is first opposed by civil restraint. Certainly one may say, "Freedom to speak or write can be taken from us by a superior power, but never the freedom

26. ibid.   27. VIII, 140; *Ethics*, 299.
28. VIII, 142; *Ethics*, 301.   29. VIII, 144–6; *Ethics*, 303–5.

to think." But how much, and how correctly, would we think if we did not think as it were in common with others, with whom we mutually communicate! Thus one can well say that the external power which wrests from man the freedom publicly to communicate his thoughts also takes away the freedom to think – the sole jewel that remains to us under all civil repression and through which alone counsel against all the evils of that state can be taken.

'Secondly, freedom to think will be taken in such a sense that the constraint of conscience is opposed to it, where without any external power some citizens set themselves up as guardians in matters of religion. Instead of arguing, they know how, by prescribed formulas of belief accompanied by scrupulous fear of the danger of private inquisition, to banish all rational examination by making an early impression on the mind.

'Thirdly, freedom in thinking means the subjection of reason under no other laws than those it gives itself. Its opposite is the maxim of a lawless use of reason (in order, as genius supposes, to be able to see further without the restriction imposed by laws). The natural consequence is that, if reason will not subject itself to the law it gives itself, it will have to bow under the yoke of laws which others impose on it, for without any law whatsoever nothing, not even the greatest nonsense, can play its hand very long. Thus the inevitable consequence of declared lawlessness in thinking (an emancipation from restriction of reason) is that freedom to think is finally lost. Since not misfortune but arrogance is responsible, it is, in the true sense of the word, squandered.

'The course of the matter is approximately this. The genius enjoys himself at first in his daring flight, for he has thrown off the harness with which reason had guided him. By authoritative decrees and great promises he soon enchants others and seems to himself to be seated on a throne which slow plodding reason so poorly adorns, even though he still speaks its language. We ordinary men call the then assumed maxim of invalidity of supremely legislative reason by the name of "fanaticism"; those favourites of kindly nature, however, call it "illumination". Because a confusion of tongues must soon arise among them, and because reason alone can validly command for everyone, each must now follow his own inspiration. So inner inspiration must finally cede to facts fabricated by external evidence, freely chosen traditions to documents of enforced authority, until the complete subjugation of reason under supposed facts, i.e., superstition, ensues. For superstition can at least have a lawful form and thus bring about a state of peace.

'Although human reason always strives for freedom, when it once breaks its fetters, its first use of a long unaccustomed freedom degenerates into abuse and a mistaken confidence in its freedom from all limitation, it falls into a persuasion of the exclusive sovereignty of speculative reason, which assumes nothing except what can justify itself on objective grounds and dogmatic convictions, and it boldly denies everything else. The maxim of the independence of reason from its own need (renunciation of rational belief) is now called "disbelief". It is not a historical disbelief, for one cannot think of it as intentional or even as responsible (because everyone must believe a fact which is sufficiently confirmed just as much as a mathematical demonstration, whether he will or not); it is a "rational disbelief", an unfortunate state of the human mind, which first takes from the moral laws all their effect on the heart as incentives, and then destroys all their authority, occasioning a turn of mind called "free-thinking", i.e., the principle of not acknowledging any duty. Here the authorities take a hand, so as to prevent the utmost disorder even in civil affairs; and as the handiest but most energetic means is to them the best, they completely destroy the freedom to think and subject it, like other pursuits, to the government. And so freedom in thought finally destroys itself when it wishes to proceed independently of the laws of reason.

'Friends of the human race and of that which is holiest to it! Assume what appears most believable to you after careful and honest testing, whether it be facts or principles of reason; but do not wrest from reason that which makes it the highest good on earth, i.e., the prerogative of being the ultimate touchstone of truth. Otherwise you will become unworthy of this freedom and certainly lose it, and you will bring this misfortune on the heads of that blameless portion of mankind which was well inclined to make use of its freedom in a lawful manner towards the good of the world.'

The last twenty-five years have shown us how penetrating Kant's vision was and how close are the ties which link irrationalism and the mystique of intuition and feeling with the suppression of individual liberties.

IV

Some important terminological and philosophical questions remain to be examined in this introductory chapter.

First of all, the word 'reason' itself. Because of the predominant influence of the neo-Kantians, who had no understanding of what Kant meant by it, the sense of this term has greatly altered. Today, 'reason' is understood as a purely theoretical faculty of knowledge, or at the most, practical wisdom. Kant's view was quite different; even at the outset reason was not purely speculative, and from 1790 it becomes an exclusively practical faculty of knowledge. As a table in the *Critique of Judgement*[30] indicates, its principle is not nature's conformity to law, but the final goal of human freedom. It might best be described as the communicable mental faculty which leads us to strive towards the realization of man's highest ends. It might be even better expressed by the word 'spirit' or by Hegel's 'logos', had not the nineteenth century weakened and blunted the meaning of those concepts also. I shall of course keep to Kant's own term; hence the need for clarification.

Universitas and *universalitas* (community and universality): Emil Lask was the first to point out the overriding importance of these two concepts for the understanding not only of Kant's thought but of modern philosophy in general. It will scarcely be possible here in a few lines to set out more than the bare essentials of the question. This requires an understanding of that fundamental phenomenon of bourgeois individualist society which Marx called 'com-

30. V, 198; *Aesth. J*, 39.

modity fetishism' and Lukács 'reification'.[31] I shall try to be
as clear as possible.

Man does not create his knowledge completely independently. He depends upon the given, whether this is denoted
by 'sensation' or by some other term. This implies that
radical rationalism is untenable.

It is not easy to establish what this 'given' is. Lask remarks with reason that it can only be determined negatively
as that which is not formed, which has no form; but the
moment we speak of or even think of it, we give it a form. I
shall thus refer to it as the matter of knowledge and shall
leave open the question of whether it is purely qualitative
and accessible to feeling alone, as with Bergson's *données
immédiates*, or a 'stream of thought' as with William James,
or again, something already structured as with the gestalt
psychologists. In any case, it seems probable that in an
asocial being (an animal or a newborn child) there can be
no question of a distinction between theory and practice,
between knowing and doing. This distinction appears with
social life, and with it appears the possibility of a division
between theory and practice: *experience*. Social life implies
common action and the division of labour; it presupposes
the possibility of communication. Now the given, matter
without form, changes with each individual; there are no
two identical perceptions. If two people are in a room, each
sees the same table in a different way, according to whether
it is to the left, to the right, in front of or behind him.

Communication, however, presupposes at least that each
transform his own immediate given, his own matter, in such
a way that the other understands what is communicated to
him and can relate it to his own given, to the matter of his
own immediate apprehension; but it also implies that each
should be able to understand the matter of his own acquaintance as a special case of knowledge held in common and his

---

31. The most important texts on this subject are found in Hegel's critique
of Kant and Fichte, in Marx's *Critique of Hegel's Philosophy of Right* and in
Capital, and in all the works of Lukács, but especially in the essay on 'Reification and the Consciousness of the Proletariat'. Important elements for the
understanding of reification in logic and the theory of knowledge are found
in Lask's *Die Logik der Philosophie und die Kategorienlehre (Werke,* vol. 11).

own knowledge as dependent upon that of all other men. *Experience* is the name given to the result of this transformation of matter which, it must be stressed, leads at least to the possibility of mutual communication, but which could eventually lead to genuine knowledge held in common. I shall refer to the general principles of this transformation of formless *matter* into *experience* as 'form'.

It follows that *for a being living in society radical empiricism is untenable*. It would lead not only to solipsism but indeed to the renunciation of all thought. It follows equally that life in society dissolves the original and immediate unity of sensibility and individual action. Between the two is interposed the transformation of the immediate given into communicable knowledge: the *theoretical* world. The unity of theory and practice can now only be re-established on a higher basis in and for the community (Lukács's 'true consciousness').

I have already said that the formal principles of experience – henceforward I shall use the Kantian term 'categories' – are not rigid and eternal. Between the minimum which renders understanding between individuals possible and the maximum which would correspond to an ideal community, there are of course a number of possible basic types. The investigations of recent years have shown that the predominance of a system of categories at a particular place and time is largely[32] sociologically determined, that is to say, determined by the social structure. The philosopher or epistemologist is naturally interested in past systems of categories (see, for example, the studies by Durkheim and Lévy-Bruhl on the thought of primitive peoples), but he is interested above all in those of contemporary man and – in so far as he can say something about them – those of an ideal community.

But since this community is still unknown to us, and since it is only partially realizable at the present time (according to Lukács, for example, in class solidarity), we

32. But not exclusively: there are also general characteristics of human nature which are independent of the social order. However, I cannot here go more deeply into the rather complex questions raised by a sociological theory of knowledge. My exposition must thus remain schematic and incomplete.

can express only vague generalities as to its categories of thought. For example,

(a) This thought *could not be purely empirical*, since there could be no such thing, *nor purely rationalist*, since it must, on the contrary, keep very close to the given, the external world. It would probably resemble a kind of empiricism. For if we accept that a higher community will re-establish for the human community the unity between thought and action which today is lacking for the individual, we must equally accept that its categorial forms will be easily adaptable to the transformation into experience of *any* given or possible matter.

(b) Similarly, the radical separation between form and content, subject and object, which characterizes the thought of individualist man will have to be overcome, although one may well ask whether these oppositions will ever *completely* disappear. Today the sole element common to all members of our society is form, whilst content is the individual element which separates them. In a higher community, where selfish interests no longer set men or human groups against one another, this difference will also disappear: *form and content will be common to all men.*

(c) Today in every field (knowledge, morals, law, etc.) form is *reified and rigid*. It must set itself against the centrifugal and egoistical tendencies of the individual. In a higher community, it will become more supple, more living, and will adapt itself better both to man and to the given, to the subject and to the object, for it is none other than the expression of their mutual relations. Moreover, it must be stressed that neither the form nor the matter of knowledge is independent in relation either to the *subject* or to the *object*, being merely the expression of their unity in man's activity, in his *action*.

(d) Today, form is *abstract* and, as *universality*, is in opposition to concrete and *individual* content. In a higher community, matter and form will be subjectively united in a concrete *community*, and objectively united in a concrete *universe*.

(e) Today form is either law-governed but not free (logical, scientific or juridical laws), or law-governed and free but not actual, an *ought* without an *is* (the moral law), whilst matter (the given, dispositions) is actual but opposed to law and devoid of freedom. Only in their union can the basis of a perfect community be established: a *universal and free reality* which is both law-governed and common to all men.

Starting from this, the most important thinkers of modern philosophy (particularly Kant with the archetypal intellect, Hegel, Marx and Lukács in the dialectical method and also Lask in emanatist logic) have tried to bring more precision to this subject. They have started out from the obvious insufficiency of modern everyday thought, and especially scientific thought, of its inability to unite the general and the individual, the possible absolute with the real given. They have all recognized that this insufficiency results from the absence of the category of totality, the *universitas*, which must be fundamental to any system of thought which is to overcome this limitation. Whilst it is unfortunately not possible to dwell on this here, I shall quote a few lines from Kant on the subject of the archetypal intellect which seem to prefigure the Hegelian dialectic: 'we are also able to form a notion of an understanding which, not being discursive like ours, but intuitive, moves from the *synthetic universal*, or intuition of the whole as a whole, to the particular – that is to say, from the whole to the parts. To render possible a definite form of the whole a *contingency* in the synthesis of the parts is not implied by such an understanding or its representation of the whole.'[33] Or, in another place: ' . . . there would be no such distinction between the possible and the actual. This means that if our understanding were intuitive it would have no objects but such as are actual. Conceptions . . . and sensuous intuitions . . . would both cease to exist.'[34] This would be the maximum, the *universitas* in the realm of logic and theoretical knowledge.

We come now to the generality of existing knowledge, the *universalitas*. Any life in society presupposes a minimum of categorial forms without which men would be unable to understand one another. Where the social character of life – whatever its level – appears openly, the human

---

character of the categories will also be more or less apparent. But this is not the case in the modern bourgeois individualist social order. Here there is no visible community, save in some exceptional cases (family intimacy, friendship, etc.). The fundamental social relations of men, the relations of production, are those of buyers and sellers of commodities, and only the antagonism resulting from the desire to buy cheap and to sell dear is permitted to enter into consciousness. What unites men in spite of everything, the fact that the buyer has no meaning unless there is a seller and *vice versa,* must appear in spite of and against their consciousness and in a reified form. The fact that production is, in spite of everything, a social fact is expressed only in the *prices* of commodities. On the stock market, 'wheat rises', 'steel falls', and so on. Man has disappeared.

Lukács has sought to show how this reification manifests itself in every sphere of life. It is bound also to appear in logic and the theory of knowledge. Here it is called 'innate ideas', 'recollection', '*a priori*', and so on – *universalitas,* universality in its divers forms. I do not wish to be misunderstood here. In any social order there will always be judgements to which all men adhere. But if these judgements (or their 'meanings') lose all connection either with the empirical given (as with Descartes or in Kantian apriorism) or with concrete man (as with Rickert, Lask or Husserl), this is a reification of truth and of thought in general.[35] Just as on the stock market wheat and steel rise or fall of themselves, so with Rickert a meaning is of itself 'true' or 'false' and all connection with man is rejected as psychologism.

In the great classics this reification takes another form. Here judgement is separated not from the subject but from matter, from the sensible. Universal mathematics

35. A reification which is also sometimes to be found in socialist writers, particularly when they deal with philosophical questions and are neo-Kantians. For example, Max Adler writes: 'It sounds paradoxical, but arises from the very essence of the critique of knowledge, when we say: in a consistent theory of knowledge, 'man' has no further place, being only the content of knowledge, just as, for example, in the most consistent epistemological theory of law, as constructed by Hans Kelsen, man, the subject of law, has become no more than a logical centre of legal relations' (Max Adler, *Lehrbuch der materialistischen Geschichtsauffassung,* Vol. I, p. 141).

represents the hope that, in a monadic and atomized society, individuals, though independent one from another, will nonetheless arrive in their thought at identical results.[36] Be it pre-established harmony or divine intervention, it remains no less a reification. And it is precisely because the community remains hidden and opaque that it must appear in the form of an abstract and reified external power (innate ideas, *a priori*, category, categorical imperative, etc.) and not as concrete and transparent human action.

I shall not insist here upon the ethical and practical aspect of this distinction between concrete totality (*universitas*) and reified universality (*universalitas*), since this is rather easier to understand and we shall meet it again later.

The difference between *universitas* and *universalitas*, between concrete totality and reified *a priori* universality, is one of the cornerstones of Kant's theoretical and practical philosophy. *A priori* universality is what characterizes given, limited man. To determine its possibilities and its limits is one of the most important tasks of the critical philosophy; the totality, the *universitas*, is today only given on the formal level (space and time) and could find its perfect realization only in a higher, suprasensible state, in the archetypal intellect, in the holy will, in knowledge of the thing in itself, and so forth. Kant clearly did not transcend reification,[37] but he described it with precision and defined its limits.

Some (Rickert and Lask) see this as his greatest merit; others (Hegel and Lukács), as a reason for the sharpest criticism. One might just as well take him to task for having written in 1790 and not in 1940, or for having lived in Königsberg and not in Paris. To me this seems quite pointless and secondary. The important thing is to separate out the authentic spirit of the critical philosophy from false or

36. It is the great merit of Max Adler to have shown this in an analysis of Kantian apriorism. See his theory of the 'social *a priori*'.

37. In any case, to transcend in thought is not to overcome. No understanding of economic facts will stop the economist talking of wheat rising and steel falling. The most precise knowledge does not stop modern physicists talking and thinking in everyday life with the old categories. Indeed, the language itself, being still adapted to the older modes of thought, would not permit them to do otherwise.

erroneous interpretations and according to our powers and abilities to continue on the path opened by Kant.

V

It remains now to trace the general lines of Kant's system, for within the confines of this work there can be no question of a detailed exposition.

One might begin this exposition in various ways. It would best correspond to the logic of the system to begin with the practical side, although, under the influence of his consideration of Hume, Kant himself started with the theoretical part, and indeed with the question of experience, where Hume had raised his problems. Kant was well aware of this when he wrote: 'It seems difficult to present in so small a space the great manifold of metaphysics in its entirety and according to its sources. But in fact the organic connection of all the faculties of knowledge under the supreme government of reason makes this easy, since it is possible to start from divers points and to follow the whole circle according to one principle. The difficulty thus lies only in choosing from which point to begin. It seems to me advisable to begin with that which first awakened my interest in the grounding of metaphysics (freedom, in so far as it is manifest through moral laws), for the solution of the associated problems requires a complete anatomy of our faculties of knowledge, and thus the whole circle can be followed. Here is given a concept of the suprasensible with its reality (though only practical).'[38]

In spite of this, I shall nevertheless begin with the theoretical part, in order not to depart more than is absolutely necessary from the tradition established by the neo-Kantians. However, I shall use a division proposed several times by Kant himself. In the *Logic*,[39] he writes:

'Philosophy in its ultimate meaning (according to the

38. XX, 344–5.

39. IX, 24. See also III, 523; *Pure R*, 635; B 733, and the letter to Stäudlin of 4 May 1793 (XI, 429; *Phil. Corr*, 205).

universal concept of reason) is the science of the relation of all knowledge and every use of reason to the final goal of human reason, to which as the supreme goal all other ends are subordinate and in which they must be united.

'The field of philosophy in this cosmopolitan sense may be reduced to the following questions: [40]

1. What can I know?
2. What ought I to do?
3. What may I hope for?
4. What is man?

'The first question is answered by *metaphysics*, the second by *morals*, the third by *religion*, and the fourth by *anthropology*. In the end, all may be reckoned to anthropology, since the first three questions relate to the fourth.'

In this work, I shall follow that division. It is necessary only to point out:

(a) With regard to the first question, that for Kant metaphysics has two parts, the metaphysics of nature and the metaphysics of morals, and that the reply to this question must thus embrace the whole analysis of *existent man*, in respect to both theory and practice.

(b) With regard to the third, that in the development of Kant's system the philosophy of history was added to that of religion.

(c) That to the first and the third questions must be added aesthetics, which unifies them, if only subjectively.

---

40. In the *Critique of Pure Reason* only the first three appear.

Chapter 2

What Can I Know?

It must be emphasized from the beginning that the essence of Kant's answer to this question can be formulated in two basic points:

1. There is in man a principle which impels him to aspire ceaselessly towards a higher state, *qualitatively* different from his present one, and it is only through this that he can accomplish his true destiny.

2. Present-day man (for Kant, man in general) is limited and cannot attain this unconditioned.

In developing these two ideas, Kant lays the philosophical foundations for the most profound and radical critique ever made of bourgeois man. Perhaps the reader will allow me to explain how I first came to understand this. It was in a class-room, where I had just been outlining the general principles of Kantian ethics. A pupil delivered a vehement speech against this morality according to which, he said, his father, a most respected citizen, would be an immoral man. This was quite unacceptable to him. When, astonished, I asked him how he had come to that conclusion, the young man explained that his father, a shopkeeper, was every day in contact with a large number of people whom he did not otherwise know and who for him were no more than the means of earning a living and feeding his family. It would never have occurred to him to treat all these unknown people as ends in themselves.

I must admit that I was taken aback by this reply. But my astonishment only increased when, on returning home and leafing through the writings of Kant, I found that Kant's first example of an immoral man corresponded more or less exactly to what my young pupil had said. On the tenth page of the *Groundwork of the Metaphysic of Morals*,

the following passage appears: 'For example, it certainly
accords with duty that a grocer should not overcharge his
inexperienced customer; and where there is much competi-
tion a sensible shopkeeper refrains from so doing and keeps
to a fixed and general price for everybody so that a child
can buy from him just as well as anyone else. Thus people
are served *honestly*; but this is not nearly enough to justify
us in believing that the shopkeeper has acted in this way
from duty or from principles of fair dealing; his interests
required him to do so. We cannot assume him to have in
addition an immediate inclination towards his customers,
leading him, as it were out of love, to give no man preference
over another in the matter of price. Thus the action was
done neither from duty nor from immediate inclination,
but solely from purposes of self-interest.'[1]

My young pupil, who had certainly never read a line of
Kant, had nonetheless perceived the logical consequences
of Kant's thought more clearly than most of the neo-
Kantians. This is clearly no arbitrary example: the 'honest'
tradesman formed the basis of the bourgeois individualist
social order which was then emerging in Europe and which
still reigns today. The example relates to the *very essence*
of this society, not to a secondary phenomenon.

I

It is man's destiny to aspire towards the absolute. This is the
basic postulate of the critical philosophy, the point of
departure which Kant cannot and does not wish to prove.
In Kantian language, it is a postulate which has no 'deduction'.

In the *Critique of Pure Reason*, Kant does not make this
explicit at the outset,[2] no doubt because, under the immediate influence of Hume's arguments, he wishes first to
take away from the understanding any claim to prove the
impossibility of the unconditioned. In the preface to the second

1. IV, 397; *Moral Law*, 65.
2. Though this is amply remedied later in the book.

edition, however, he at least partially rectifies this omission with a brief remark: 'For what necessarily forces us to transcend the limits of experience and of all appearances is the *unconditioned*, which reason, by necessity and by right, demands in things in themselves, as required to complete the series of conditions.'[3] And in the *Critique of Practical Reason* Kant asserts very clearly at the outset that one cannot prove 'the supreme principle of practical reason', viz. that the will is determined only by law, by the concept of a 'supersensuous nature'.[4] This principle has no deduction. Again, 'the moral law is given, as an apodictically certain fact, as it were, of pure reason, a fact of which we are *a priori* conscious, even if it be granted that no example could be found in which it has been followed exactly'.[5]

Kant uses a large number of expressions designating the unconditioned: the suprasensible, the highest good, the totality, the *universitas*, the noumenon, the thing in itself, the archetypal intellect, the holy will, the intuitive or creative understanding and so forth. It would be an interesting and useful task to investigate how far each of these expressions corresponds to some aspect of the comparison between the unconditioned and present-day man. However, we may spare ourselves that labour, for it is clear that all these concepts are closely linked in Kant's philosophy and share the same human and existential function.

It is only in terms of this first postulate that we can understand the meaning of the two pairs of concepts which form the very basis of the critical system: *Thing in itself* and *Appearance*, *Freedom* and *Necessity*.

II

Thing in itself and Appearance. Kant has often been accused of having admitted without good reason the existence of things in themselves, as distinct from their appearances, and for having illegitimately used the category of causality

---

3. III, 13–14; *Pure R*, 24; B xx.   4. V, 45; *Prac. R*, 46.
5. V, 47; *Prac. R*, 48.

to this end. However, the texts seem to me very clear: 'The undetermined object of an empirical intuition is entitled *appearance*.'[6]

1. The accent here is on '*undetermined*' and '*empirical*'. It follows, reversing the assertion, that the *completely determined* object of a *non-empirical* intuition is the thing in itself. And, indeed, that is what the texts say. For example, 'to know a thing completely, we must know every possible predicate, and must determine it thereby, either affirmatively or negatively. The complete determination is thus a concept, which, in its totality, can never be exhibited *in concreto*. It is based upon an idea, which has its seat solely in the faculty of reason.'[7] 'If, therefore, reason employs in the complete determination of things a transcendental substrate . . . this substrate cannot be anything else than the idea of an *omnitudo realitatis*. . . . But the concept of what thus possesses all reality is just the concept of a *thing in itself* as completely determined.'[8] (This quotation shows once again that, in the knowledge of the thing in itself, we are dealing with the category of totality which, according to Kant, is lacking in human knowledge, and which Hegel and Lukács will seek to include in such knowledge.) The entire *Critique of Pure Reason* is permeated with the idea that the thing in itself could be known only by an intellectual intuition and not by empirical intuition.

2. Human knowledge, the result of the union of sense and understanding, cannot attain the unconditioned, the completely determined.

3. But from the knowledge of appearance, which alone is accessible to us, we have no right to deduce the existence of things in themselves; indeed, '*Understanding* and *sensibility*, with us, can determine objects *only when they are employed in conjunction*. . . . If . . . anyone still hesitates . . . let him attempt. . . . The attempt must therefore be made with a synthetic and therefore transcendental principle, as, for instance . . . "Everything contingent exists as the effect of some other thing." . . . Now whence, I ask, can the under-

6. III, 50; *Pure R*, 65; B 34.   7. III, 386; *Pure R*, 489; B 601.
8. III, 387–8; *Pure R*, 490; B 603–4.

standing obtain these synthetic propositions, when the concepts are to be applied, not in their relation to possible experience, but to things in themselves (noumena)? . . . The proposition can never be established, nay, more, even the possibility of any such pure assertion cannot be shown.'[9]

4. Knowledge of things in themselves would only be possible through another kind of intuition, *qualitatively* different from that of given empirical man. The *understanding* as a purely theoretical faculty, tied to experience, cannot determine whether such an intuition exists or is even possible. For it, the suprasensible remains a problematic notion.

5. But if the unconditioned did not exist and if the intuition of given empirical man were the only possible one, then human reason would not be able to fulfil its destiny. Since the understanding can say nothing about the existence or non-existence, the possibility or impossibility of the suprasensible, reason can and must legitimately accept its *possibility* as a transcendental idea. (I should have liked to say a 'practical postulate', but at this stage Kant still distinguished between 'practical' and 'speculative' ideas, a distinction which the internal logic of the system does not require and which Kant virtually abandoned nine years later in the *Critique of Judgement*. In the latter, reason is a purely practical faculty of knowledge).

6. Once the thing in itself is accepted as a transcendental idea, it also becomes the cause of appearances, that which appears in appearances, and so on. Those are the passages repeatedly quoted by the critics. But this is to overlook the fact that such passages are not concerned to provide a proof for the existence of things in themselves: they presuppose, on the contrary, that the thing in itself has already been accepted as a transcendental idea. The proof itself is always based upon the fact that if human reason were to accept the contrary hypothesis it would be unable to fulfil its destiny, and therefore even to strive after it. It is unnecessary to dwell upon that mythical object which could not be known

9. III, 213–14; *Pure R,* 274–5; B 314–15.

by *any* subject. This is but a chimera in the minds of certain critics; there is no trace of it in the writings of Kant.

III

Freedom and Necessity. I must admit that Kant seems to me to have given to this problem the clearest and least ambiguous answer of any that I have found in the whole history of philosophy. It provides the only possible basis for any philosophy of history, whether materialist or idealist, as well as for any scientific sociology, and for the human sciences in general, in so far as they make any claim to be *sciences* rather than vulgar materialist metaphysics or intuitionist flights of fancy. But since the methodological distortions of the human sciences today make the understanding of this problem so difficult, I shall try here to set out Kant's point of view as I understand it, as clearly as possible and in a purely systematic way, without cumbrous scholarly references.[10] At the end I shall point out where I have perhaps departed from a strictly scholarly interpretation.

We have seen that in the precritical period[11] Kant already distinguished three different spheres of the given: the mechanical, the biological and the spiritual. This last, in the critical philosophy, eventually becomes the intelligible world of freedom.

In the *mechanical sciences*, the understanding deals with objects determined solely by the past. If we neglect the present influences of life and mind, previous events in the world completely determine the present state and motion of every particle of inert matter. Kant knows, of course, and tells us repeatedly, that our limited conceptual knowledge can never achieve the complete determination of even a single inert object. Nevertheless, it is here that the abstract conceptual knowledge of the understanding comes closest to the concrete given.

10. The most important texts are as follows: III, 360; *Pure R*, 461; B 556 et seq. v, 89; *Prac. R*, 92 et seq. 'Critical elucidation of the analytic of pure practical reason.' v, 357 et seq.; *Tel. J.*

11. See *The only possible ground* and *Dreams of a Visionary.*

In biology, in the knowledge of the organic world, the situation is quite different. Here, not only is the whole determined by its parts, but the parts in their functions and connections are also determined by the whole.[12] The organic individual appears as 'possessing an intrinsic finality'; in it, 'every part is reciprocally both end and means'.[13] Now, our understanding is unable to grasp the whole before the parts other than 'by analogy with the causality that looks to ends'. We can only understand a whole which determines its parts and their reciprocal relations if we also assume the existence of a transcendent being in whose consciousness there already exists in advance a concept of this whole according to which it consciously organizes the parts.

Thus, any mechanical explanation of organic life is insufficient. To it must be added another, teleological principle by virtue of which we think of nature as a conscious producer, as 'possessed of a faculty of its own for acting *technically*'. However, this can only be a problematic regulative principle of reflective judgement; it must never become a constitutive principle of determinant judgement. We must consider the organic as though there were a goal intrinsic to nature, but we must never assert that this is in fact the product of an intentionally working cause. For we can imagine that a higher understanding which knew the whole before the parts could likewise understand the organic immanently, without transcendent mediation. The teleological viewpoint in biology can thus only be a necessary aid to our limited analytic understanding, but not a means of really understanding organic life.

According to Kant, there is for us only one possible way of constructing experience on the basis of the empirically given. This is by establishing connections and explaining them as in the mechanical sciences. We must use the same

12. Of course, I am speaking here not of the universe but of the totality of an organic individual or, occasionally, of the species.

13. An interesting question which Kant does not deal with explicitly, and which still remains obscure today, is that of the extent to which mechanical causality could be defined as determination by the past, organic causality as determination by the present, and mental causality as determination by the future.

method in the realm of organic life and proceed as far as possible on this road towards the explanation of phenomena. Only when this no longer suffices, when we encounter a unity and a structure which are no longer or not at present amenable to mechanical explanation, must we make appeal to a teleological view of phenomena, though not to teleological explanation.

Here, an important methodological question arises. Kant asks and answers it in his treatment of freedom, but I should like to consider it forthwith, since I believe that an analogous solution is possible here. Between the realm of inert matter, where the whole is determined by the parts and the present by the past, and the realm of organic life, where the totalities of individual organism and species determine the parts and where, consequently, the present is at once cause and effect, there is an essential qualitative difference. No motion and no composition, however complicated, of particles of inert matter could ever produce a living organic individual.[14] Nevertheless, there is in nature continual interaction between inanimate objects and living beings.

But how, given this interaction, is it still possible to submit the whole of nature to deterministic explanation? Do we not frequently encounter, in popular treatments of the subject, the claim that the least interruption of mechanical causality would suffice to remove all possibility of deterministic or even scientific explanation? It is therefore important to stress that this claim is *incorrect*, and it seems to me not the least of the merits of the critical philosophy that it was the first to recognize this.

14. Of course, biologists must never abandon the search for the means of producing life from inert matter. Kant implicitly demands this when he says that 'mechanical explanation must be extended as far as possible'. If it were successful, nothing essential to Kant's position would be changed. There would then be only two radically separate spheres, that of matter and that of mind, as with Descartes. Between inert matter and organic matter there would still remain a qualitative difference, though not a sharp one, admitting of gradations and borderline cases. One thing must nevertheless be clear; the problem of the production of life is a problem for physics and chemistry; for the biologist, life will always remain a premiss of his science. As yet, however, we have little with which to confront Kantian scepticism; in fact, in a hundred and fifty years biology has made little *decisive* progress towards the experimental solution of this problem.

It is nevertheless true that the least possibility of *arbitrariness*, of *absolute* indeterminacy, would suffice to make any coherent scientific explanation impossible. But the organic (and, as we shall see later, the mental) is neither arbitrary nor absolutely indeterminate. It is, on the contrary, subject to an order which is strict and rigorous, albeit not mechanical. Moreover, all serious advocates of the teleological point of view are perfectly well aware of this. In a teleological order, for example, things and events would be as necessary as in a mechanical one; their necessity would merely be determined by the future, by the goal, and not, as in a mechanical order, by the past. Chance, as Bergson has clearly shown, is merely one order seen from the point of view of another which is different from it.

In addition to the mechanical order to which, according to Kant, inert matter is subject, and the teleological order governed by future goals which, he says, has a *constitutive* value only for the practical realm of reason and freedom,[15] there may exist yet another order, almost incomprehensible to our limited understanding, that of living matter dominated by the totalities of the organic individual and the species. Today we should probably also add the strict order of statistical probability which, according to most physicists, governs inert matter at a certain level.

Now all these different orders *can be seen from the point of view of a single one of them*, so long as all the factors ruled by the other orders are regarded as constants which must naturally be known as precisely as possible, but which cannot be further reduced or explained. In scientific thought and in everyday life we often come across comparable examples of the integration of different orders into a particular one; thus, for example, scientific psychology and sociology can establish more or less exact causal laws precisely because they accept as a fact, as a constant which is not to be analysed or explained, that man is an intellectual being whose actions are governed, to a greater or lesser extent, by conscious and voluntary goals. For such sciences, it is simply a question of establishing as precisely as possible the

15. And *not* for the organic realm.

influence of external conditions on the consciousness, the wills and the actions of men, and conversely, the influence of this consciousness, of these wills and actions, on the surrounding environment. Such a task is obviously much more difficult than, but not essentially different in nature from, that of the natural, and even the physico-chemical, sciences.

That is why the human sciences must proceed not by feeling or intuition but by an *empirical* and, so far as circumstances permit, *experimental* study. Given its much more complex subject-matter, however, this study can as yet achieve only a less precise and less rigorous knowledge than that attained by the natural and physico-chemical sciences.

Again, there are technical and practical rules which are governed by their goal and by the future; they can even be found collected in books, for example, in a political manual, a medical treatise or a cookery book. Now in these works, mechanical or organic causality is integrated only implicitly, as a constant which is not to be reduced or explained but only to be known as precisely as possible. For the goal of a practical and technical rule is to show how a man can attain his ends, *in spite of or by means of* these other orders. That the politician or the doctor is a man who, as such, can fall in love or die, that the house where one is cooking may collapse as the result of an earthquake – the authors of such works are certainly not unaware of these things, but it would be out of place to speak of them in a treatise on politics, medicine or cookery; they are more or less precisely known constants which it is unnecessary to analyse in more detail.[16] Similarly, because of the interaction

16. In answer to the possible objection of certain 'Marxists' who are as frightened of the word 'constant' as the rationalists are of 'variable', I should like further to note:

(a) that this 'constancy' is nothing but the order of change, an order which man necessarily assumes in his every action;

(b) that this order can never be known definitively but always with a greater or lesser degree of precision, and that because of this, knowledge of it must be continually improved by the analysis of concrete situations.

Hegel and Marx rightly struggled against every attempt at schematization here. But general rejection of the postulate of regularity means the renuncia-

of the different orders such technical rules must obviously be much more complex and less precise than purely practical or ethical norms which disregard any influence of sensible reality on the pure will.

In the case of the relations between the statistical probabilistic order of quantum physics and that of classical mechanical causality, the question should be even simpler, for here there are no longer two essentially different orders, the latter being only a special case of the former.

After these observations on the relations between the mechanical and organic orders, it should be easier to grasp Kant's conception of practical and intelligible freedom. Man's destiny is to aspire to a higher state, to the unconditioned. Each of his actions may be accomplished with the aim of realizing this destiny, in which case the action is free; equally, it may have another motive and another causality, in which case it is not free. There is no third possibility.

We know from the existence of the moral law that human freedom is possible and real. The moral law is the *ratio cognoscendi* of freedom, which is in turn the *ratio essendi* of the moral law. Whilst he is under no illusions about man in bourgeois individualist society and is indeed rather inclined to pessimism, Kant never ceases to emphasize that in empirical reality there is perhaps no single action which is truly free. However, this is not a refutation of freedom as such; for every man, even one who has never performed a moral and truly free action, recognizes an imperative, a moral law, and thus at least the possibility of acting freely. Above all, however, it must be stressed that the realm of freedom and reason is not that of the arbitrary, but constitutes for man an *order* which is strictly determined by the future and by the supreme goal.

tion of all science and all effective action: I should no longer be able to cross the road for fear that a primeval monster might spring up and carry me off into some bewitched world. To break off all contact with reality and to construct such an Alice-in-Wonderland world is indeed mystical romanticism. Historical materialism must obviously assume a constant which is postulated but never entirely known. It is on this very point that superficial critics have accused it of self-contradiction.

Kant calls the aspiration towards the absolute which is immanent to man his *intelligible character*. It is found whenever and wherever a man exists; thus it is not created, does not vary and remains extra-temporal. We grasp it directly as soon as we have regard to the *ought*, to moral action. However, on the theoretical and contemplative level, it is inaccessible to us, since everything empirically given is subject to biological and mechanical causality and is therefore appearance. Thus on the theoretical level only the *empirical character* of man can be grasped. His intelligible character, the aspiration towards a higher state, constitutes the practical realm of mind. This is a new, third order in addition to mechanical causality and organic life; so far as we know positively today, no known complexity of inert or organic matter can give rise to a glimmer of mind.[17] Mind is something original and qualitatively new.

The actual empirical actions of man thus belong to two qualitatively different spheres, that of the practical *autonomy* of the spirit and that of mechanical and biological *heteronomy*. Kant calls the first *causality through freedom*, since the determining principle of action is internal and situated in the intelligible world, in the future (in the realization of the kingdom of ends); the second he calls heteronomy, because the action is determined by the external

17. Of course, positive science here also proceeds from the hypothesis that somewhere one day life was born of dead matter and at a later stage mind from biological organization. Kant shows his awareness of this (many passages in his works remind one of Darwinism) and indeed tacit approval of it in saying that the attempt to provide scientific explanation for everything must not be circumscribed. However, he obviously doubts whether it can ever be anything more than a working hypothesis; and indeed today, 140 years after Kant's death, our treatment of these questions remains at the stage of research and hypothesis.

Let us suppose for a moment that science manages experimentally to create life from dead matter and to explain how mind arises from the organic. Would this change our problem in any way? Scarcely. The first question is physico-chemical, the second biological. The biologist as such does not seek to create life: he presupposes it in his science. The historian or sociologist does the same for mind. There would thus still be three *essentially* and *qualitatively* different spheres, which would no longer be rigidly separated from one another but would overlap in certain cases, and in place of the philosophy of Kant, there would be the confirmation of its continuation in the dialectic of Hegel and Marx.

world and by the past. Thus every human action can be considered from two different points of view:

1. It can be seen from the theoretical and contemplative point of view of the empirical and deterministic human sciences. Here, intelligible freedom constitutes an implicit presupposition, a constant which, just because it is a constant, is not always expressed explicitly. Since the realm of intelligible freedom is not arbitrary but constitutes a rigorous order, since it is a matter not of chance but of *causality through freedom*, it might be possible to calculate with precision not only the influence of any given temporal and empirical phenomenon upon the *empirical operation* of the intelligible will but also the degree of assistance or resistance with which the world affects the realization of its goals. In more modern language, if we suppose that all the empirical elements are known (which is of course never possible in practice), past empirical phenomena could in each case be related to the empirical action being performed through the formulation of a mathematical function in which the intelligible character, human freedom, would figure implicitly as a constant. Precisely because it is a constant, it is in permanent danger of disappearing in reification. The empiricist sociologist finds this constant neither essential nor interesting. He is content to discover more or less precise laws connecting consecutive events. But this can never satisfy the philosopher.

To illustrate this difference, the example of a falling stone which Kant borrows from Spinoza could hardly be bettered. There are still empiricist sociologists today who maintain that the only difference between mechanical causality and human causality lies in the fact that the one is unconscious whilst the other is conscious. If it were conscious, a falling stone would believe that it was freely following its trajectory. Kant seizes upon this example to make his conception clear. The will of the stone would arise only when it was thrown,[18] but in man there is a primal free will which, although it can obviously be hindered by external empirical influences,

18. To be precise, it should perhaps be added that the stone's will to follow gravitation would itself arise externally from the existence of another mass.

cannot be suppressed. The most evil empirical action is still the result of a twofold determination: that of the intelligible free will and that of the empirical influence of the external world. This intelligible world of freedom constitutes the presupposition (one could perhaps say the *a priori*) of all the human sciences and separates them from the natural sciences, just as the implicit presupposition of life separates biology from chemistry and physics.

2. Human actions can, however, be experienced from a quite different point of view, from the ethical and practical point of view. This completely changes the picture. Here, each man immediately experiences his intelligible freedom. He feels that there is a supreme norm which *should* determine his actions; anything else is seen merely as a favourable circumstance or an unfortunate hindrance in relation to their realization. Everything mechanical or biological figures here only as a more or less precisely known constant, to be used or overcome in order to achieve one's ends. At most, the empirical can affect the manner and degree of this realization; it can never dominate or limit the freedom of the will. Pure will always remains free. It is determined by nothing external in the past or the present, but exclusively by its goal. The realm of freedom is the realm of the future, just as the realm of mechanical causality is the realm of the past.[19]

Having set out schematically the basic elements of the problem of freedom, I must add one or two rather more scholarly considerations. What I have said is at variance on one point with a strictly scholarly interpretation of the texts. The idea of a constant which I have used does *not* appear in

19. Two further observations must be added here:

(a) Of the two points of view (the contemplative and the practical) the latter is the most perfect for humanity. In extreme cases, the pure theoretician can completely disregard mental life, whilst the practical man must know the real connections as precisely as possible in order to achieve his ends.

(b) We are now able to appreciate the essential difference between the human sciences (history, sociology, etc.) and the philosophy of history. The former are theoretical and, like all contemplative visions, dominated by the past or at most by the present. The philosophy of history considers every event in relation to the realization of supreme human ends. It is practical and directed towards the future. Thus all the so-called 'logical contradictions' of historical materialism disappear (see Chapter 4, Section 111).

Kant; it is reified. With him, the two ways of seeing (practical and contemplative) appear as radically separate. Neither of the two shows through even weakly in the other in the form of a constant, although a large number of texts clearly tend in the direction of my account. Nevertheless, Kant's fundamental theses on this question seem to me correct, viz.:

1. Man is free, and his will can and must be determined exclusively by his intelligible goals.

2. From the contemplative and theoretical point of view, human actions can be regarded as mechanically determined by the past.

3. There is no contradiction between these two claims.

What seems to me incorrect is the claim that it is impossible for man to unite theory and practice. But this limitation of Kant's thought is explicable in terms of the social situation of Germany in his time. The unity between his theoretical views and their realization in action could not be achieved by the German bourgeoisie; that is why it appeared something of a mystery on the theoretical level. In any case, I do not believe that any philosophical system, either before or after Kant, has shown such profound insight into the problem of human freedom.[20]

IV

A question almost as difficult as the preceding one is that of the doctrine of the radical evil in man. On this topic I shall attempt to demonstrate that:

(a) The doctrine of the radical evil is not a foreign body in Kant's philosophy. It is not only justified but even necessary for the coherence of the system. It is certainly not a concession to the Christian religion.

---

20. Lukács in his book opposed any separation of theory from practice. But in the heat of the battle he did not see that once action is no longer individual but social, and thus necessarily *conscious*, a theoretical and deterministic science of man becomes absolutely necessary. Its possibility must therefore be explained and given epistemological foundations. Most other Marxists have merely undertaken sociology without the philosophy of history, allowing human freedom to disappear – a reification far more serious than Kant's.

(b) However, the obscurity of the relations between free-dom and necessity discussed earlier prevents Kant from integrating the doctrine of the radical evil into his system. That is why it may sometimes appear as a kind of 'concession'.

Since the texts are particularly clear,[21] I can be brief. The radical evil consists in 'the indwelling of the evil principle with the good . . . in human nature'. There exists in man both a 'predisposition to good' and a 'propensity to evil'. A being in which only the good principle acted would be a holy will. But man is also exposed to the influence of his sensuous nature, to heteronomy. To the extent that this heteronomy opposes free will as a principle which can be and has been conquered, man is certainly not a holy will, but nor is he thereby evil – only weak, or, one might say, limited. But his sensuous nature does not operate mechanically: 'freedom of the will is of a wholly unique nature in that an incentive can determine the will to an action *only so far as the individual has incorporated it into his maxim*'.[22] Consequently, for a sensuous inclination to lead to action it must first be accepted by the conscious will, incorporated into its maxim. Men have two kinds of maxim:

(a) Good ones, which enjoin them to be determined exclusively by intelligible ends.

(b) Bad ones, which enjoin them to be determined by other motives.

We thus have the following systematic classification of possible kinds of will:

1. The holy will, determined *exclusively* by good maxims.

2. The good human will, which contains the two kinds of maxim, but in which the good ones overcome the evil ones.

3. The evil human will, which also contains the two kinds of maxim, but in which the evil ones overcome the good ones.

4. The diabolical will, determined exclusively by evil maxims.

---

21. *Religion within the limits of reason alone*; *Werke* VI, 17–55.
22. VI, 23–4; *Religion*, 19.

'The wickedness (*vitiositas, pravitas*) or, if you like, the corruption (*corruptio*) of the human heart is the propensity of the will to maxims which neglect the incentives springing from the moral law in favour of others which are not moral.'[23] Externally, of course, such actions may be perfectly 'legal'. It is natural that in his thoroughgoing critique of contemporary man,[24] Kant should find in him a radical propensity to evil. He provides a telling critique of the man who has 'good morals' but who most of the time is not 'moral' and acts according to the letter rather than the spirit of the law. The details belong to anthropology and not to philosophy. I shall be content to quote a single passage as an example: 'A member of the British Parliament once exclaimed, in the heat of the debate, "Every man has his price, for which he sells himself." If this is true (a question to which each must make his own answer), if there is no virtue for which some temptation cannot be found capable of overthrowing it, and if whether the good or evil spirit wins us over to his party depends merely on which bids the most and pays us most promptly, then certainly it holds true of men universally, as the apostle said: "They are all under sin, – there is none righteous (in the spirit of the law), no, not one." '[25] One could hardly be more categorical.

However, the titles of the two following chapters, 'Concerning the conflict of the good with the evil principle for sovereignty over man' and 'The victory of the good over the evil principle, and the founding of a kingdom of God on earth' express the second element in Kant's thought, the aspiration towards a better world and the hope for its realization. I shall return to this later.

23. VI, 30; *Religion*, 25.
24. To avoid continual repetition, let me say here for the last time that Kant is always concerned with man in general. In fact, however, he describes the man of the bourgeois individualist social order then arising. As with all human types, such a man no doubt embodies certain elements conditioned by his historical situation and certain elements of man in general. The dependence of knowledge upon social conditions results from the inability of ideologists belonging to a particular social group clearly to perceive the frontier between the two.
25. VI, 38–9; *Religion*, 34.

So far, all seems clear. But it is now that the difficulties begin. For given Kant's sharp separation of intelligible freedom, comprehensible only on the practical level, from the influence of sensibility, which is limited to the world of appearances, it is not possible to see how the intelligible good principles and the heteronomous evil principles can compete with one another for control over man, or more especially how heteronomous motives become maxims of a will which is both immoral and free. Indeed, there is no room for evil either in the sensible, where it would be merely an obstacle, or in the intelligible, which is the domain of practical freedom alone. It is unnecessary to go into the details of Kant's development of this point. The conclusion is clear: 'the rational origin ... of the propensity to evil remains inscrutable to us'.[26] 'Evil could have sprung only from the morally-evil (not from mere limitations in our nature); and yet the original predisposition ... is a predisposition to good; there is then for us no conceivable ground from which the moral evil in us could conceivably have come.'[27]

V

In the first part of this work I quoted Kant's phrase according to which 'everything depends on our seeking out the *data* of the problem, how is the soul *present in the world, both in material and in non-material things*', and a further passage which teaches us 'that the human soul, once freed from its connections with external things, would be completely unable to change its internal state'.

In this chapter I have so far spoken of 'man' in the singular. This was necessary since exposition must begin somewhere. It was understood, however, that this isolated man does not exist, that man can only 'have an I' *in and through* community with other men and their common relations with the external world. So I shall now speak of the human community, and since I wish to stay as close as possible

to the Kantian and neo-Kantian tradition, I shall begin with
the epistemological aspect of the problem. Unfortunately,
neo-Kantianism had disastrous effects here too. Our first
task must therefore be to restore to the basic questions their
original significance.

For Descartes, Leibniz, Hume, all the great classical
philosophers, the theory of knowledge starts out from the
question summed up in Kant's brilliant formula: 'How are
synthetic judgements *a priori* possible?' That is to say: how
are judgements which 'extend our knowledge and yet are
necessary and strictly universal' possible?

To understand the meaning and the importance of this
question, we must consider in more detail certain points
which have already been mentioned several times in this
work. In any human society there must be a minimum of
common theory, feelings and moral standards for life in
common (and such life is, above all, action) to be possible.
A pack of wolves, a hive of bees or a colony of ants does not
form a society in that their communal existence is based
solely upon instinctive mutual adaptation and not upon
common thought and action.

This idea is one of the foundation-stones of Kant's philosophy. He repeatedly asserts that a number of autonomous
monads can never form a world, unless their mutual relations are already given with the existence of each one of
them. In this lies Kant's superiority over all the dogmatic
rationalists who preceded him and who admitted only an
external connection between individuals (pre-established
harmony, occasional causes, etc.). Here we are at the centre
of the problem. For it was neither by chance nor through
lack of penetration that Descartes, Leibniz and Malebranche
failed to understand the internal cohesion of the parts in
the whole. Their failure was conditioned by the social situation of the bourgeoisie whose ideology they expressed.

The bourgeois social order, by its basic structure, tends
to destroy or at least to disguise all community between
individuals. Of course, there remain various particular concrete communities which constitute the life of each separate
individual, but in the final analysis these appear as fortuitous. Man is divided, and the parts which connect him with

a concrete community appear as appendices of what he 'fundamentally' is. Man in general remains outside any community. As a German or an Englishman, he belongs to a nation, as a father to a family, as a football player to a club, but as a *man* he seems to be something quite independent, a being without any relations, entirely self-sufficient.

We must not forget, as so many Marxists do, the positive influence of this fact upon the development of the human spirit. I have already noted in the first chapter how it was trade, the production of commodities for the market, and the individualism which developed from it which opened up to man one of the most important conquests of the human spirit, individual freedom. I should like here to point out that it was also trade which made possible the birth of philosophical thought on the Asiatic coasts of Ionia and later in Athens and Magna Graecia – not, of course, in the sense that philosophy is a product of trade, but because in a society based upon buying and selling the concrete features and relations of the particular individual give way to the general and abstract features of buyer and seller. Thus thought too could be directed towards the general and abstract features of 'man'. It is because the Athenian or the Spartan, the rich man or the poor man, the man or the woman had disappeared before the general character of buyer or seller that thought could pose the general problems of man as such.

This was a great victory of the spirit over the biological and the collective.[28] Man had finally reached the basic problems. Philosophy was born. Since then, philosophy has only been able to survive where it was possible to focus attention upon man as such and to understand his peculiarities on the basis of man in general. (For example, in the Middle Ages there was a genuine Christian philosophy, since in certain of its forms Christianity is a universal and generally human religion.)

28. I use the word 'collective' in contrast to 'community'. This contrast corresponds in part to Kant's distinction between the 'anthropological' and the 'philosophical', to Hegel's 'in itself' and 'in and for itself' and to Marx's and Lukács' distinction between false and true consciousness.

Expressions such as German or French, bourgeois or proletarian philosophy only have a meaning to the extent that they merely indicate a philosophy which arose among the Germans or the French, the bourgeoisie or the proletariat, or a philosophy whose insights were made possible by the social or economic situation of these groups. They cannot indicate that the philosophy is concerned only with problems peculiar to the French or to the Germans, to the bourgeoisie or to the proletariat, nor that its results would be valid only for them. In that sense a German or bourgeois or proletarian philosophy would be as contradictory as a square circle, At most it could be called ideology, or political propaganda.[29]

All this, however, forms only one aspect of individualist ideologies. We come now to the other aspect, to reification. If the individualist world-views put man as such at the centre of interest and thus made philosophy possible, they also emptied him of any concrete relation or community. The world of the dogmatic rationalists was a world of

29. This is why there can be no question of a philosophy of intuition or of life. Life, the biological, is insufficient for philosophy; for philosophy to be possible, it must first be transformed and appear in the higher form of the human community, of reason, of mind. There was much truth in the intuitionist critique of abstract rationalism, and I shall return to this later. But the intuitionists did not represent progress in the investigation of these problems; they provided no living and concrete content for the abstract form of reason. On the contrary, they represented a regression of such proportions that the collective and the biological replaced the intellect and philosophy was no longer possible. From this point of view there is no essential difference between 'race' for the National Socialists and 'instinct' for Bergson.

Kant had seen just this danger; hence his categorical rejection of any feeling which does not arise from 'reverence for the law'. To put it simply: the man who helps another solely because he likes him, because he knows him or because he is a *Volksgenosse* might behave quite differently towards one who lacks these properties. He may remain silent in the face of all kinds of barbarity and injustice; he may give it his blessing; or indeed even participate in it. It is no coincidence that most of these 'philosophers' approve in their way of friendship and love of the fatherland or the family, but reject the love of humanity as something abstract and inauthentic. But it is precisely the aspiration towards a universal human community (in Kant reified as 'reverence for the law') which raises all other feelings from the strictly biological level to that of the intellect. Without this effort they become brute passion, clannishness, chauvinism, and so on. Of course, Kant's law is largely abstract and reified, but that is another question. However abstract and reified the form in which spirit appears in a world-view, it is still *spirit* and must not be replaced by the collective or the biological.

independent monads with only their form in common. Even this common form appeared as a mysterious and supra-sensible reality whose origin could not be seen, much less understood (as innate ideas, recollection of another exis-tence, *a priori*, etc.). Now, all great philosophies have in common the effort to grasp man as a whole in both form and content. That is why the question of the relation between abstract form and concrete content became the central problem of classical philosophy.

I have already noted the two directions in which classical philosophy attempted to unite form with content. Rational-ism was an attempt to absorb the whole of content into pure form (universal mathematics) and thus to make the *purely formal* community of individuals a material community comprehending the whole of human thought. Empiricism, on the contrary, tried to dissolve form in content, in the hope of being able to found a community which, if not necessary, was at least actual. Kant was the first great philosopher ruthlessly to dispel these two illusions and to give a precise picture of man in the bourgeois individualist social order.

We can now understand the meaning of the question which forms the foundation of classical philosophy: 'How are synthetic judgements *a priori* possible?' How do *isolated and independent* men who take no account of one another and who recognize their own reason as the sole judge and the highest court of appeal not only understand one another, but *necessarily* understand one another? What is that mini-mum of shared presuppositions which must be recognized even by two men with diametrically opposed views if they are to communicate and to conduct a conversation (in the widest sense of the term)? What is that minimum of com-munity which exists in any dialogue and makes men not independent monads but members of a greater whole, of one community, of one world?

The significance of the first text quoted in this work now becomes clear – Kant's treatment of the three forms of egoism (theoretical, aesthetic and practical egoism), whose analysis must be in part 'metaphysical' and in part 'anthro-pological'. The question of metaphysical egoism, the question 'whether I, as a thinking being, had reason to accept, apart from my own existence, the existence of a corpus of other beings in community with me (called the universe)' – this question is identical in its theoretical part with that of the possibility of synthetic *a priori* judgements, and it finds in this formula its clearest and most concise expression.

How far *can* egoism 'of the understanding, taste and practical interest' be taken? To answer this question Kant wrote the three *Critiques*, the *Groundwork of the metaphysics of morals*, and the *Metaphysical Rudiments of Natural Science*. How far, within these possible limits, egoism *in fact* goes in a given place and at a given time is a question of empirical anthropology. Kant brought to it some clarification, but he consciously left to his successors the task of providing the answers.

I could now regard this point as clarified and pass on, had not the neo-Kantian interpretation given rise to grave misconceptions which oblige me to examine at least its essential features rather more closely. The neo-Kantians would no doubt regard my position as yet another instance of that much-derided view, 'psychologism'. Disregarding the particular views of nineteenth- and twentieth-century German professors on the theory of knowledge and considering only their interpretation of Kant's philosophy, the following points are to be observed:

1. It is clear even to most of the neo-Kantians that 'remnants' of this 'fatal psychologism' are woven into and dominate the whole of Kant's work.

2. When read in context, most of the passages quoted to show that Kant at least attempted to transcend psychologism actually have the opposite effect. I quote just one example of this.

In a famous passage of the *Critique of Pure Reason*,[30] Kant takes issue with those who regard the concepts of the understanding as merely 'subjective dispositions of thought, implanted in us from the first moment of our existence'. This would certainly lead to harmony between our thought and the laws of external nature, but the categories would lack

30. III, 128–9; *Pure R*, 174–5; B 167–8.

'the necessity . . . which belongs to their very conception'. At first sight, this passage seems to support those logicians who completely separate 'logical necessity' from man. Reading right to the end, however, we learn that 'This is exactly what the sceptic most desires. For if this be the situation, all our insight, resting on the supposed objective validity of our judgements, is nothing but sheer illusion; *nor would there be wanting people who would refuse to admit this subjective necessity*,[31] a necessity which can only be felt. Certainly a man cannot dispute with anyone regarding that which depends merely on the mode in which he himself is organized.'

Kant is thus concerned with necessary agreement between men. This passage, like all those used in the polemic against psychologism, signifies simply that the categories of the understanding, together with everything *a priori*, are human and intellectual factors, not biological ones. A pack of wolves or a swarm of bees does not constitute a community. It is obvious that community requires more than fortuitous resemblance or external harmony; the elements must be conditioned in their very existence by the totality. In synthetic *a priori* judgements the community is postulated from the outset. The categories are, in spite of their reification, the theoretical expression of the human spirit and the human community.

Nevertheless, there is a partially correct side to the neo-Kantian interpretation. The two marks of pure knowledge, of knowledge *a priori*, are *necessity* and *universality*. Apart from the human, transcendentally subjective character which I have just mentioned, they both also have an objective character. They create from sensible impressions the object of knowledge – experience. The categories of the understanding determine the given (albeit not wholly). This aspect of the *a priori* elements (the only one which the neo-Kantians have generally noticed) is of course also present in Kant as well as the other. The connection between the two poses a difficult problem which may be formulated as follows: how do the *a priori* categories which

31. My italics.

make communication and understanding between men possible nevertheless refer necessarily to something outside man, to an object? Why can two men only understand one another by speaking of a third element, an object?

For classical philosophy, which thought of theoretical man as contemplative, as a *spectator*, this question was difficult to resolve. For us today it is a little clearer. In freeing the *a priori* from reification, in relating it to the real human community, we know that this community can only be based upon human activity, upon the common action of men. Now all action involves the transformation of the external world. It must relate to a common object. The function of theoretical knowledge is precisely to transform the unformed immediate given, which differs from one individual to another, into a common object. For Kant, however, knowledge and action, theory and practice, were almost totally separate; the impossibility of uniting them constituted indeed, as I have often repeated, the upper limit of his philosophy. In this context, the relation between the human aspect and the objective aspect of knowledge could only become incomprehensible, and thus in his system the two elements coexist without any connection.

But it is the mark of the truly great thinker to be aware, if only confusedly, of the limits of his vision, whilst for the *epigoni* everything seems clear and unproblematic. In this respect, a letter from Kant to J. S. Beck[32] on 'the "original activity" (the relating of a representation, *qua* determination of the subject, to an object distinguished by it, by which means it becomes a cognition and is not merely a feeling)' seems to me particularly important, especially since the freer form of a letter allows us better to grasp how Kant himself actually saw things.

'One cannot actually say that a representation *befits* another thing but only that . . . a relation to something else . . . *befits* the representation, whereby it becomes *communicable* to other people . . . we can only understand and communicate to others what we ourselves can *make*, granted that the

32. Letter to Beck of 1 July 1794; *Phil. Corr*, 216–17.

manner in which we intuit something . . . can be assumed to be the same for everybody. . . .

'The synthesizing itself is not given; on the contrary, it must be done by us: we must *synthesize* it if we are to represent anything as *synthesized* (even space and time). We are able to communicate with one another because of this synthesis. The grasping (*apprehensio*) of the given manifold and its reception in the unity of consciousness (*apperceptio*) is the same sort of thing as the representation of a composite (that is, it is only possible through synthesis), if the synthesis of my representation in the grasping, and its analysis in so far as it is a concept, yield one and the same representation (reciprocally bring forth one another). This agreement is applied to something that is valid for everyone, something distinguished from the subject, that is, an object, since it lies exclusively neither in the representation nor in consciousness but nevertheless is valid (*communicable*) for everyone.

'I notice, as I am writing this down, that I do not even entirely understand myself and I shall wish you luck if you can put this simple, thin thread of our cognitive faculty under a sufficiently bright light. Such overly refined hairsplitting is no longer for me.'

For the *epigoni*, in contrast, everything is clear. It was sufficient to reject *communication* between men as inessential 'psychologism' and to 'transcendentalize' 'doing' after their fashion, so that nothing remained but the object, the experience. Kant's problem had disappeared.

VI

I hope that Kant's formulation of the problem is now clear. His answer, however, is no less important. I have already referred to the three principal features of that answer:

1. *Against Hume and empiricism* Kant shows that the ability of men to communicate with one another and to agree at least in their general categories of thought is not a contingent circumstance, but part of the very essence of man. There are synthetic judgements *a priori*.

2. *Against Descartes, Leibniz and dogmatic rationalism* he shows that for man (read given man) this necessary agreement is restricted to the formal. Any hope that it might become complete and material without a qualitative change in the world is but an optimistic illusion.

3. Despite this insight, Kant always held fast to the idea of a higher knowledge in which content would also be universal and necessary. This is revealed in concepts such as the original understanding, intellectual intuition, the thing in itself and complete determination. They are to be found throughout the *Critique of Pure Reason*, even if they are only problematic concepts – as problematic as the transition to a higher form of community and of life was for the German bourgeoisie of the time.

In this section I shall concentrate upon the second point, the limitation of human knowledge. Here Kant shows a brilliant grasp of the essential points. Synthetic judgements *a priori* are purely formal. There is no universal criterion of truth. 'It is obvious however that . . . it is quite impossible, and indeed absurd, to ask for a general test of the truth of such content. A sufficient and at the same time a general criterion of truth cannot possibly be given.'[33] Kant is here still concerned with general logic, but the same idea is immediately carried over to the transcendental level, for otherwise 'the understanding is led to incur the risk of making . . . a material use of its pure and merely formal principles'.[34]

The whole of the sociology of knowledge is based upon this idea. Consider the implications of this: the theoretical community of men is only necessary to the extent that it is purely formal. Materially, this community is only a more or less accidental fact. All the empirical sciences belong to the sphere of that 'egoism of the understanding' whose actual extent is to be determined by anthropology. That two and two make four, that every property belongs to a substance, that everything empirical has a cause, these are propositions which every man accepts and must accept by virtue of his life in society. (If from a taste for paradox he denies them

33. 111, 79; *Pure R*, 97–8; B 83.   34. 111, 82; *Pure R*, 100; B 88.

verbally, he must nevertheless presuppose their truth in his activity.) This is enough to assure the possibility of communication between individuals. But it goes no further. For in the case of a proposition with the slightest material content, no man can be obliged to accept it if it is not obvious to him or if it is in opposition to the interests of his social group. There is no material criterion of truth; even if there is something which all men accept as true, each recognizes only his own understanding as the supreme court of judgement.

The most cursory glance at the present state of the sciences shows that these are no mere academic propositions. In the natural sciences, where the interests of all men are more or less the same and where selfish interests collide less often, the sum of universally acknowledged truths is greatest. In the human sciences, however, where the economic, social and religious interests of different groups come into play, the situation is truly catastrophic. '*Einfühlungspsychologie*', 'history as art', and so on – the terminology alone indicates the conscious renunciation of universality. One need only consider a few specific instances, such as the history of the French Revolution, the sociology of the state or the theory of value, to see the most diverse and contrasting opinions all being presented with the same conviction. And where interest requires it, this chaos can also infect the natural sciences, as with racial theories in biology.

So long as a higher form of knowledge, that is to say, a higher form of real human community, has not been achieved, the possibility of genuinely scientific knowledge will depend upon the anthropological and in the last instance fortuitous circumstance that in a given sphere social interests coincide. Elsewhere, particularly in the human sciences, scientific knowledge remains a problematic concept, a question which cannot easily be resolved. For present-day man, there is no criterion of truth which is both material and universal.[35]

35. My own position here can be briefly set out as follows:

(a) The only possible criterion of truth is action, practice.

(b) In a society where it is not the community, the *we*, but the individual, the *I*, which constitutes the subject of action, the criterion of truth can only

VII

I must here add a few further remarks on Kant's theory of knowledge.

The majority of rationalist philosophers recognize only the division of the faculty of knowledge into sensibility and understanding. Kant was the first great modern philosopher to make the threefold division: sensibility, understanding and reason. At first sight, this division appears clear: the given material, the application of limited form by given man, and the ideal totality as a regulative idea. But the division is complicated by the fact that sensibility is not only content but in part also form, pure intuition (space and time). This may be explained in terms of Kant's basic idea, namely that no power in the world could unite completely autonomous and independent elements into a single whole. Even what is given by the senses cannot be entirely atomized and monadic, for it would then be impossible to grasp it in a single apperception, in consciousness. Pure intuition, space and time, constitutes precisely that formal totality which is the first condition of knowledge by the understanding and reason.

Three important points must be stressed here:

1. Space and time are given to us as formal wholes, sensible impressions as the autonomous elements which form the content of these wholes. 'The proposition that the totality of all conditions in space and time is unconditioned is false. For if all things in space and time are conditioned (internally), no totality of them is possible. Thus those who accept an absolute whole composed merely of conditioned conditions contradict themselves . . . and yet space is to be seen as such a whole, as is elapsed time.'[36]

2. It follows that knowledge relating to sensible impressions is methodologically quite distinct from knowledge

---

be individual and cannot have universal validity. In so far as limited groups (classes, nations, etc.) constitute the subject of action, there arise class ideologies and national ideologies which may be true or false according to whether or not they have the whole of humanity as an end.

36. XX, 288.

relating solely to pure intuition (space and time). In the first, representations are subsumed under the concepts of the understanding. It is abstract – in Lask's terminology, analytic. Representations are determined by it without complete determination, the concrete, being attained. The concept 'man' signifies only the common properties obtained through the analysis of a whole series of representations subsumed *under* it. In the second, the whole is given before the parts. Concepts are therefore merely rules for the construction of the parts. Here knowledge no longer proceeds by *subsumption under* concepts, but by *construction of* concepts. It is thus concrete, emanatist, and within the framework of the purely formal attains the individual and concrete representation. The concept 'square' is not an abstract summary of the properties common to all squares, but a rule according to which squares can be constructed within the given totality of space. Although as Lask rightly notes the analysis of mathematical thought is for Kant a secondary consideration, these ideas are nevertheless developed clearly and unambiguously at several points in the *Critique of Pure Reason*.

3. What remains unclear is how, whilst space and time are totalities *in* which (and not under which) sensible representations are contained (and not subsumed) they are nevertheless not themselves given as wholes but rather constituted only in human action, in composition or construction. I do not feel that Kant entirely overcomes this difficulty.

With regard to the transcendental deduction of the categories, whilst I do not wish to enter into the protracted debate extending from the neo-Kantians right up to Heidegger's most recent book, I should like to emphasize two points.

1. Kant is in no way refuted by the fact that the later development of science has modified the number and content of the categories. He knew perfectly well that one cannot deduce 'such and so many' categories; they are simply given. The deduction concerns only the justification and the necessity of *form as such*, not of its specific structure, for 'this peculiarity of our understanding, that it can produce

a priori unity of apperception solely by means of the cate-gories, and only by such and so many, is as little capable of further explanation as why we have just these and no other functions of judgement, or why space and time are the only forms of our possible intuition'.[37] Now, that which is in-capable of explanation is merely a fact which might have been otherwise.

2. An idea which continually returns in Kant's philosophy is that the consciousness of 'I am' is not an intuition but only an intellectual representation and 'has not, therefore, the least predicate'. It is entirely empty and can only acquire content through knowledge of the external world. For 'outer experience is really immediate, and . . . only by means of it is inner experience – not indeed the consciousness of my own existence, but the determination of it in time – possible'.[38] On the other hand, 'the original synthetic unity of transcendental apperception', that is, the union of all the divers representations of intuition in 'the act of appercep-tion, "I think"' is necessary for both outer and inner experience.

The transcendental deduction is ultimately developed as follows:[39]

1. 'The exposition of the pure concepts of the understand-ing . . . as principles of the possibility of experience.' In other words, it is only by logical and scientific thought, by the empirical employment of the categories, that man can attain experience.

2. 'but of this[40] [experience – L.G.] as the *determination* of appearance in space and time *in general*'

3. 'and this determination in turn as ultimately following from the *original* synthetic unity of apperception, as the form of the understanding in its relation to space and time, the original forms of sensibility'. In other words, the union of representations in the 'act of apperception, "I think"' only takes place in the employment of the categories for experience in accordance with the understanding.

37. 111, 116; *Pure R*, 161; B 145–6.   38. 111, 192; *Pure R*, 245–6; B 277.
39. 111, 129; *Pure R*, 175; B 168–9.   40. (Translation slightly modified.)

In this exposition, the terminology of which may at first sight appear complicated, an idea is expressed which still retains its value and importance today, namely, that the act 'I think' and indeed any content-full determination of consciousness, of the 'I am', is inseparable from knowledge through the understanding and through reason. This is the *philosophical foundation* of Kant's reply to the philosophy of feeling, the political aspect of which we have already encountered in the article against Jacobi. When external and internal reality is no longer thought by means of the concepts of the understanding but is directly lived, then together with the 'I think' any more precise determination of the 'I am' also disappears (Scheler calls this '*sich in eins fühlen*'). This is merely the philosophical and psychological aspect of the disappearance of individual freedom to which the Jacobi article referred.

VIII

Let me now briefly and schematically sum up the essential features of Kant's theory of knowledge:

1. Man's destiny is to strive towards the unconditioned. In epistemology, this unconditioned would be the exhaustive determination of the given, knowledge of the totality, of the thing in itself.

2. This ideal knowledge would realize the theoretical totality with regard not only to the object (as universe), but also to the subjects (as perfect community). Thus, at least from the theoretical and contemplative point of view, a material and necessary human community would be established. There would be a material criterion of truth.

3. But human knowledge is limited. It can only attain a purely formal and empty totality with respect both to the object, the universe (space and time), and to the subjects, the human community (pure intuition and *a priori* categories).

4. Although the idea of a close connection between the subjective totality (the human community) and the objective totality (the universe) dominates Kant's theory of know-

ledge, the nature of this connection is not entirely clear to him. I think the reason for this lies in his inability to attain a clear picture of the relations between thought and action, between theory and practice.

5. The problem of the content of the totality (of concrete community and empirical experience) can only be dealt with case by case, according to the anthropological and empirical circumstances.

6. But for man to approach the unconditioned, the totality content must first be given to form, since even the formal totality does not exist independently of man but only in his action, in the unification of the manifold given in a single *experience*.

7. By the empirical employment of the categories of the understanding, by the unification of sensations in a single experience, the consciousness of the 'I am' receives a concrete and intuitive content; the individual becomes a rational and spiritual being, albeit a limited one – a man. It is only on the basis of this empirical experience in conformity with the understanding that man achieves the membership of a community (albeit a reified and formal one) which is necessary to his essence. But the content-full material community remains a function of the concrete anthropological and empirical conditions, that is, from the point of view of freedom and reason, it remains something whose realization is in the last instance contingent, but which must be sought necessarily.

8. On the basis of these assumptions, the principal task of the critique of pure reason consists in the struggle against two dangerous illusions which could lead man to betray his destiny and to abandon the search for the absolute, namely:

(a) *the transcendental employment of the categories*, the idea that the human faculty of knowledge, such as it is and without qualitative change, can attain the absolute, the illusion of all dogmatic metaphysics, and

(b) *sceptical empiricism*, the contrary affirmation, according to which the unconditioned, the totality in general, is unreal and inaccessible to any kind of knowledge. If this were the case, the aspiration towards a higher state would become meaningless: speculative ideas would lose their regulative meaning and practical postulates their practical meaning.

In the first case, man would be a god and there could be nothing higher *than* him; in the second, he would be a demon or an animal and there could be nothing higher *for* him. However, he is neither the one nor the other, but something intermediate – a being who must realize his destiny.

With this world-view common to the greatest thinkers and poets of the bourgeoisie, to Racine and Pascal in France, to Goethe and Kant in Germany, classical thought and art reached the summit of their achievement. Thereafter, there were only three possible paths: (1) the return to classical individualism (a path which was partially open in countries where bourgeois society still represented the future, for example in Germany: Fichte, Nietzsche); (2) the path towards decadence, towards an *apologia* for the existing order; and (3) beyond individualism, the path which leads to a philosophy of the *we*, and of the human community.

IX

Having reached the practical philosophy, I can now be much briefer. In its essentials it is analogous to the theoretical philosophy, although of course important differences remain. This is not, as is often claimed, the result of a particular predilection for symmetry on Kant's part. It is simply that in the two cases the same subject-matter and the same questions are considered from two different angles. The practical philosophy, like the theoretical philosophy, is concerned with man in bourgeois individualist society (for Kant, of course, man in general) and his relation to the community. It must be noted, however, that reification here takes less opaque forms as a result of the obvious priority of the subject over the object on this level.

The point of departure is the aspiration towards the unconditioned, towards the totality, of which I spoke at the beginning of this chapter. The radical atomism of all material human relations comes next. At first sight, there can here be even less question of community than on the theoretical level. The theoretical community was endangered by the absence of any *material* criterion of truth and thus of anything which could require men to agree as to the content of their thought. Kant had demonstrated at least the possibility of community through the existence of a *formal* criterion of truth.

On the practical level, however, the problem seems far more serious. Here one can no longer ask what could require men to desire the same things, for it is precisely when and because they desire the same things that conflict, the absence of community, becomes most obvious.[41] 'Though elsewhere natural laws make everything harmonious, if one here attributed the universality of law to this maxim, there would be the extreme opposite of harmony, the most arrant conflict, and the complete annihilation of the maxim itself and its purpose. . . . In this way a harmony may result resembling that depicted in a certain satirical poem as existing between a married couple bent on going to ruin, "Oh, marvellous harmony, what he wants is what she wants"; or like the pledge which is said to have been given by Francis I to the Emperor Charles V, "What my brother wants (Milan), that I want too."'

Here the two dangerous illusions which the critical philosophy must combat also appear.

(a) To dogmatic rationalism corresponds the Stoic morality according to which ideal harmony, the absolute, can be attained by independent individuals relying only upon themselves and upon their own reason.

(b) To sceptical empiricism corresponds utilitarianism, the Epicurean philosophy in all its divers forms, which rejects all *a priori* values of reason, but which expects from the sensibility of individuals not, it is true, a necessary community, but at least an actual one.

The sole difference is that whereas in the speculative field the most powerful and dangerous enemy was philosophical rationalism, in the practical field it is utilitarianism. Here again, the first task is to oppose utilitarianism by demonstrating that men are not independent monads but even now

41. v, 28; *Prac. R*, 27–8.

form a community, albeit a purely formal one – that there are practical synthetic judgements *a priori*. The function of formal unification (which in the theoretical part was that of pure intuition and the categories of the understanding) is here fulfilled by the only practical synthetic proposition *a priori*, the categorical imperative: '*Act only on that maxim through which you can at the same time will that it should become a universal law.*'[42]

This categorical imperative is present in every man without exception, even when it operates against him. 'If we now attend to ourselves whenever we transgress a duty, we find that we in fact do not will that our maxim should become a universal law – since this is impossible for us – but rather that its opposite should remain a law universally; we only take the liberty of making an *exception* to it for ourselves (or even just for this once) to the advantage of our inclination. Consequently, if we weighed it all up from one and the same point of view – that of reason – we should find a contradiction in our own will, the contradiction that a certain principle should be objectively necessary as a universal law and yet subjectively should not hold universally but should admit of exceptions.'[43]

By the fact that each man recognizes it (even if he usually gives it a *contradictory content*), the categorical imperative unites all men in a formal whole. By it each man is bound, consciously or unconsciously, to other men in each of his own actions, as in the judgements he makes upon the actions of others. But this imperative is purely formal, for every material and particular motive is contrary to it and can only put men in opposition to one another and atomize the community. 'If a rational being can think of its maxims as practical universal laws, he can do so only by considering them as principles which contain the determining grounds of the will because of their form and not because of their matter.'[44]

Hegel and Lukács have objected that the examples chosen by Kant surreptitiously introduce a determinate content

42. IV, 421; *Groundwork*, 88.   43. IV, 424; *Groundwork*, 91–2.
44. V, 27; *Prac. R*, 26.

into the form. For example, Kant writes that it would always be immoral and in contradiction with the categorical imperative to accept a deposit and subsequently to deny that one had done so and refuse to return it. Kant's critics see in this the introduction of a concrete capitalist institution into the general human and supratemporal form, for 'if there were no such thing as a deposit, where then would be the contradiction?'

Elsewhere such accusations are probably justified. This is hardly surprising, since even the greatest thinkers are subject to illusions resulting from the social conditioning of their thought. In this particular instance, however, a passage in one of Kant's letters shows that he has clearly seen the difference between the material historical order and the purely formal characteristics common to all orders. He writes:[45] 'As for the question, Can't there be actions that are incompatible with the existence of a natural order and that yet are prescribed by the moral law? I answer, Certainly! If you mean, a *definite order of nature*, for example, that of the present world. A courtier, for instance, must recognize it as a duty always to be truthful, though he would not remain a courtier for long if he were. But there is in that *typus* only the form of a *natural order in general*, that is, the compatibility of actions as events in accord with *moral laws*, and as [events] in accord with *natural laws*, too, but merely in terms of *their generality*, for this in no way concerns the special laws of any particular nature.'

It is clear that Kant here introduces into the 'natural order in general' much of the content of the ideal society he dreams of, and indeed, that ideal society is also historically conditioned. But he has at least clearly seen the methodological problem. Moreover, with regard to the example referred to above, Kant could have replied to his critics that a deposit may exist wherever men possess objects of any kind (even if only objects for consumption). Furthermore, even if the case arises only rarely, it would always be immoral to deny having received in deposit an object which one has in fact received.

45. Letter to J. S. Beck of 3 July 1792; *Phil. Corr,* 192-4.

In the relations between form and content, however, there is a great difference between the practical and theoretical spheres. In the latter, the function of combining the material of sensible impressions into universal experience was fulfilled by form. Between form and matter there was no contradiction. The two being, as it were, complementary, neither could have an autonomous existence; together, however, they constituted human thought as it is encountered in everyday life and in the empirical sciences.

In the practical sphere, the situation is quite different. Here there is a radical contradiction between form and matter, and each can develop only at the expense of the other. Anything a man does for pleasure or from inclination undermines the community, even if his action appears outwardly to conform to the categorical imperative. For once an action has a material motive, it is at most 'legal', and there is a risk that the man might act in just the opposite way in the absence of that motive. Today, universality can only arise in so far as everything material is excluded from the motives of action and respect for the law remains the sole motive.

The most violent objections have been made against Kant's formalism. (He is accused, for example, of emptying man of all content.) But he could have replied to all his critics that it was hardly his fault if with man as he is given all content leads to contradiction and atomism. Neither is it his fault if the sole link which subsists between men is the purely formal moral law, to which most of them pay only lip-service, each expecting obedience to it from others whilst infringing it in his own actions. Kant cannot be blamed if men constitute merely anthropological communities (nation, class, family, etc.) which are dependent upon concrete empirical conditions and are usually in conflict to boot.

Kant's practical writings are shot through with awareness of the tragic limitation of man, of his divided existence, eternally torn between a *material* but atomistic and egoistic aspiration towards happiness and a *purely formal* morality. That is why the moral law is an imperative, an 'ought', and not an 'is', as it would be in the case of a holy will. In talking of the highest good, of the kingdom of God, Kant continually speaks of a world where 'ought' and 'is', moral and natural totalities, would be one, where to merit happiness through one's moral acts would bring actual happiness in its train. But if the world as it is actually given is not like this, that is no fault of Kant's. It is the role of a great philosopher neither to embellish what is, nor to accept it. Kant did neither. That is why he became one of the greatest thinkers of modern philosophy.

Moreover, he was aware of another essential fact. He recognized that the two elements which constitute contemporary man – material sensibility (heteronomy) and formal respect for the law (autonomy) – are not equivalent before reason. The first (to which all the philosophers of feeling and of life pay homage) is in fact man's limitation, that which opposes him to other men, which destroys the community and ultimately abolishes the distinction between man and beast. That is why he fought it so fiercely even in its seemingly highest expressions, and even today it must be stressed that he was right. The man who helps others solely from feeling or desire may tomorrow commit the most immoral acts for the selfsame reasons. The second element, on the other hand, the categorical imperative, intelligible freedom, is precisely that which frees man from the biological, albeit only formally. It points the way towards something higher and better and allows man to hope for an essentially and qualitatively different future world, in which matter will no longer be opposed to form and both will unite in the perfect totality of the highest good.

But what practical conclusions can present-day man draw from these truths? Once aware of his intelligible freedom, what can he do to approach the highest good and to further its realization? What ought I to do? – we shall study this, the second question of Kant's philosophy, in the next chapter.

Chapter 3

What Ought I to Do?

I

It was only in asking this question – and by the way in which it asked it – that the critical philosophy became one of the great expressions of the tragic vision of the world, that it became a 'metaphysics of tragedy'.

That it could never pass from the *I* to the *we*, that in spite of Kant's genius it always remained within the framework of bourgeois individualist thought, these are the ultimate limits of Kant's thought. And nowhere are those limits expressed in such a clearly tragic way as in this question, for nowhere is the community so absolutely necessary as in *action*. What can *I* do? If we reflect on the fact that we are here concerned with the overcoming of human limitations, then so long as the question is asked *in this form*, so long as the subject of the sentence is *I*, there is only one possible answer: *Nothing which can really overcome this limitation.*

That is why in the critical philosophy (as in all tragedy) the question of *doing*, of action, was no longer an attempt really to overcome the obstacles, really to resolve the problems; it no longer concerned the *realization of the whole*, but only the meaning of *individual existence*. It had become the question of *duty*. 'This question is answered by morals.' However, the proposition *I ought* is not in the future tense, but – as is too often forgotten – in the present; the real future would be *I shall*. In the critical philosophy, where man's limitation and the problem of his destiny predominate, only secondary importance is ultimately accorded to the philosophy of history; there is only a *present*, *duty*, and an *eternity*, *religion*, but no *future*, no *history*; this is the clearest expression of that ultimate limit beyond which, despite all his efforts, Kant was never able to pass.

However, there being no means of escape is not of itself tragic. For many people, life today offers literally no means of escape; there is no means whereby they can fulfil themselves and give authentic meaning to their existence. But this lack of prospects is not of itself tragic. It becomes so only when it confronts a man who cannot exist where there is no means of fulfilling himself, a man for whom human values are a living reality, that is to say, for whom they must *always* and *necessarily* be transformed into actions. Where these 'values' remain only thoughts and feelings and are not transformed into *actions*, there is no tragedy. But neither is there any philosophy, for nothing remains but words.[1] Kant, however, was a truly great philosopher; that is why, in spite of there being no means of escape, he not only asked this question but made it the centre of his system, and that is why the lack of prospects became tragic.

For Kant the question 'What ought I to do?' has only one sense: What ought I to do *to realize the absolute, the perfect totality, knowledge of the universe and the kingdom of ends?* This provides the only authentic meaning for human life whereby man can rise above the physical and the biological.

Kant's reply is brief and straightforward, consisting of *one* premiss and *one* conclusion.

The premiss: It must be shown (and is shown in the first two *Critiques*) that the totality is not impossible, that a hope exists – be it ever so small – of attaining and realizing it. For no man could consciously and unreservedly commit his existence to the pursuit of a goal which he knew to be necessarily unattainable.

The conclusion: If there remains *the slightest hope* that somewhere, one day, in an intelligible world the absolute can be realized, then *act as if the maxim of your action were to become through your will a universal law of nature*, that is, act *as if* the realization of the absolute depended only upon that single action which you are about to perform, as if it depended only upon *your* will and *your* action.

But Kant knows full well – and herein lies the tragedy – that in reality it does not depend only upon any single action.

---

1. That is why there is no romantic tragedy, but only romantic drama.

For the individual, for the man who acts, however, that is of no consequence. From the moment he accepts the existence of the slightest hope, he has no further choice. All that tends towards the totality, towards the unconditioned, is for him *autonomy*, spirit and reason, the meaning and the realization of life. All else, even the slightest compromise, is *heteronomy*, unfreedom and unreason, betrayal of one's own destiny. 'As if through your will' – in those five words Kant expresses in the clearest and most precise manner the grandeur and the tragedy of human existence.

'Through your will' expresses the grandeur of man. When he acts nothing external can determine his will or change its course, there can be no compromise, no distraction, for the fate of the community and of the universe, the absolute, depends upon that will alone.

'As if' – that is the tragic limitation, for nothing essential in the external world really depends on this individual action. It will not change the world, still less other men. At most the individual will fulfil his own destiny, and even this only partially and imperfectly. He is now 'worthy of happiness' but not really 'happy', since for that the realization of the 'highest good' would be necessary.

Here it must again be stressed that although for Kant what matters is a 'good will' rather than effective action, this does not mean that man can rest content with pious wishes. For Kant a good will is always directed exclusively towards reality[2] and realization. The will remains good only if *despite all a man's efforts* external obstacles prevent action, but not if weakness or hesitation infect that will itself. Indeed, for Kant the connection between will and realization is so natural that the problem is how a man can will something which cannot be realized.[3]

2. Of course 'reality' here means not the empirical given but the realization of the intelligible totality.

3. 'I have been taken to task for adopting a similar procedure (*Critique of Practical Reason*, Preface, p. 16) and fault has been found with my definition of the faculty of desire, as a *faculty which by means of its representations is the cause of the actuality of the objects of those representations*: for mere *wishes* would still be desires, and yet in their case every one is ready to abandon all claim to being able by means of them alone to call their object into existence. But this proves no more than the presence of desires in man by which he is

The answer to the question 'What ought I to do?' lies, obviously, in the field of ethics. But the radical dualism of the critical philosophy (at least in its first decade) is such that we also find certain elements of the answer to this question in the *Critique of Pure Reason*. I shall briefly enumerate the most important points.

II

With regard to theoretical activity, the answer seems clear. We must strive towards knowledge of the *universitas*, towards total determination, and never be satisfied with the given empirical knowledge provided by the understanding, although we know that without an abuse of the categories such knowledge is beyond the capabilities of empirical man. This is the theory of the 'regulative employment' of the ideas of pure reason.

We have already seen how this principle completely changed its meaning in the writings of the neo-Kantians, how for Cohen it became a matter of 'rules and indications', 'points of view' and 'maxims', and how the *qualitative* difference between the two forms of knowledge was transformed into a purely *quantitative* difference.

Here I should like to mention a point of terminology to which Kant devoted several pages of the *Critique of Pure Reason*[4] and which has been almost entirely neglected by the neo-Kantians – the problem of infinite regress. 'Mathematicians speak solely of a *progressus in infinitum*', and they are perfectly right in that, but 'Quite otherwise is it with the problem: how far the regress extends, when it ascends in a series from something given as conditioned to its conditions.

in contradiction with himself. . . . But why our nature should be furnished with a propensity to consciously vain desires is a teleological problem of anthropology. It would seem that were we not to be determined by the exertion of our power before we had assured ourselves of the efficiency of our faculty for producing an object, our power would remain to a large extent unused. For as a rule we only first learn to know our powers by making trial of them. This deceit of vain desires is therefore only the result of a beneficent disposition in our nature' (v, 177–8; *Aesth. J,* 16–17).

4. III, 348 ff.; *Pure R,* 449 ff.; B 536 ff.

Can we say that the regress is *in infinitum,* or only that it is indeterminately far extended (*in indefinitum*)?'

After a long development, Kant concludes that 'the totality of the composition of the appearances of a cosmic whole' is a *progressus in indefinitum,* whilst 'the totality of division of a whole given in intuition' is a *progressus in infinitum,* that is to say, we can never assert that qualitatively superior knowledge of the totality, of the thing in itself, is attainable only at infinity. All that we can and must say is that our efforts to attain it can only assure an indeterminately extended progression, a *progressus in indefinitum.* In contrast to this, the progression from a given totality to its parts and to its content is a *progressus in infinitum,* since every totality, even the formal totality of space and time, is infinitely rich in parts. Obviously, the neo-Kantians were bound to regard this merely as a sterile and scholastic play on words.

III

Kant has been criticized for having propounded an ethical system which is purely formal and devoid of content. This criticism seems to me to be without foundation. It is not Kant's ethic which is an empty form but that of actual man in bourgeois individualist society.

In ethics, too, we are concerned with the questions which I referred to at the beginning of this work. How far can practical egoism go? How far does it actually go? The first question is metaphysical, the second anthropological. The metaphysical answer is this: however far practical egoism *actually* goes, there is a limit beyond which it *cannot* go. For the most evil and selfish of men at least *recognizes* a universal moral law, though he may disregard it in his every action and merely expect others to conform to it. By virtue of this general recognition of a categorical imperative, all men belong to a single whole and constitute a community, albeit a purely formal one. It is formal because *in reality* the content of this imperative varies from place to place and from time to time in *the concrete consciousness* of men. The content of the moral law at any given time or place is a question for anthropology; its answer determines the actual extent of practical egoism.[5]

Of course, Kant's system does not deprive morality of content. On the contrary, just as on the theoretical level the authentic meaning of human life is to strive from the formal totality, from empirical spatial and temporal experience, to the *content-full totality* of the *universitas* and noumena, so on the practical level the *duty* of man is to take the *content-full totality* as his sole guiding principle and to act *as if* its realization depended upon his present action alone.

There is an essential difference between theory and practice. In the first, form and content are complementary. Pure intuition and the categories of the understanding determine empirical representations, albeit not completely. That is why progress towards the content-full totality is a *progressus in indefinitum*, *within* human experience. Man's limitation is expressed in the fact that there is no universal material criterion of truth but only a formal one.

In ethics, the position is quite different. Here there is a radical and insurmountable contradiction between the general form of the categorical imperative and any particular given matter. Every material motive of the will is a product of selfish 'interest' and therefore opposed to the generality of the imperative. There is thus a contradiction which, if it cannot be resolved, can at least be integrated into the empirical existence of men through ignorance or inconsistency, through the illusion that the categorical imperative could admit of an exception for oneself, that is to say, through 'false consciousness'. It is only when every particular empirical motive has been excluded, when every selfish interest has disappeared, that one can give to the purely formal categorical imperative the only content appropriate to it.[6] There is thus a material criterion of good and evil in morals. Man's

5. In Lukácsian terms, one might say that the answer belongs to the sociology of the countless forms of 'false consciousness', but that for Kant this consciousness is determined by reference to the whole of humanity, rather than to a social class (and by means of that to humanity) as it is for Lukács.

6. There is only *one* 'true consciousness' but there are infinitely many forms of 'false consciousness'.

limitation lies in the fact that this criterion either remains unconscious or is disregarded in real concrete action.

As for Kant's critics, if his ethical system was not sufficiently clear to them they had only to look in Kant's own works to find the explicit assertion that his ethic *is not purely formal*. One could hardly expect to find this assertion in Kant's analysis of given empirical man, but only when he poses the question 'What ought I to do?' We read, for example, in the *Groundwork of the Metaphysics of Morals*[7] that 'the principle of morality' has three forms, which 'are at bottom merely so many formulations of precisely the same law', but that there is 'a difference between them, which, however, is subjectively rather than objectively practical'. They correspond to '1. a *form*', '2. a *matter*' and '3. a *complete determination* of all maxims'. This is the old tripartite division with which we are familiar from the Dissertation, a division into 'form', 'matter' and 'ideal content-full totality'.

We know the general form of the categorical imperative. What, then, is the *content* of this formula, the matter of the maxims which should direct man's actions? Clearly, it can only be a categorical rejection of individualist man as he is today. Indeed, Kant succeeds in concentrating into a few words the most radical condemnation of bourgeois society and in formulating the foundations for any future humanism: *'Act in such a way that you always treat humanity, whether in your own person or in the person of any other, never simply as a means, but always at the same time as an end.'*

Once we realize that this formula condemns any society based on production for the market, in which other men are treated as means with a view to creating profits, we see the extent to which Kant's ethic is an ethic of content and constitutes a radical rejection of existing society.[8] Moreover, and no less radically, it lays the foundations for any true humanism in establishing the only supreme value upon which

7. IV, 436; *Groundwork*, 103–4.
8. For the benefit of those 'Kantians' living in Germany today [1945], I should like to repeat that this is the formal condemnation of *any* oppression or humiliation of a man, whatever his race or nationality (the sole exception being punishment for *individual* crimes).

all our judgements must be based. That supreme value is humanity in the person of each individual man – not just the individual, as in rationalism, nor just the totality in its different forms (God, state, nation, class), as in all the romantic and intuitionist doctrines, but the *human* totality, *the community embracing the whole of humanity* and its expression in *the human person*. 'Complete determination', the totality, would be the realization of a 'kingdom of ends', that is to say, the very reverse of present-day society where, with the exception of a few rare and partial communities, man is never more than a means.[9]

Finally, one last formula drawn from the *Metaphysics of Morals*.[10] There too we learn that ethics gives us 'a *matter*', 'an *end* of pure reason', which 'so far as men are concerned, it is a duty to have'. To the question 'What ends are also duties?' Kant gives the short but precise reply: 'They are *one's own perfection* and the *happiness of others*.' When we consider how the thoughts and actions of men in capitalist society are entirely dominated by the profit motive, that is to say, by attempts to augment their *own* happiness whilst requiring perfection in *others*, it is clear that the contrast could hardly have been expressed more concisely and absolutely.

How can the enthusiasm for Kant's ethics professed by so many German academics be reconciled with the *Gleichschaltung* of such a large number of them at the decisive moments of recent history since 1914? Such a question is outside the scope of this book; I leave it to their own consciences and to the judgement of the reader.

IV

Kant's answer to the question 'What ought I to do?' led to a view which could be described as tragic pessimism. All

9. This is well expressed in the old saying that even the king is only the first servant of his state (and not of his people). Today the industrialist becomes a servant of his own firm, the worker a servant of a machine which is not even his own. This is the general phenomenon of reification.

10. VI, 379 ff.; *Metaph. II*, 38 ff.

that I can do is *imperfectly* and *partially* salvage my own existence from the general limitation and immorality. To overcome this limitation in reality is beyond the powers of men. As I have said, Kant never passed from the *I* to the *we* as the subject of action; confined within an individualistic framework, he continued to conceive the possibility of harmony and concord between men in terms of *universalitas*, of universality, rather than *universitas*, real and concrete community.

For this reason I attach great importance to a passage in *Religion within the limits of reason alone* where the subject of action appears as *we*. The passage concerns the true church which is to bring about the kingdom of God on earth. Of course, the importance of such a passage must not be exaggerated. It is at most the one swallow which does not make a summer but which is nonetheless its herald. In view of the later importance in Hegel and Marx of these as yet inchoate ideas, I quote the passage here:[11]

'To found a moral people of God is therefore a task whose consummation can be looked for not from men but only from God himself. Yet man is not entitled on this account to be idle in this business and to let Providence rule, as though each could apply himself exclusively to his own private moral affairs and relinquish to a higher wisdom all the affairs of the human race (as regards its moral destiny). ... The wish of all well-disposed people is, therefore, "that the kingdom of God come, that his will be done on earth". But what preparations must they now make that it shall come to pass?

'An ethical commonwealth under divine moral legislation is a *church* which, so far as it is not an object of possible experience, is called the *church invisible*.... The *visible church* is the actual union of men into a whole which harmonizes with that ideal ... The true (visible) church is that which exhibits the (moral) kingdom of God on earth so far as it can be brought to pass by men. The requirements upon, and hence the tokens of, the true church are the following:

1. *Universality*, and hence its numerical oneness; ...

11. VI, 101–2; *Religion*, 92–3.

2. Its *nature* (quality); .i.e., *purity*, union under no motivating forces other than *moral* ones (purified of the stupidity of superstition and the madness of fanaticism).

3. Its *relation* under the principle of *freedom*; both the internal relation of its members to one another, and the external relation of the church to political power – both relations as in a *republic. . . .*

4. Its *modality*, the *unchangeableness* of its *constitution*, yet with the reservation that incidental regulations, concerning merely its *administration*, may be changed according to time and circumstance; . . .

'An ethical commonwealth, then, in the form of a church, i.e., as a mere *representative* of a city of God, really has, as regards its basic principles, nothing resembling a political constitution. For its constitution is neither *monarchical* (under a pope or patriarch), nor *aristocratic* (under bishops and prelates), nor *democratic* (as of sectarian *illuminati*). It could best of all be likened to that of a household (family) under a common, though invisible, moral Father, whose holy Son, knowing his will and yet standing in blood relation with all members of the household, takes his place in making his will better known to them; these accordingly honour the Father in him and so enter with one another into a voluntary, universal, and enduring union of hearts.'

Chapter 4

What May I Hope for?

It is not always easy to grasp the existential sense this question has for one who asks it. In everyday life, the force of habit is so great that all too often everything which relates to humanity as a whole and to authentic man disappears from view. Or if these ideas occasionally reappear, they are for the most part mere phrases, words devoid of any real and living meaning.

Of course, universal human values such as freedom, justice and love of one's fellow men do not lose all their influence on the individual and his actions – this would be impossible – but their existence becomes latent; it is veiled and reified by the automatism of everyday life and the immediately given. This occurs the more easily in that every-day relations with the immediately given are one aspect of the whole life of man and as such generally appear and operate under the same name as universal human values. It will always be the mark of a just man that he neither deceives nor consciously hurts another. But today justice seems to consist of *no more* than that; it does not matter to the individual if somewhere in the world thousands of men whom he does not know and with whom he has no personal relations are imprisoned or killed while he remains silent, or at most deplores it occasionally over a cup of coffee.

It will always be a part of freedom that one should be able to choose the place of one's Sunday outings, or a part of love for one's fellows that one should help the poor. But today this seems to suffice. Of what consequence is it if somewhere a few hotheads disappear because they have spoken too loudly of the rights of man and of human solidarity, or if millions suffer from hunger or die in poverty? If, then, a man whose words are not put into action, whose spirit has only the unconscious existence of the 'in itself' and not of the consciously 'for itself', whose human nature has become abstract and hidden behind the concrete appearance of the employee, the civil servant, the businessman, the scientist or the industrialist, if such a man (and today we are all to some extent such men) asks the question 'What may I hope for?' this can only be an empty phrase unless it refers to the economic prospects of the months to come or to the next wage increase.

But for the man who takes human spiritual values seriously, and with whom they are transformed into action, this question has a quite different existential importance, for it determines the meaning and the content of his life. That is why it is so important for him not to be deceived by any illusion, whether it be positive or negative. For when optimism and pessimism become existential, when pessimism leads necessarily to despair and optimism can only be based upon the legitimate hope of realizing universal human values, then nothing is more important for man than to seek valid reasons for this hope, reasons which can determine his actions and give content to his life.

It must not be thought that where there is the slightest hope there can no longer be tragedy. On the contrary, that hopeless pessimism which abandons the search may be *Existenzphilosophie*, mysticism, or romantic *mal du siècle*, but it has nothing to do with classical thought or the tragic vision. Tragedy only exists when man searches with all his powers for a means of escape and where he is ready to set his life upon the weakest and flimsiest hope before he will acknowledge the void. Only in grasping this can we understand the philosophy of Kant or classical thought in general.

'This question is answered by Religion.' Such is the basis of Kant's answer; but in the shadow of religion, two other important elements appear in the critical system: aesthetics and the philosophy of history. Although for Kant, given the historical conditions of his time, the philosophy of history could only be of secondary importance, in the later development of humanism (with Hegel, Marx, Lask and Lukács) it has come ever more to the fore and has replaced the philosophy of religion. Since I am here engaged on a work of philosophy and not of Kant scholarship, I feel justified, in the light of my own philosophy and of the development of humanism after Kant, in placing the philosophy of history at the end of my study as the culmination of the critical philosophy, the element which opened out towards the future.

Did not Kant himself teach that it is never the past but only the future which can and must determine the value of any theoretical or historical study?

THE PRESENT – BEAUTY

In the first years of the critical period, Kant had seen in contemporary, empirical man only his theoretical and practical limitations. It is in a letter of 1787[1] that he first announces that he has discovered 'a kind of *a priori* principle different from those heretofore observed' and is working on a 'critique of taste'. This heralds his third principal work, the *Critique of Judgement*. As in the preceding pages, I cannot and do not intend to give a detailed analysis of this work. However, the reader will miss it the less in that the critique of taste is clearly and simply set out in two hundred pages which he will have no difficulty in reading for himself. I shall thus be content to enumerate a few main ideas in order to show the position and importance of aesthetics in the critical system.

The basic points of Kant's analysis of aesthetic judgement may be formulated as follows:

1. In the aesthetic field, empirical man living today can already overcome his limitations and attain the totality.

2. But aesthetic judgement in its different forms, and the feelings of pleasure and displeasure which correspond to it, do not relate to the reality of objects but only to their *form* or to the *symbolic expression* of the suprasensible. Aesthetic judgement is *subjective*.

Let us examine some aspects of this analysis a little more closely.

---

1. Letter to Reinhold of 28 and 31 December 1787, *Phil. Corr*, 127.

(a) *Judgements of taste are subjective*. The *Critique of Judgement* begins with these words: 'If we wish to discern whether anything is beautiful or not, we do not refer the representation of it to the Object by means of understanding with a view to cognition, but by means of the imagination (acting perhaps in conjunction with understanding) we refer the representation to the Subject and its feeling of pleasure or displeasure. The judgement of taste, therefore, is . . . aesthetic – which means that it is one whose determining ground *cannot be other than subjective*.'[2] A judgement of taste 'denotes nothing in the object', but in it the subject feels himself and the manner in which he is affected by the representation.

Section 2 bears the title: 'The delight which determines the judgement of taste is independent of all interest', where interest is 'the delight which we connect with the representation of the real existence of an object'.[3] It is this absence of interest which distinguishes pleasure in the beautiful from pleasure in the agreeable or the good, both of which are connected with the existence of the object. It might be added that this also distinguishes it from the true, for through the distinction between the actual and the merely possible or impossible, theoretical judgement is also connected with the existence of the object. The subjectivity and disinterestedness of judgements of taste explains why here 'Critique takes the place of Theory',[4] so that whereas there are three Critiques, there is only a Metaphysics of Nature and of Morals, but no metaphysics of the beautiful.

Here I should like to add two further observations:

(i) Kant's analysis refers only to one form of aesthetic judgement, that of beauty, but it clearly remains valid for the other two, for the sublime and for the symbolic expression of the suprasensible, although it is not explicitly repeated with respect to them.

(ii) This analysis of the beautiful as a representation which relates to the subject and which does not denote a conceptual property of the object is, to my knowledge, one

2. V, 203; *Aesth. J*, 41–2.   3. V, 204; *Aesth. J*, 42.
4. V, 170; *Aesth. J*, 7.

of the first *analyses of reification* in philosophy.[5] I think it is thus important to mention its affinity with the later analysis of commodity fetishism in Marx and with the general reification of mental life in Lukács.

(b) *A judgement of taste is always a singular judgement*. 'In their logical quantity all judgements of taste are *singular* judgements. . . . For instance, by a judgement of taste I describe the rose at which I am looking as beautiful. The judgement, on the other hand, . . .: Roses in general are beautiful, is no longer pronounced as a purely aesthetic judgement, but as a logical judgement founded on one that is aesthetic.'[6] Again, this holds for all three forms of aesthetic judgement. This reveals an important difference between aesthetic judgements and theoretical thought. One of the principal limitations of the latter was that it always remained on the level of general abstract scientific laws without ever being able to attain the individual. Aesthetic judgements, on the other hand, have nothing in common with abstract laws and are always concerned with the concrete individual.

(c) For the theoretical understanding, there was only one way of understanding the individual and concrete whole – the teleological conception. This, however, could only be *regulative* and not constitutive, for the goal and the being postulated as the conscious creator of things in accordance with this goal (God) were not objectively given. Judgements of taste overcome this limitation, for '*Beauty* is the form of *finality* of an object, so far as perceived in it *apart from the representation of an end*.'[7] Finality without an end, this concept whose theoretical impossibility debars our understanding from a more profound knowledge of organic reality (and even from exhaustive knowledge of empirical reality in general)[8] is one of the four constitutive moments of aesthetic judgement and of the beautiful.

5. Just as Marx shows that price, which at first sight seems to be an objective property of a commodity, is in reality only a human and social valuation of it, so Kant shows that beauty, which at first sight seems to be an objective property of a beautiful object, is in reality a human valuation of it.

6. v, 125; *Aesth. J*, 55.   7. v, 236; *Aesth. J*, 80.

8. Both the understanding of organic beings and the complete determination

(d) Thus our understanding could never attain complete determination, if only because we can have complete knowledge only of *a priori* form and not of its empirical content. Now, as we shall see later, it is form alone which is the object of judgements of taste; that is why these judgements *in so far as they remain judgements of taste* and refer in no way to the empirical content or to its real existence, can attain complete determination (aesthetic and not conceptual) of the object.

(e) In the field of ethics, the practical ideas of reason were goal-directed and completely determined; the limitation consisted in the fact that for man they were not a reality but a duty – a requirement, a hoped-for end, but not its realization. This limitation is also overcome by the finality of the beautiful. Aesthetic judgement in all its forms always refers to a *given* object of the imagination which is thus present, if only subjectively, and not to a duty or a concept. On the theoretical level, the subject was inadequate to the object, since his thought and knowledge could never exhaust the riches of reality; on the ethical level, the object was inadequate to the subject, since reality could never meet the requirements of the categorical imperative and the highest good; on the aesthetic level, however, the only adequacy possible for concrete, empirical man is achieved, the only true unity of subject and object – though admittedly only a subjective unity which does not require the real existence of the object. It follows, as Lukács rightly notes, that so long as man does not forsake aesthetic judgement for theoretical or ethical judgement, he is wholly drawn into this judgement, and that the aesthetic object also constitutes a totality, a world which neither has nor can have any connection with other objects outside it.[9]

(f) *The ideal of beauty.* 'Properly speaking, an *idea* signifies a concept of reason, and an *ideal* the representation of an

---

of physical objects would be accessible to a constitutive teleological conception. Since, however, *no objective end* is given to us and our understanding cannot conceive of *finality without an end*, the teleological point of view must remain regulative for our limited understanding.

9. See G. Lukács, 'Die Subjekt-Objekt-Beziehungen in der Aesthetik', *Logos*, VIII.

individual existence as adequate to an idea.'[10] This concept of an ideal, that is to say, of a being which embodies the ideas of reason, appears twice in the critical philosophy. In the *Critique of Pure Reason*, the ideal of reason is placed in the intelligible world, where alone the ideas of reason can be realized. *The ideal of pure reason is God.* But in aesthetics, where empirical man can even now attain the absolute, the totality, albeit only subjectively, the ideal is at one with reality. *The ideal of beauty is man.*[11]

Thus Kant takes in aesthetics the decisive step which Feuerbach and more especially Marx were much later to take in ethics and epistemology: the humanization of the transcendent. Once man can attain the unconditioned, there is no longer any room for God. For humanist thought a transcendent God had been, in the final analysis, only a substitute for man. Man had left heaven to God only because he could neither do without it nor occupy it himself. Every important step in the history of humanism, from Kant's aesthetics to the anthropology of Feuerbach and of Marx, has also been a step towards the secularization of the world and the humanization of heaven.

The most critical antithesis is not that between revealed religion and the atheism of the unbeliever. For the spiritual always involves faith in higher universal human values, and the hope of realizing them. Without faith, man would not be a rational being, and would become scarcely distinguishable from an animal. In this *very wide* sense, we can say that religion is universally human. But what religion? Modern humanism is an attempt to replace the positive religions of a transcendent God by an immanent religion of man and of the human community. Kant's society of citizens of the world or Marx's socialist society are but new realist and humanist forms of the ancient dream of the kingdom of God, and every step away from reification and towards the humanization of the earth is at the same time a step towards the secularization and the humanization of heaven.

10. V, 232; *Aesth. J*, 76.
11. Between the two, Kant also has a third, the ideal of the wise man (III, 384; *Pure R*, 486; B 597).

'*Wir wollen hier auf Erden schon das Himmelreich errichten*', wrote Heine, and thus expressed the essential content of modern humanism. What distinguishes the great philosophers of this tradition from lesser thinkers is that the former take both parts of that line equally seriously – both '*auf Erden*' and '*das Himmelreich*' – and admit no compromise and no illusions.

But here too Kant's analysis was clear and precise, for he spoke of contemporary individualist and selfish man, who cannot attain the totality either in thought or in action. All that his successors have been able to add is the prospect of a future which has yet to be created. In aesthetics, however, the only sphere in which present-day man can, if only subjectively, attain the absolute, there is no longer any room for God. Even the most pious and religious of artists, whenever they wished to express the idea of God *in their art*, have had to represent a man.[12] The ideal of theoretical and practical reason is God. The ideal of beauty is man.

(g) I have repeatedly stressed that man can attain the totality only in and through the community. Therefore, if contemporary individualist man can even only subjectively attain the totality in aesthetic judgement, he must there also realize, if only subjectively, a perfect community. (This is possible in that the main obstacle to human community – that of selfish interests connected with the existence and enjoyment of real objects – is here absent.)

Indeed, we find in the *Critique of Judgement* not only a great many scattered passages relating to the aesthetic community but also a number of sections in the Analytic of the Beautiful and in the Deduction of Pure Aesthetic Judgements which are devoted to it. Let me first quote the titles:

'19. The subjective necessity attributed to a judgement of taste is conditioned.'

'20. The condition of the necessity advanced by a judgement of taste is the idea of a common sense.'

'21. Have we reason for presupposing a common sense?'

---

12. From the point of view of positive religion, the ancient Jews were quite right in forbidding any graven image of God. Art deepens religious feeling only in diminishing transcendence.

'22. The necessity of the universal assent that is thought in a judgement of taste, is a subjective necessity which, under the presupposition of a common sense, is represented as objective.'

'39. The communicability of a sensation.'

'40. Taste as a kind of *sensus communis.*'

'However, by the name *sensus communis* is to be understood the idea of a *public* sense, i.e. a critical faculty which in its reflective act takes account (*a priori*) of the mode of representation of every one else, in order, *as it were*, to weigh its judgement with the collective reason of mankind. . . . This is accomplished by weighing the judgement, not so much with actual, as rather with the merely possible, judgements of others, and by putting ourselves in the position of every one else, as the result of a mere abstraction from the limitations which contingently affect our own estimate.' 'We might even define taste as the faculty of estimating what makes our feeling in a given representation *universally communicable* without the mediation of a concept.'[13]

We have already encountered a public sense in epistemology (space, time, the categories) and in ethics (the categorical imperative). The *a priori* was indeed distinguished by its universal validity. What distinguishes the aesthetic *sensus communis* from the speculative and practical *a priori*? The theoretical *a priori* was completely reified. Space, time and the categories appeared in experience as completely objective. (Their subjectivity was only revealed in transcendental analysis.) The theoretical *a priori* was *actual* but *not free*. The moral *a priori*, on the other hand, expressed the freedom of the subject but required the renunciation of sensibility, of his relations with the concrete empirical given, and the highest good was only a hope for the suprasensible and for eternity. The aesthetic *sensus communis* is free from all these limitations. Each man's judgements of taste are free; they cannot be disputed; the man who cannot see the beauty of a rose will never be persuaded of it. But such judgements are lawlike, in that they require the general recognition of all men. The union of *spontaneous freedom* and *the universal validity of law* constitutes the ideal community. On the theoretical level, we can only hope for it from the archetypal understanding, and in ethics from God's realization of the highest good. In aesthetic judgement, it is given to us here and now.

Here and now, but only subjectively; for the *sensus communis* weighs judgements 'not so much with actual, as rather with the merely possible, judgements of others'. Man feels at one with others only in so far as he remains within aesthetic judgement. In reality, aesthetic judgements diverge, since, as Lukács notes, aesthetic judgement is only a part of concrete man as a whole, and a real and perfect community is only possible for him if it is simultaneously realized in every field. It follows from this that aesthetic egoism cannot exist. Kant himself draws this conclusion in the *Critique of Judgement*: 'The import of the judgement of taste . . . cannot be *egoistic*, but must necessarily, from its inner nature, be allowed a *pluralistic* validity. . . .'[14] It is thus all the more astonishing that in the *Anthropology* he refers to aesthetic egoism. But it is also noteworthy that the only example given is that of the man who applauds himself 'however bad others may find his verses, paintings or music, or however much they may find fault or mock them'.[15] This is the Oronte of Molière's *Misanthrope*, and we know that in his case an interest, vanity, is at work; thus his judgement is certainly egoistic, but it is no longer purely aesthetic. Aesthetic judgement is pluralistic 'from its inner nature'.

I hope that these remarks have clarified at least the general lines of the position and significance of aesthetics in the critical philosophy. I must now briefly mention the forms of aesthetic judgement. They are three (of which one contains two subdivisions). The first two are concerned exclusively with *form* and are set out explicitly in the Analytic: (1) *the beautiful*; (2a) *the mathematically sublime*. The aesthetics of content is found in (2b) *the dynamically sublime*, which is set out explicitly in the Analytic, and in (3) *the symbolic expression of the suprasensible* which continually recurs in Kant's

14. v, 278; *Aesth. J*, 132.   15. VII, 129–30.

analysis without, however, being expressly mentioned as an independent form of aesthetic judgement.

(a) *Beauty* characterizes a manifold given in sensation or in imagination, whose form is compared by reflective judgement 'with its faculty of referring intuitions to concepts', and thus 'imagination (as the faculty of intuitions *a priori*) is undesignedly brought into accord with understanding (as the faculty of concepts)'. This 'unity of imagination and understanding' arouses a feeling of pleasure which is 'exacted from everyone' and which is connected with the representation of the object.[16]

It must be emphasized here that beauty, or more precisely 'free beauty (*pulchritudo vaga*)',[17] consists in the agreement between the *form* of a manifold in the imagination and the understanding as the faculty of concepts *in general*, but not between the *empirical content* of this manifold and its unity under a *determinate* concept of the understanding. For this would be a theoretical and not an aesthetic judgement. Beauty is the *ability* of a manifold to be determined *in virtue of its form* by a conceptual unification, but not its actual determination by a concept, which would be a theoretical judgement.

This analysis further explains not only the difference between theoretical and aesthetic judgement, but also their affinity. A scientific analysis or an elegant and well-conducted proof is of course a purely theoretical operation, but it almost always awakens in us an aesthetic pleasure as well. For in unifying a given intuitive content in a determinate conceptual form it awakens our faculty of reflective judgement, which judges only *the adequacy of the form of the manifold brought under the concepts of the understanding in general*.

(b) *The sublime*, in contrast, is all that by its magnitude (the mathematically sublime) or by its might (the dynamically sublime) 'may appear ... to contravene the ends of our power of judgement, to be ill-adapted to our faculty of presentation, and to be, as it were, an outrage on the imagination'.[18] For in so far as our relation to such an object

16. v, 190–91; *Aesth. J*, 30–32.   17. v, 229; *Aesth. J*, 72.
18. v, 245; *Aesth. J*, 91.

is not determined by interest (such as when we fear the raging ocean), it makes us conscious of the moral and intellectual superiority of the ideas of our reason over purely physical or biological nature. 'It is . . . for us a law (of reason), which goes to make us what we are, that we should esteem as small in comparison with ideas of reason everything which for us is great in nature as an object of sense; and that which makes us alive to the feeling of this supersensible side of our being harmonizes with that law.'[19]

Whatever the magnitude or the might of nature, it has no power over us as reasonable beings, and for just this reason its magnitude and might make us conscious of the infinitely greater magnitude and might of our own moral ideas. 'The *beautiful* is what pleases in the mere estimate formed of it. . . . The *sublime* is what pleases immediately by reason of its opposition to the interest of sense.' 'The beautiful prepares us to love something, even nature, apart from any interest: the sublime to esteem something highly even in opposition to our (sensible) interest.'[20] Beauty is the accord between imagination and understanding, the sublime the relation of imagination to reason. 'This, now, is the foundation of the necessity of that agreement between other men's judgements upon the sublime and our own, which we make our own imply. For just as we taunt a man who is quite inappreciative in forming an estimate of an object of nature in which we see beauty, with want of *taste*, so we say of a man who remains unaffected in the presence of what we consider sublime, that he has no *feeling*. But we demand both taste and feeling of every man, and, granted some degree of culture, we give him credit for both. Still, we do so with this difference: that, in the case of the former, . . . we make the requirement as a matter of course, whereas in the case of the latter, . . . we do so only under a subjective presupposition (which, however, we believe we are warranted in making) namely, that of the moral feeling in man. And, on this assumption, we attribute necessity to the latter aesthetic judgement also.'[21]

19. v, 257; *Aesth. J*, 106.   20. v, 267; *Aesth. J*, 118–19.
21. v, 265–6; *Aesth. J*, 116–17.

(c) *The symbolic expression of the suprasensible*. This third form of aesthetic judgement appears most clearly in the section dealing with man as the 'ideal of beauty'. We learn here[22] that man alone 'among all the objects in the world' admits of an idea of beauty. 'Two factors are here involved. *First*, there is the aesthetic *normal idea*. . . . *Secondly*, there is the *rational idea*. This deals with the ends of humanity so far as capable of sensuous representation, and converts them into a principle for estimating his outward form, through which these ends are revealed in their phenomenal effect.' The ideal of beauty 'consists in the expression of the *moral*, apart from which the object would not please at once universally and positively'.[23] Thus the second last section of the *Critique of Aesthetic Judgement* is entitled 'Beauty as the symbol of morality'. For Kant, of course, 'moral' does not mean just any narrow 'morality', but only the realization of man's authentic destiny.

In 1917, Lukács wrote that 'the *Critique of Judgement* contains the seeds of a reply to every problem of structure in the sphere of aesthetics; aesthetics need thus only clarify and think through to the end that which is implicitly there to hand'.[24] Although he seems since to have changed his opinion, this remains for me the best characterization of the work. Many ideas are not fully worked out in it, and many are to be found only implicitly. But the essence of aesthetic judgement is there grasped for the first time with a depth which to my knowledge has not been attained since, let alone surpassed. However, what especially interests me is the question of the significance of the aesthetic for the existence of present-day man.

And we have just heard Kant's reply. It is a *consolation*, an *alleviation*, but certainly not a way of *overcoming* man's limitation and its tragic implications. For the unconditioned, the totality which man can attain in aesthetics is subjective; it is merely a form or a *symbolic expression*, not an objective and material reality encompassing the whole man. A single

---

22. V, 233; *Aesth. J*, 76–7.   23. V, 235; *Aesth. J*, 79.
24. *Logos*, VII, p. 8.

line from Goethe's *Faust* sums up the content of the *Critique of Judgement* better than any theoretical analysis:

Am farbigen Abglanz haben wir das Leben.

ETERNITY – GOD, IMMORTALITY

In expressing his opposition to the Stoics and the Epicureans, Kant frequently calls himself a *Christian*, and his appeal to *religion* for the answer to the question 'What may I hope for?' indicates the immense importance of religion in the critical system. What, then, is the place of faith in a transcendent God in Kant's philosophy? Before answering this question, I should like to clarify it in two respects.

1. If we claim that Kant's thought is *philosophical*, it is pointless to ask whether and to what extent it is also religious (in the broadest sense). For it seems to me that the very essence of religion lies in *belief* in the sacred, in certain supreme values, and in the *hope* of their realization.[25] Now when we conceive of religion in this way, any really philosophical vision of the world must be religious. Even thinkers such as Spinoza or Marx who, *from the point of view of any particular positive religion,* are 'unbelievers', appear as men of deeper religious feelings and a more powerful religious faith than many of their 'theological' opponents. The only difference was (and is) that their vision of the world is an authentic religion of the universe (Spinoza) or of the human community (Marx), whilst their Jewish or Christian adversaries professed an all too often external and superficial faith in a transcendent God. It should also be clear that the great religious figures of history – the prophets, St Augustine, Joachim of Fiore, Aquinas, Thomas Münzer, or Pascal – have far more in common with Spinoza, Kant or Marx than with Max Scheler or many a modern theologian.

2. Therefore, the question asked in this section has nothing to do with Kant's attitude to the rites and dogmas of

25. This definition of religion is not far from that of so 'scientific' a sociologist as Emile Durkheim.

positive Christian religion. There too the answer is clear: *Kant rejected all positive religion*, and of all the positive religions Christianity appeared to him merely as the one which least overstepped the bounds of reason. He thus saw in it at most a temporary educative function, leading humanity towards the practical and moral religion of reason. In the last analysis, however, it was not the truth, but rather a kind of lesser evil. (These remarks apply, of course, only to the traditional positive Christian religion with its ceremonies, its mysteries and its prayers, not to Christianity *as Kant himself understood it*, a purely practical and moral religion recognizing no ontological, physical or metaphysical God but only the practical postulate of his existence.)

Although circumstances obliged him to be prudent, Kant more than once expressed his position quite clearly, and in spite of its purely terminological concessions, *Religion within the limits of reason alone* is one of the most radical critiques of any positive and revealed religion (including Christianity) ever written.[26]

Having clarified these two points, I can now tackle the most important problem posed by Kant's religious philosophy: Why should he so often and so insistently call himself a *Christian*? But before attempting to answer this question, I must set out, if only schematically, the principal elements of Kant's philosophy of religion.[27]

1. The theoretical and speculative dialectic of reason 'compels us to seek the key [to the antinomy]. . . . This key, when once found, discovers that which we did not seek, and

---

26. Elsewhere in Kant's writings there are many passages which are barely concealed attacks against all positive religions and their churches. I have already quoted the introduction to *Dreams of a Visionary*. Let me add to this a passage from the *Critique of Practical Reason*. 'Mohammed's paradise or the fusion with the deity of the theosophists and mystics, according to the taste of each, would press their monstrosities on reason, and it would be as well to have no reason at all as to surrender it in such a manner to all sorts of dreams' (v, 120–21; *Prac. R*, 125). It should be clear to the reader that here, without in the least distorting Kant's meaning, Mohammed and the theosophists may be replaced by any one of many analogous religions.

27. The principal relevant texts are the Dialectic of the *Critique of Practical Reason* and *Religion within the limits of reason alone*. Both works (and indeed all Kant's writings in answer to the question: What may I hope for?) are extremely clear and accessible.

yet need, namely, a view into a higher immutable order of things in which we already are, and in which to continue our existence in accordance with the supreme decree of reason we may now, after this discovery, be directed by definite precepts.'[28] We know that this key to the antinomy is the distinction between the thing in itself and appearance, but that for the theoretical and speculative understanding anything suprasensible (the thing in itself, freedom, God) is a *problematic concept* of which neither the existence nor the non-existence may be asserted.

2. But we also know that the simple fact that the *impossibility* of the suprasensible cannot be proved by the understanding must suffice for man to live his life in conformity with the supreme determination of reason and to 'act as if the maxim of his action were to become through his will a universal law of nature'.

3. But man can really 'act as if . . .' only if the realization of the suprasensible does not remain for him a simple *problematical and theoretical possibility*; he must really believe in its realization. For Kant is far too great a thinker to admit the *radical separation of thought from action as even possible*. This point calls for several observations. We have already seen how often, in his analysis of theoretical and practical reason, Kant encounters this separation in the life of present-day individualist man.

A large number of critics (among them Lukács) have accused him of taking this separation of theory from practice much too far instead of abolishing it, such an abolition being the principal task of any serious philosophy. To this one can reply that the relevant passages contain the analysis of individualist man as he was in Kant's time and is still, and not man as he ought to be; Kant was describing *real men* and not *ideal man*. To overcome the contradiction between thought and action in the life of men, it is necessary, in Marx's famous phrase, not merely to interpret the world, but to change it. It is also important to emphasize that even in Kant's analysis of present-day man this separation is never carried right through to its limits. Even if we neglect

28. v, 107–8; *Prac. R*, 111–12.

their purely subjective unity in aesthetics, there remain two decisive points where theory and practice, thought and action, are united.

(a) In the Dialectic of Pure Reason, where Kant more than once asserts that it is only because theoretical knowledge *cannot* prove the impossibility of the suprasensible that man can fulfil the practical determination of reason. For no one can commit his existence to a goal the realization of which he knows with certainty to be impossible.

(b) In the Dialectic of Practical Reason, in the passage quoted above, where Kant admits that the *duty* to 'act as if' the suprasensible would be realized by our action is 'inseparably' linked with *belief* in the realization of this suprasensible.

This is Kant's famous 'primacy of practical reason': we *must believe* in a certain reality even if theoretical reason can assert *nothing* about it, *because the interest of practical reason is 'inseparably' bound up with belief in that reality.* 'By primacy between two or more things connected by reason, I understand the prerogative of one by virtue of which it is the prime ground of determination of the combination with the others. In a narrower practical sense it refers to the prerogative of the interest of one so far as the interest of the others is subordinated to it.'[29] 'But if pure reason itself can be and really is practical, as the consciousness of the moral law shows it to be, it is only one and the same reason which judges *a priori* by principles, whether for theoretical or for practical purposes. Then it is clear that, if its capacity in the former is not sufficient to establish certain propositions positively (which however do not contradict it), it must assume these propositions just as soon as they are sufficiently certified as belonging inseparably to the practical interest of pure reason. It must assume them indeed as something offered from the outside and not grown in its own soil. . . . It must remember that they are not its own insights but extensions of its use in some other respect, viz., the practical; and that this is not in the least opposed to its interest, which lies in the restriction of speculative folly.'[30]

29. v, 119; *Prac. R*, 124.
30. v, 121; *Prac. R*, 125–6 (translation slightly amended).

Two questions remain open: (a) What is this practical unconditioned *in whose realization reason must believe*? and (b) Why must the belief in its realization be a belief in a supernatural and transcendent God rather than belief in a historical and immanent future for humanity?

I continue my schematic exposition:

4. Practical reason 'seeks the unconditioned for the practically conditioned (which rests on inclinations and natural need); and this unconditioned is not only sought as the determining ground of the will but . . . as the unconditioned totality of the object of the pure practical reason, under the name of the *highest good*'.[31] This practical unconditioned described in philosophical terms as the *highest good*, or in theological terms as the *kingdom of God*, consists in the union of *virtue* and *happiness*. 'That virtue (as the worthiness to be happy) is the supreme condition of whatever appears to us to be desirable . . . and, consequently, that it is the supreme good have been proved in the Analytic. But these truths do not imply that virtue is the entire and perfect good as the object of the faculty of desire of rational finite beings. For this, happiness is also required, and indeed not merely in the partial eyes of a person who makes himself his end but even in the judgement of an impartial reason, which impartially regards persons in the world as ends-in-themselves.'[32]

The common fault of the Stoics and Epicureans was to regard one of these two elements of the highest good as contained in the other. For the Stoic, virtue itself implies happiness; for the Epicurean the search for happiness constitutes the whole of virtue. 'The Epicurean said: To be conscious of one's maxims as leading to happiness is virtue. The Stoic said: To be conscious of one's virtue is happiness. To the former, prudence amounted to morality; to the latter

---

31. V, 108; *Prac. R*, 112. Kant here also defines the 'science' of philosophy as 'instruction in the concept wherein the highest good is to be placed and in the conduct by which it is to be obtained'. This shows once again to what extent the neo-Kantians in wishing entirely to abandon the doctrine of the highest good falsified and trivialized Kant's thought.

32. V, 110; *Prac. R*, 114.

... morality alone was true wisdom.'[33] For Kant both these points of view are regrettable and dangerous illusions. 'We cannot but regret that these men ... unfortunately applied their acuteness to digging up an identity between such extremely heterogeneous concepts as those of happiness and virtue.'[34] 'The maxims of virtue and those of one's own happiness are wholly heterogeneous ... they strongly limit and check each other in the same subject.'[35]

When we consider Kant's definition of virtue as 'the maxim of which you can will that it should become a universal law', it must be recognized that this opinion is well-founded. For the fundamental limitation of man in bourgeois individualist society is precisely that for him virtue and happiness are incompatible. So long as the *individual*, the *I*, is the subject of action, the search for happiness is not universal but egoistic, and as such, contrary to virtue. The universal remains for him a duty which he can fulfil only in renouncing all content, his sensuous nature, his inclinations, that is to say, in renouncing his happiness. The union of these two heterogeneous elements of the highest good thus presupposes a radical change in the community, a qualitatively different universe, the kingdom of God.

5. We must thus, for reasons 'belonging inseparably to the practical interest of pure reason', *believe* in the coming realization of this qualitatively superior society, of the highest good, of the kingdom of God.

The question remains: Why must we believe not in a *human, historical* and *immanent* realization in the *future*, but in a *superhuman* and *supernatural* realization in *eternity*? Why must practical interest lead reason *not to a philosophy of history but to a transcendent religion*?[36] This question is all the more natural in that Kant's works contain almost all the basic elements of a philosophy of history, but without their carrying sufficient existential weight to replace the philosophy of religion. Kant hoped for a historical develop-

---

33. V, 111; *Prac. R*, 115.   34. V, 111; *Prac. R*, 116.
35. V, 112; *Prac. R*, 117.
36. I use the word 'transcendent' here in its usual sense. For Kant it had another meaning: practical postulates were 'transcendent' for speculative reason, but 'immanent' for practical reason.

ment towards a better community, towards a society of
citizens of the world, towards perpetual peace, and that
hope is clearly expressed in his works. But it never became
strong enough to render superfluous the practical postulate
of a superhuman being who would bring about the eternal
realization of this higher community: the kingdom of God.
What was later to seem obvious to Marx and Lukács seemed
impossible to Kant, for all that he had clearly perceived and
analysed the problem. But why?

I believe the only serious answer to that question lies in
the social situation of Germany and particularly of Prussia
at that time, in their economic and political backwardness,
and in the weakness of the progressive forces, which made
any hope in a *historical* future appear largely as illusion or
utopia. The 'theories of progress' so widespread at the time
reduced to apologies for existing society, belief in a world
which would improve slowly and 'naturally' of itself. In the
ideology of the Enlightenment, progress had become a
natural law rather than the object and task of the philosophy
of history. For this ideology suppressed the two basic foundations of such a philosophy, namely the *qualitative difference*
between present and future, and the *need for action*.[37] It is
no wonder, then, that Kant found all these theories of progress prejudicial to 'morality'.

At the basis of Kant's religious philosophy stand two
assumptions:

(a) The impossibility for our reason of *adequate* belief in
a historical development towards a higher social order, and

(b) The incompatibility of the ideologies of natural progress with the requirements of morality.[38]

---

37. For this reason, the neo-Kantians are much closer to the Enlightenment
than to Kant.

38. ' . . . our reason finds it impossible to conceive, in the mere course of
nature, a connection so exactly proportioned and so thoroughly adapted to
an end between natural events [virtue and happiness] which occur according
to laws so heterogeneous. . . . But now a determining factor of another kind
comes into play. . . . The command to further the highest good is objectively
grounded (in practical reason), and its possibility itself is likewise objectively
grounded (in theoretical reason, which has nothing to say against it). But as
to the manner in which this possibility is to be thought, reason cannot objectively decide whether it is by universal laws of nature without a wise Author

On this basis, the *practical postulates* of the immortality of the soul and the existence of God become for Kant the only *adequate* reply to the question 'What may I hope for?' The second assumption is a well-grounded philosophical analysis, but the first derives from the concrete historical conditions of Kant's time. Not even the greatest and most profound thinkers can free themselves from the conditions in which they live.

6. Kant has three 'postulates of pure practical reason':[39]

I. 'Immortality', which 'derives from the practically necessary condition of a duration adequate to the perfect fulfilment of the moral law', that is, from the soul's need for an infinite span of time in order to attain the complete fulfilment of the moral law.

II. 'Freedom', which is 'the necessary presupposition of independence from the world of sense and of the capacity of determining man's will by the law of an intelligible world'.

III. 'The existence of God' which is 'the necessary condition of such an intelligible world by which it may be the highest good'.

To show, however, the ultimate inadequacy for *positive* religion of such a purely *practical* God, it suffices to point out that:

(a) Kant's God is a practical postulate with no physical or metaphysical existence. His reality is purely moral and practical, a consequence of the *a priori* concept of duty.

(b) But we read in the *Metaphysics of Morals* that there are two kinds of duty, duties of *justice* and duties of *virtue*, and that man has no duties of justice towards God.[40]

As for duties of virtue, the two-page chapter devoted to them bears the title 'The Doctrine of Religion, as the Doctrine of Duties to God, Lies Beyond the Bounds of Pure

---

presiding over nature or whether only on the assumption of such an Author. Now a subjective condition of reason enters which is the only way in which it is theoretically possible for it to conceive of the exact harmony of the realm of nature with the realm of morals as the condition of the possibility of the highest good; and it is the only way which is conducive to morality' (V, 145; *Prac. R*, 150–51).

39. V, 132; *Prac. R,* 137.   40. VI, 241; *Metaph. I*, 47.

Moral Philosophy'. I quote only the following passage: 'But as for the *material* aspect of religion, the sum of duties *to* (*erga*) God or the service to be rendered him (*ad praestandum*), this could contain particular duties ... these duties would belong only to revealed religion, which would, therefore, also have to presuppose the existence of this Being, not merely the Idea of him for practical purposes, and to presuppose it, not arbitrarily, but rather as something that could be presented as given immediately or mediately in experience. But such religion still comprises no part of *pure philosophical morality*, no matter what other grounds it might have. Thus *religion*, as the doctrine of duties *to* God, lies entirely beyond the bounds of pure philosophical ethics, and this fact serves to justify the author of the present [ethical treatise] for not having followed the usual practice of bringing religion, conceived in that sense, into ethics.'[41]

A transcendent superhuman God who has only *practical* and *moral* reality but who *lacks independent moral existence* since there are no duties towards him, a God who is thus only a practical postulate of the only duties which really exist, duties 'of men towards men' – a more unreal God could scarcely be imagined. This is easily understood if we remember that in Kant's philosophy God is merely an expression of that absolute which man can neither renounce nor attain himself, a heavenly substitute for man who is thus in continual danger of being overthrown when, with the progress of human life and thought, man finally claims his rights.

Having delineated the basic features of Kant's philosophy of religion, we must now ask how, in spite of his negative attitude towards positive traditional Christianity, Kant could call himself a *Christian*.

It is significant that this claim is most often made (particularly in the posthumous writings) when Kant wishes to mark himself off from the Stoics and Epicureans. For the elements which distinguish the critical philosophy from those two views are precisely those which it shares with Christianity. Moral Stoicism and Epicureanism, like the corresponding epistemological doctrines, rationalism and empiricism, maintain that today's individualist man can attain the absolute or at least the maximum humanly possible. Thus any superior community, any better world, *qualitatively* different from that of today becomes superfluous. On the religious level, this assertion becomes the doctrine that the kingdom of God can be achieved now, on earth, and *in the present form of the human community*.

That is why debates over the religious attitudes of philosophers such as Descartes or Fichte seem to me futile. Their *personal* convictions or sincerity are of little philosophical importance. However, it is a logical consequence of most of the systems of classical Greek philosophy, and of almost all those of modern philosophy before Kant, which, in the final analysis, constitute no more than a renaissance of the Greek systems, that God can have no really *human* function – that is to say, no truly religious function. All that remains to him is the maintenance of harmony between the isolated and autonomous individuals who constitute the community, or between the atomistic elements which make up the universe. The God of Descartes is the guarantor of eternal truths; the God of Leibniz is responsible for the pre-established harmony of monads; the God of Malebranche acts, but only as nature acts, through a *general* will; the God of Spinoza is finally to be identified with nature. It is clear to any genuinely religious man that none of these functions is truly transcendent, and that none of these conceptions of God has anything in common with that of the Christian revelation.

That is why, despite the Platonism and Aristotelianism of the scholastics, Christian philosophy constitutes a vision of the world which is essentially *new* and *different* from that of the ancients; Kant is perfectly correct when he writes in the *Critique of Practical Reason*: 'If I now regard Christian morals from their philosophical side, it appears in comparison with the ideas of the Greek schools as follows: the ideas of the Cynics, Epicureans, Stoics, and Christians are, respectively, the simplicity of nature, prudence, wisdom and holiness. In respect to the way they achieve them, the Greek schools differ in that the Cynics found common sense suffi‎

cient, while the others found it in the path of science, and thus all held it to lie in the mere use of man's natural powers.'[42]

Kant's attitude towards all these philosophies is in all essentials identical with that of Christianity. To this extent, *but only to this extent*, he is justified in calling himself a Christian. Both world-views see man as a limited being whose authentic destiny is to strive towards the unconditioned, the totality, the highest good, the kingdom of God, without ever being able to attain it by his own efforts. Both *believe* in a superhuman aid by which alone man can realize his destiny. 'Christian ethics, because it formulated its precept as pure and uncompromising (as befits a moral precept), destroyed man's confidence of being wholly adequate to it, at least in this life; but it re-established it by enabling us to hope that, if we act as well as lies in our power, what is not in our power will come to our aid from another source, whether we know in what way or not.'[43]

Christian philosophy and the critical philosophy are thus alike to the extent that they share a common conception of man, of his relation to the unconditioned and of the possibility of his realizing his authentic destiny. But here also begins their essential difference.[44]

For if we examine the Christian philosophy of the middle ages we find everywhere the same conception of the relations between faith and knowledge, a conception common to all the scholastic systems whatever their other differences. The Christian thinker of the middle ages begins with *faith* which, based on revelation, is not subject to doubt. This primary faith in the existence and omnipotence of God is then reconfirmed through knowledge of the created world, and renders possible the understanding of the universe and of man. In all the famous scholastic tags – *fides quaerens intellectum, credo ut intelligam*, and so on – faith is the rock upon which rational understanding is based. Kant's train of thought, however, takes quite the opposite direction. It

---

42. V, 127–8; *Prac. R*, 132 n.   43. V, 128; *Prac. R*, 132 n.

44. I am here referring, of course, to the relations between Kant's world-view and that Christian philosophy which admits the existence of an ontological and transcendent God.

starts out from man's rational knowledge, the human community and the universe. Because man can fulfil his authentic destiny only if his hopes for the realization of the highest
good are justified, because he is limited and cannot attain
this realization by his own efforts, rational knowledge of
the world must be supplemented by the practical postulate
of rational religion. The *fides quaerens intellectum* has become an *intellectus quaerens fidem*. It is faith which is a supplement to reason, and not, as in scholastic Christianity,
rational knowledge which is a supplement to and a confirmation of faith.

At first sight, however, this may seem unimportant. When
rational knowlege and faith agree, what does it matter which
is the premiss and which the conclusion? But only at first
sight: for knowledge is not fixed and eternal. Deeper and
more precise knowledge of man and the universe can reveal
new and *immanent* ways of overcoming a limitation which
had been thought radical and absolute. Thus the agreement
between rational knowledge and faith breaks down. This
process has occurred twice in the history of Western thought.
The first occasion was the development from medieval
Christian philosophy through the Renaissance to classical
rationalism and the empiricism of the seventeenth and
eighteenth centuries; the second was the development of
the dialectical humanist philosophy of Kant through Hegel
to Marx and Lukács. It is in the light of the difference between these two developments that we can best understand
the difference between their two points of departure.

For the medievals, the Christian faith formed an independent premiss based only upon revelation. When later
rational knowledge began to follow its own development,
and even to come into conflict with faith, there arose first
of all the 'double truth' position of the Averroists (in the
universities of Paris and Padua, for example). Faith and
reason now each had its own independent vision of the
world, well-grounded in its own sphere, but contradicting
that of the other. As the need for a unified system of thought
obliged the most important thinkers to opt for one or the
other of the two positions, this choice could only be made

by a brutal and revolutionary decision, by abandoning what had previously been a basic premiss.

But the atomistic and, in the end, radically non-Christian world-views continued to develop, and the closer they came to precise knowledge of man, the more they became aware of the limitations of the individual.[45] The natural result of this has often been a return to Christianity or at any rate to religion. Thus Spinoza, Goethe, Racine, Pascal and Kant all returned to a religion of the supra-individual, the last three indeed to Christianity. From the philosophical point of view, however, the Christianity of the great classical thinkers and poets was fundamentally different from that of the middle ages, for the revolution brought by the Renaissance and by rationalism remained a permanent part of the European mind. *Knowledge of man* was now the *premiss* and the *point of departure*; *faith* in a superhuman and transcendent God was only a *consequence*.

And as with Hegel and Marx knowledge of man and of the human community progressed and the idea of a higher form of human community showed how the limitations of individualist man might be overcome *immanently*, so the philosophy of religion gave way to the philosophy of history without the need for any modification of the premises or any choice between two autonomous and independent truths; for Kant's philosophy of religion already implied as a natural and inevitable consequence the immanent religion of a higher, authentic human community – socialist thought.

THE FUTURE – HISTORY

The simple fact that most of Kant's writings on the philosophy of history are to be found not in the principal philosophical works but in a series of lesser pieces[46] leads to the

45. Who to them, of course, appeared as man as such.
46. The most important texts relating to the philosophy of history are: 'Idea for a universal history with a cosmopolitan purpose' (1784), 'Review of Herder's ideas on the philosophy of human history' (1785), 'On the common

question: what is the role of history in Kant's philosophical system?

The above-mentioned fact is certainly not to be explained by saying that the questions treated in these texts do not belong to philosophy in the strict sense and thus have no place in the main works. On the contrary, I shall attempt to show that the same questions are involved here as in the philosophy of religion, and that the logical structure of the answers to the problems of the philosophy of history is closely related to that of those in the philosophy of religion. Even less can it be explained, as is all too often attempted, in terms of Kant's lack of interest in history. For in the works not belonging to the critical system itself, scarcely any subject occupies a more important place; moreover, these few short works already contain almost all the fundamental categories of the later philosophy of history of Hegel, Marx and Lukács.[47]

It seems to me rather that this is a very clear example of how the decisive limitations of a great thinker are not individual and personal, but determined by the social conditions in which he lives. Kant is not lacking in understanding of the problems of the philosophy of history or of the different possible answers to them. Indeed, all the basic elements are worked out by the inner logic of his system. But the social and political situation in which he lived was such that he could not attribute to history sufficient existential reality to introduce it at the heart of his philosophy.

A great thinker is not solely concerned with the logical structure of his system, nor with developing new and original ideas. He is concerned above all to grasp what is essential and of decisive importance for man. And it is in this that he ultimately depends upon economic and social conditions. For human existence is that of a person as a part and an expression of the community. Now, the community evolves

---

saying "This may be true in theory, but it does not apply in practice"' (1793), 'Perpetual Peace' (1795) and 'The Contest of Faculties' (1798) [all except the second translated in *Polit*].

47. Apart from the concept of class, of course; the economic and political state of Germany was still too backward for this. In France it had already been discovered by the Physiocrats.

slowly under the influence of many complex and inter-woven factors, and the work of even the greatest thinker is only one of these factors, and indeed one whose action is extremely slow. Thus, however great his influence, a philo-sopher can never cause an idea to acquire decisive impor-tance for the men of a country and of an age in spite of and against social and economic conditions. As with the scientist or the artist, his greatness lies in his becoming the spokes-man of humanity and in his expressing man as he really is, with his real problems, his tasks and his means of achieving them.

Even a philosopher of genius is not a prophet. Prophets belong to revelation. The philosopher is a man who tries to explain himself to himself and to explain to his contempor-aries the meaning of life, the destiny of man, and the means open to man for the fulfilment of that destiny. He tries to formulate the dreams and hopes of a human community and in doing so to make it conscious of them; he tries to open for man the road to himself, that is, to the community and the person. In short, he is a man who seeks 'instruction in the concept wherein the highest good is to be placed and in the conduct by which it is to be obtained'. And if he suc-ceeds in this, even in part, he will perhaps, in spite of all these restrictions, have accomplished a task superior to that of the prophet.

I should now pass to the exposition of Kant's philosophy of history. Unfortunately, however, in the course of the last seventy years this concept has been used in so many dif-ferent ways that it is not easy at first sight to give it a precise and determinate meaning. Today the expression 'philosophy of history' may denote general sociological laws, like the Marxist theory of the importance of productive forces in historical development, or theological theories as in Bossuet's *Discours sur l'histoire universelle*, or indeed methodological analyses of the historical sciences. Sometimes the phrase is even used of epistemological studies such as Rickert's work on concept-formation in the historical sciences.

Of course, up to a certain point every scientist is free to choose his own terminology. However, where words already exist in previous usage, it would be wrong to use others without due cause, and thereby to encourage confusions of a kind all too prevalent in the human sciences. Today we have the word *sociology* to denote the positive science which investigates the general laws of social development. It should thus be clear that historical materialism and historical idealism are sociological rather than philosophical theories.[48] Similarly, everything concerning the methods of the historical sciences belongs to applied logic[49] and everything concerning concept-formation to epistemology.

What, then, is left for the philosophy of history? Let us recall Kant's definition: philosophy is 'instruction in the concept wherein the highest good is to be placed and in the conduct by which it is to be obtained'. That seems to me also to define the object of the philosophy of history. Just as the philosophy of religion speaks of God as creator of the highest good, and of the conduct by which we can participate in it, so the philosophy of history has as its object the following question: to what extent can history *qua* development of the human community lead to the realization of the highest good, and by what conduct can we now, in our present life, accomplish our destiny and attain the highest good?

The philosophy of history must thus answer an ethical question and is a part of practical philosophy, whilst the problems listed above were of a scientific and theoretical kind. Of course, theory and practice are inseparable, since an action which aims at realization presupposes the most accurate possible theoretical knowledge of reality. Indeed, this theoretical knowledge must be true, since errors and illusions can only hinder action. But the agent does not take up an indifferent and contemplative attitude towards theoretical knowledge. He hopes that it will not prove to him the impossibility of achieving his goals (for then he would have to renounce his action), but rather that it will show him that they are probably and even certainly realizable.

48. Moreover, among the most important historians to have shed light on the influence of economic conditions on social and political life, some, such as Pirenne or Marc Bloch, completely reject the Marxist philosophy of history.
49. I shall not here go into the problem of the degree to which the methodology of the human sciences differs from that of the natural sciences.

There thus exists no more senseless objection to the philosophy of history than that based upon the claim that there is a contradiction involved in seeking objective historical factors favourable to a goal which one wishes to bring about oneself. Hundreds of examples from everyday life suffice to show the untenability of this argument. Does not the doctor who wishes to cure a patient look for factors in his biological constitution which may hasten or even bring about a cure? Having found such factors, does he renounce all treatment? Does not an architect who wishes to build a house look for solid ground capable of supporting it? When he has found such ground, does he then return home and wait for the house to build itself? Let us take an even more obvious example. We are at present living through one of the most terrible wars of history; for five years we have heard the leaders of both sides demonstrating to their followers that victory is certain for technical, strategic, moral and even religious reasons. But it has not crossed their minds that, in the light of such proofs, they should lay down their arms and wait for victory. All of these people – the doctor, the architect, the military leader – are guilty of the 'contradiction' repeatedly attributed to the philosophy of history in general and to Marx in particular. The critics overlook two important facts, namely:

(a) That human actions are included as decisive factors in the laws of social development which guarantee the realization of the ideal, just as the activity of the doctor, the builders and the soldiers is understood in the examples above;

(b) That when success appears probable or certain, the agent's courage and his desire to act increase, which in turn increases the probability of realization of the ideal until it becomes a certainty.[50]

---

50. There is, of course, the danger of illusions, conscious or unconscious, intended or unintended. We often read into the facts what we wish to find there, or claim to have established the facts we require although we have not actually done so. In the claims of military leaders propaganda plays a considerable part, as it does also in everyday political struggles. But in the long run, illusions are always costly pleasures. Whatever the masses may be told, the leader himself must be clearly acquainted with the real situation. By

The philosophy of history is a combatant – a combatant in the struggle for an ideal human community, for a higher and more authentic life. Since, like the doctor, the architect and the soldier, it is active, it too will be guilty of the 'contradiction', despite all protestations at its 'lack of logic'.

I have defined the philosophy of history as the search and the hope for the unconditioned in the temporal development of the human community. Logically, there should thus be two kinds of philosophy of history, since time has two directions, the past and the future. A pessimistic and reactionary philosophy of history would find the unconditioned only in what has been, in what is irretrievably past and can only be remembered; an optimistic philosophy would pin its hopes upon the future which we shall ourselves create.

Let us consider the first. There is no doubt that such views have existed and still exist today. We need only consider 'historicism' and the historical school which sees some value in every ancient institution and in every past event simply because it is historical. Similarly, there is romanticism with its enthusiasm for the middle ages. However, I doubt whether this can be called a philosophy. Philosophy is the search for universal human values, and hitherto every past event and every historical fact has been particular and limited.[51] If such an attitude, which looks exclusively towards the past, is nevertheless to arrive at universal values, it must abandon the real, the historical, and turn to the 'original', to revelation or to myth, that is to say, to the

---

means of illusion or deception he can buy time, but he cannot escape from a hopeless position. Once he realizes that the situation is hopeless, he must abandon the struggle (assuming that he acts only in order to attain his goal and not for other motives).

The philosopher of history as such has no part in everyday politics; he is concerned with the struggle as a whole, with the possibility, the probability or the certitude of attaining the highest good. For him, intended illusions are senseless and involuntary ones extremely dangerous.

If, then, we are dealing with a genuine philosophy of history and not with one of those 'interesting' and 'ingenious' works which one so often encounters in this field, the sociological thought will there be as rigorously scientific as possible in spite of the primacy of the practical.

51. Especially in Germany. The French might point to the Revolution and the Declaration of the Rights of Man.

imagination. It must take the road which has always been taken by the principal proponents of reactionary world-views. (One need only consider the later Schelling, or romanticism, or, in our time, the great upsurge of studies on myths – Lévy-Bruhl and the 'primitive mentality' – or the importance Heidegger attaches to imagination and the first of Sartre's philosophical works, *L'Imagination* and *L'Imaginaire*.)

If, therefore, the philosophy of history is to relate to real history, there remains only the second alternative, whose major representatives are Kant, in part Hegel, Marx and Lukács. And thus we arrive at a conclusion which may at first sight seem paradoxical: *as a human value, history, for man, denotes not the past but the future*. Only when this is understood is it possible to understand the great works of German humanism in the philosophy of history. For it explains why in those works,[52] in Kant's writings on the philosophy of history, in Marx's *Capital* and in Lukács' *History and Class-consciousness*, the authors speak almost exclusively of the present and above all of the future.[53]

History as future. This idea is much too important for modern humanism and, if we consider the literature of the human sciences over the last seventy years, much too new and unusual not to dwell on it a little longer. It is clearly incomprehensible for an individualist conception of the world which accepts the idea that the individual can attain the absolute. For such a conception any future is a purely individual one, the *I* is the sole subject of thought and action, the community, like the physical world, is only the *object* of individual action or of theoretical and contemplative knowledge. Thus there can only be empirical history, relating the events of the past, seeking causal connections between them

52. With the exception of those of Hegel: with him, the two attitudes referred to above coexist, though they are hardly combined into a synthetic unity. Thus the work of Hegel could lie at the origins not only of the historical school, but also of the young Hegelians and of Marxism.

53. In German, there are two words: *Historie* and *Geschichte*. The first characteristically denotes only the *past*, whilst the second denotes the *future*, and also the past in so far as it is regarded from the point of view of hope in the future. One speaks of a *historische Schule* and of *Geschichtsphilosophie*. The reverse would be impossible, if only for linguistic reasons.

and if possible establishing general sociological laws. There is empiricist or rationalist sociology and historiography, but not empiricist or rationalist philosophy of history.

Nor can there be a philosophy of history for the mystical doctrines of intuition or feeling. For here, since the subject tends to disappear, to merge with the universe and the spiritual, the essential difference between the human and the biological or physical disappears with it. (This constitutes a major difference between Kant and Herder.) If these philosophies are evolutionary, then the evolution is biological, as with Bergson, or cosmic, as with Schelling, but never historical. And as, in these world-views, external reality tends in general to lose its real significance, past history itself becomes more and more subordinate, something of importance only as an expression of the absolute.

It is only in a philosophy of the human community, where it is not the *I* but the *we* which forms the subject of thought and action, that the philosophy of history becomes the centre of the philosophical vision. For the *we*, for the community, history and the future are identical. Every past event which essentially concerns a particular community is *historical (historisch)*; every future event is *historic (geschichtlich)*. The past can only become *historic* in so far as it is important for the future of the community and is considered from this point of view.[54]

A future which assures future generations of a better and happier life will today, in the struggle for its realization, give

54. Here it must be noted that Kant was aware of this distinction between philosophical history with a cosmopolitan purpose and history conceived purely empirically, and that he indeed emphasized the usefulness and the necessity of the latter: 'It would be a misinterpretation of my intention to contend that I meant this idea of a universal history, which to some extent follows an *a priori* rule, to supersede the task of history proper, that of *empirical* composition. My idea is only a notion of what a philosophical mind, well acquainted with history, might be able to attempt from a different angle' (VIII 30; *Polit*, 53). It is a distinction which must not be forgotten. History in the second sense (*Geschichte*) is the future of the human community and also the investigation and evaluation of the past from the point of view of a hoped-for future which is to be created by common action. History in the first sense (*Historie*) is the purely scientific and empirical investigation of the past. Both are useful and indeed indispensable, but it is essential not to confuse them.

meaning and content to personal and individual life. History as 'the concept wherein the highest good is to be placed', historical action as 'the conduct by which it is to be attained', these, I feel, constitute the sole object of any true philosophy of history.

I shall rest content here, as I have hitherto, with a schematic exposition of Kant's philosophy of history without entering into details and without bringing sociological questions into the topics for consideration.[55]

55. To avoid distortion of the picture, I must point out that the historical conditioning of Kant's thought is much more marked in his treatment of concrete sociological and political questions and also in such matters as his analysis of the virtues, considered separately, or in his consideration of particular scientific questions, than in his strictly philosophical works. As an example, I shall here examine in more detail one problem which illustrates the enormous differences in concrete anthropological and political questions between Kant, Marx and Lukács. I choose the problem of the practical and political possibilities for the realization of a republican state and a society of citizens of the world, a problem with which Kant was frequently concerned.

Logically, a republic might come about in two possible ways. It could be achieved either from *above*, by the will of the monarch (or of the rulers) or at least with his consent, or from *beneath*, against his will, by the people. For Kant, the first possibility is clearly the more desirable. This is only natural given the weakness of the progressive popular forces in the Germany of his time. On the other hand, he is only too well aware that rulers are as selfish as other men and that there is little chance of achieving a higher form of society by their conscious and virtuous action. 'Thus while man may try as he will, it is hard to see how he can obtain for public justice a supreme authority which would itself be just, whether he seeks this authority in a single person or in a group of many persons selected for this purpose. For each one of them will always misuse his freedom if he does not have anyone above him to apply force to him as the laws should require it. Yet the highest authority has to be just *in itself* and yet also a *man*. This is therefore the most difficult of all tasks, and a perfect solution is impossible' (VIII, 23; *Polit*, 46).

There remains then the possibility of independent action by the people against the monarch. This question of revolution from beneath continually occupied Kant and its solution was made more difficult in his last years with the occurrence of the French Revolution. The more enthusiastic Kant became over the French Revolution and the more strongly he defended it, the more categorically he rejected the idea of popular revolution in other monarchies, that is to say, in Prussia. (On this point, however, it is difficult to determine what in Kant's writings springs from the genuine internal necessity of his thought and what is to be explained in terms of prudential and external considerations.) Kant was thus faced with the difficult task of finding a consistent position combining approval of revolution in France and condemnation of it in Prussia. Thus many of the texts, at least at first sight, seem contradictory. I quote two examples: 'The rights of man are of more importance than order and calm. Great order and calm may be based on general

In this order of ideas, two facts are conspicuous:
(a) The resemblance between the structure of Kant's philosophy of history and that of his philosophy of religion.
(b) The resemblance between this philosophy and the later philosophy of history of Hegel, Marx and Lukács.

1. The most important category of the philosophy of religion was the idea of the highest good, the union of virtue

---

oppression. And disorders in the commonwealth which arise from the desire for justice are passed over' (xv, No. 1404). 'There can therefore be no legitimate resistance of the people to the legislative chief of state. . . . It is the people's duty to endure even the most intolerable abuse of supreme authority. The reason for this is that resistance to the supreme legislation can itself only be unlawful. . . . An alteration in a (defective) constitution of a state, which may sometimes be required, can be undertaken only by the sovereign himself through reform, and not by the people through a revolution' (vi, 320–1; *Metaph. I*, 86–8).

But to avoid any misunderstanding of his position with respect to the French Revolution he immediately adds the following remark: 'Moreover, if a revolution has succeeded and a new constitution has been established, the illegitimacy of its beginning and of its success cannot free the subjects from being bound to accept the new order of things as good citizens, and they cannot refuse to honour and obey the suzerain who now possesses the authority' (vi, 322–3; *Metaph. I*, 89).

Or on another occasion: 'If, however, a more lawful constitution were attained by unlawful means, i.e. by a violent *revolution* resulting from a previous bad constitution, it would then no longer be permissible to lead the people back to the original one, even although everyone who had interfered with the old constitution by violence or conspiracy would rightly have been subject to the penalties of rebellion during the revolution itself' (viii, 372–3; *Polit*, 118).

Kant's views on the right of the people to defend its liberties by force can be summed up as follows:

1. The people has the right to require of the sovereign that he 'should not attempt' that which does not correspond to justice.

2. The content of this right is formulated in the following phrase: 'Whatever a people cannot impose upon itself cannot be imposed upon it by a legislator either' (viii, 304; *Polit*, 85).

3. But the right of the people is purely 'negative, that is, concerned only with judgement'; it has 'no right of constraint against him who does it an injustice'.

4. The sole guarantee of the people lies in the freedom of expression, which makes it possible to impel the government towards reforms by means of public criticism. ('Obedience without the spirit of freedom' is 'the occasioning cause of all secret societies'.)

5. The people never has the right of rebellion, not even against the most serious abuses and the harshest injustices. Rebellion, revolution, is always one of the gravest of crimes which must be severely punished – even by death. (In voicing approval of the death penalty Kant is not being particularly bloodthirsty, but simply defending the French Revolution.)

and happiness in the kingdom of God. Similarly, the most important category of the philosophy of history is the idea of a higher form of the human community and of society, the society of citizens of the world, perpetual peace, the perfect civil constitution, a league of nations and so on. Both ideas are the expressions of a higher community, qualitatively different from that which exists today. The difference is that whilst we look to the kingdom of God *in eternity*, as a result of our actions and with the assistance of God, the society of citizens of the world is anticipated *for the future*, as a result of our actions and with the assistance of the 'plan of nature' which we call fate or providence.[56]

Kant is well aware of these parallels between the philosophy of religion and the philosophy of history: 'We can see that philosophy too may have its *chiliastic* expectations; but they are of such a kind that their fulfilment can be hastened, if only indirectly, by a knowledge of the idea they are based on, so that they are anything but over-fanciful.'[57]

2. Just as with the highest good happiness was a consequence of virtue, that is to say, of the virtuous and reasonable actions of men, so the higher form of the community can only be created by human actions: 'Nature has willed that

---

6. Once the revolution has succeeded, the new government is to be obeyed for the same reason and as much as the old, and it would be equally criminal to rebel against it.

7. From the analytic point of view of formal universal law, every revolution is a contemptible crime. From the emanatist point of view of the future of the human species and of progress, revolution (or at least the French Revolution) and the fact that it finds supporters throughout the world are both gratifying and edifying (VII, 85–6; *Polit*, 183). In a footnote to this passage, Kant protests against the 'slanderous sycophants', who 'have tried to portray this innocuous political gossip as innovationism, Jacobinism and conspiracy, constituting a menace to the state. But there was never the slightest reason for such allegations, particularly in a country more than a hundred miles removed from the scene of the revolution.'

In this way the two opposed positions are combined, though not without some difficulty, into a single point of view. From the foregoing it is easy to see the extent of the influence of the historical situation of the moment on Kant's thought concerning these concrete questions.

56. However, as Kant has little confidence in history, the perfect civil constitution, the society of citizens of the world, and so on, are less perfect than the highest good. They guarantee only *universal freedom* and *perpetual peace*, whilst the highest good guarantees universal virtue and happiness.

57. VIII, 27; *Polit*, 50.

man should produce entirely by his own initiative everything which goes beyond the mechanical ordering of his animal existence, and that he should not partake of any other happiness or perfection than that which he has procured for himself without instinct and by his own reason.'[58]

3. But in Kant's individualist conception of the world, which recognizes only the *I* and not the *we*, these reasonable actions are no more adequate for the realization of the society of citizens of the world than they were in the philosophy of religion for the realization of the highest good. They constitute a *necessary* but not a *sufficient* condition for this realization.

Here again two supra-individual elements come in, corresponding to the two practical postulates of the immortality of the soul and the existence of God (the third postulate, freedom, is common to the two).

The postulate of immortality was necessary to assure men a sufficient span of time for the attainment of perfect virtue. In the philosophy of history, the same part is played by the immortality of the species. 'In man (as the only rational creature on earth), those natural capacities which are directed towards the use of his reason are such that they could be fully developed only in the species, but not in the individual.'[59] '. . . every individual man would have to live for a vast length of time if he were to learn how to make complete use of all his natural capacities; or if nature has fixed only a short term for each man's life (as is in fact the case), then it will require a long, perhaps incalculable series of generations, each passing on its enlightenment to the next, before the germs implanted by nature in our species can be developed to that degree which corresponds to nature's original intention. And the point of time at which this degree of development is reached must be the goal of man's aspirations (at least as an idea in his mind), or else his natural capacities would necessarily appear by and large to be purposeless and wasted.'[60]

The postulation of God's existence assured the realization of the highest good. Precisely the same part is played in

58. VIII, 19; *Polit*, 43. 59. VIII, 18; *Polit*, 42.
60. VIII, 19; *Polit*, 42–3.

the philosophy of history by the 'hidden plan of nature' (a concept which prefigures Hegel's 'cunning of reason'), 'to bring about an internally – and *for this purpose* also externally – perfect political constitution as the only possible state within which all natural capacities of mankind can be developed completely'.[61]

4. Just as the immortality of the soul and the existence of God did not form part of theoretical knowledge, but were rather practical postulates, so the 'hidden plan of nature' and the progress of the human species towards perpetual peace and the society of citizens of the world are necessary practical assumptions and not a part of empirical or *a priori* knowledge.

The only difference is that, in the first case, these postulates concerned the suprasensible, and thus no proof of their truth or falsity was possible, whilst in the second, in the philosophy of history, the postulates concern concrete reality, and such a proof, although extremely difficult to establish, is not inconceivable. We must then endeavour to create a 'history with a cosmopolitan purpose' which would confirm these assumptions. 'The real test is whether experience can discover anything to indicate a purposeful natural process of this kind. In my opinion, it can discover *a little*; for this cycle of events seems to take so long a time to complete, that the small part of it traversed by mankind up till now does not allow us to determine with certainty the shape of the whole cycle, and the relation of its parts to the whole. . . . Nevertheless, human nature is such that it cannot be indifferent even to the most remote epoch which may eventually affect our species, so long as this epoch can be expected with certainty. And in the present case . . . it appears that we might by our own rational projects accelerate the coming of this period which will be so welcome to our descendants. For this reason, even the faintest signs of its approach will be extremely important to us.'[62]

The following passage shows even more clearly the practical and moral character of this assumption and its affinity with the practical postulates: 'I may thus be permitted to

61. VIII, 27; *Polit*, 50.   62. ibid.

assume that . . . the human race is . . . engaged in progressive improvement in relation to the moral end of its
existence. This progress may at times be *interrupted* but
never *broken off*. I do not need to prove this assumption; it is
up to the adversary to prove his case. . . . I base my argument upon my inborn duty of influencing posterity in such
a way that it will make constant progress . . . and that this
duty may be rightfully handed down from one member of
the series to the next. History may well give rise to endless
doubts about my hopes, and if these doubts could be proved,
they might persuade me to desist from an apparently futile
task. But so long as they do not have the force of certainty, I
cannot exchange my duty . . . for a rule of expediency which
says that I ought not to attempt the impracticable.'[63]

5. The sociological aspect of Kant's writings on the philosophy of history is strictly speaking outside the terms of
this work. But I should like nevertheless to draw attention
to two points which, without any doubt, are the first seeds of
the later philosophies of history of Hegel and Marx.

(a) The 'hidden plan of nature' is the first form of Hegel's
'cunning of reason' and of Marx's historical necessity. It
guarantees the realization of the higher order to come, of the
society of citizens of the world and perpetual peace: 'Perpetual peace is *guaranteed* by no less an authority than the
great artist *Nature* herself (*natura daedala rerum*). The
mechanical process of nature visibly exhibits the purposive
plan of producing concord among men, even against their
will and indeed by means of their very discord. This design,
if we regard it as a compelling cause whose laws of operation
are unknown to us, is called *fate*. But if we consider its purposive function . . . we call it *providence*. . . . Yet while this
idea is indeed far-fetched in *theory*, it does possess dogmatic
validity and has a very real foundation in *practice*, as with
the concept of *perpetual peace*, which makes it our duty to
promote it by using the natural mechanism described
above.'[64]

(b) 'The means which nature employs to bring about the
development of innate capacities is that of antagonism within

63. VIII, 308-9; *Polit*, 88-9.   64. VIII, 360-62; *Polit*, 108-9.

society, in so far as this antagonism becomes in the long run
the cause of a law-governed social order.'[65] This '*antagonism*'
by means of which development is brought about later,
with Hegel, becomes dialectical contradiction, and with
Marx, the class struggle. It is 'the *unsocial sociability* of
men, that is, their tendency to come together in society,
coupled, however, with a continual resistance which constantly threatens to break this society up. . . . Man has an
inclination to *live in society*, since he feels in this state more
like a man. . . . But he also has a great tendency to *live as an
individual*, to isolate himself, since he also encounters in
himself the unsocial characteristic of wanting to direct everything in accordance with his own ideas.'[66]

Taken individually, men resist one another: 'It is this very
resistance which awakens all man's powers and induces him
to overcome his tendency to laziness. Through the desire
for honour, power or property, it drives him to seek status
among his fellows, whom he cannot *bear* but yet cannot
bear to leave. Then the first true steps are taken from bar-
barism to culture. . . . All man's talents are now gradually
developed . . . and by a continued process of enlightenment,
a beginning is made towards establishing a way of thinking
which can with time transform the primitive natural capacity
for moral discrimination into definite practical principles;
and thus a *pathologically* enforced social union is transformed into a *moral* whole.'[67]

The development of the relations between states through
the antagonism of wars towards the moral goal of perpetual
peace is analogous. Kant knows only too well that in his age
this sociological analysis is much more a moral and practical
hypothesis than a scientifically established fact. It is, according to him, the most important task of the philosophical
historian to provide empirical confirmation for this hypothesis. That is why he continued to search in both the past
and the present for facts which might support his analysis in
this way. And it was given to him, in his sixty-fifth year,
to witness one of the greatest events of world history, an

65. VIII, 20; *Polit*, 44.   66. VIII, 20–21; *Polit*, 44.
67. VIII, 21; *Polit*, 44–5.

event which he immediately recognized as the long-awaited decisive demonstration of the moral progress of humanity: the French Revolution.

Thus his position with regard to it was unambiguous. In backward Germany where the news of the Revolution and of its development struck like lightning and, with the Jacobin terror, most of its original supporters, Schiller, Schelling, Hegel and so many others, took fright and joined the opposition, there were a very few who, while critical of the excesses of the Jacobins, did not allow this to upset their judgement on the Revolution as a whole and its importance for humanity. Among these few were Germany's two greatest poets – Goethe and Hölderlin.[68]

No one, however, spoke out so clearly and unequivocally as the seventy-four-year-old Kant in his last published work. His words resound like the last salute of the imprisoned giant to his brothers who have broken the bars of their prison and begin now to live in freedom. It is a salute which is formulated with considerable prudence (which he himself excuses in pointing to the dangers of such an attitude) and which contains many more or less transparent reservations (thus, for example, the footnote quoted above with the 'more than a hundred miles'), for when one has oneself no chance of breaking down the prison walls, it would be foolish to irritate the guards too much. It is, however, in spite of everything, a salute which is sufficiently clear to reveal as an obvious falsification any claim that in his old age Kant allowed himself to be yoked to the wagon of German nationalism and of Prussian reaction. It is a salute which confirms again what the whole critical philosophy has demonstrated repeatedly, that those 'philosophers' who, at the decisive moment, from fear, from calculation, or through subjectively sincere but radically perverted thought have be-

68. Of course orthodox German history of ideas has always sought to disguise this fact and has treated Goethe and Hölderlin with the same ill-usage as the neo-Kantians meted out to Kant. I hope to show this in a future work on *Faust* and the attitude of Goethe towards the French Revolution. [This 'work' is 'Goethe et la Révolution Française', an essay published in Goldmann's *Recherches Dialectiques* in 1959 – Trans.]

trayed the cause of freedom and the rights of man in support of a most reactionary dictatorship which has suppressed every freedom, that such 'philosophers' have thereby lost the right to link their thought and their action in any way with the name and the work of Immanuel Kant.

And it is with the salute of this old man to the youthful freedom of the French people and to its defenders throughout the world that I shall end my exposition of his philosophy of history:

'*An occurrence in our own times which proves this moral tendency of the human race.*

'The occurrence in question does not involve any of those momentous deeds or misdeeds of men which make small in their eyes what was formerly great or make great what was formerly small, and which cause ancient and illustrious states to vanish as if by magic, and others to rise in their place as if from the bowels of the earth. No, it has nothing to do with all this. We are here concerned only with the attitude of the onlookers as it reveals itself *in public* while the drama of great political changes is taking place: for they openly express universal yet disinterested sympathy for one set of protagonists against their adversaries, even at the risk that their partiality could be of great disadvantage to themselves. Their reaction (because of its universality) proves that mankind as a whole shares a certain character in common, and it also proves (because of its disinterestedness) that man has a moral character, or at least the makings of one. And this does not merely allow us to hope for human improvement; it is already a form of improvement in itself, in so far as its influence is strong enough for the present.

'The revolution which we have seen taking place in our own times in a nation of gifted people may succeed, or it may fail. It may be so filled with misery and atrocities that no right-thinking man would ever decide to make the same experiment again at such a price, even if he could hope to carry it out successfully at the second attempt. But I maintain that this revolution has aroused in the hearts and desires of all spectators who are not themselves caught up in it a *sympathy* which borders almost on enthusiasm, although the very utterance of this sympathy was fraught with danger. It cannot therefore have been caused by anything other than a moral disposition within the human race.

'The moral cause which is at work here is composed of two elements. Firstly, there is the *right* of every people to give itself a civil constitution of the kind that it sees fit, without interference from other powers. And secondly, once it is accepted that the only intrinsically *rightful* and morally good constitution which a people can have is by its very nature disposed to avoid wars of aggression (i.e. that the only possible constitution is a republican one, at least in its conception), there is the *aim*, which is also a duty, of submitting to those conditions by which war, the sources of all evils and moral corruption, can be prevented. If this aim is recognized, the human race, for all its frailty, has a negative guarantee that it will progressively improve or at least that it will not be disturbed in its progress.

'All this, along with the *passion* or *enthusiasm* with which men embrace the cause of goodness (although the former cannot be entirely applauded, since all passion as such is blameworthy), gives historical support for the following assertion, which is of considerable anthropological significance: true enthusiasm is always directed exclusively towards the *ideal*, particularly towards that which is purely moral (such as the concept of right), and it cannot be coupled with selfish interests. No pecuniary rewards could inspire the opponents of the revolutionaries with that zeal and greatness of soul which the concept of right could alone produce in them, and even the old military aristocracy's concept of honour (which is analogous to enthusiasm) vanished before the arms of those who had fixed their gaze on the *rights* of the people to which they belonged, and who regarded themselves as its protectors. And then the external public of onlookers sympathized with their exaltation, without the slightest intention of actively participating in their affairs.'[69]

69. VII, 85–7; *Polit*, 182–3.

Conclusion:
What is Man?
Kant and Contemporary Philosophy

I hope that the preceding pages, though more a list of con-
tents than a detailed exposition of Kant's philosophy, have
nevertheless given the reader some idea both of its extraordinary riches and of its rigorous unity. In this conclusion
I wish briefly to sum up Kant's conception of man and the
place of Kant's thought in the development of modern
European philosophy.

For Kant, man is a rational being and, since reason implies universality and community, at least in part a 'social'
being. He is not an autonomous monad who is only part of
the community through his relations with other monads.
On the contrary, man is in his very existence part of a greater
whole, of a *community*, and thereby, of a *universe*.

Both this community and this universe, however, are
imperfect, for the actions of man are still dominated by
powerful instincts and selfish interests which set him against
his fellows and tend towards the disintegration of the community and the universe. Man is an 'unsocial-sociable'
being. The selfish and anti-social actions and relations of
the individual indicate his *dependence* upon his biological
nature and upon the external world and constitute his
heteronomy; his tendency to strive towards a higher, perfect
community constitutes his spiritual and rational nature,
his *freedom*, his *autonomy*.

It is the destiny of man as a rational being to strive in all
his actions and with all his power towards the realization
of a perfect community, of the kingdom of God on earth,
of the highest good, of perpetual peace. This he can only do
if the understanding does not forbid him to *believe* in and
to *hope* for the realization of this community. What now

unites men in their thoughts and their actions and constitutes their still imperfect community is universal and *a priori form*, common to all individuals (the pure intuition of space and time, the categories of the understanding, the categorical imperative), and aesthetic judgement, partly formal and partly material, but purely *subjective*. What separates them is empirical matter, differing from individual to individual (sensations, inclinations, selfish interests).

The knowledge and the actions of present-day man are thus limited, *social in their form and unsocial in their content*. His knowledge is merely an *incomplete* determination of appearances in experience, his actions selfish and contrary to the community, for which the universal is no more than a duty, a categorical imperative which is not actually followed. A higher community would make possible qualitatively superior knowledge and action, knowledge which would be the complete determination of things in themselves and a holy will for which there would no longer be an imperative or duties, but only free activity in conformity with the community. Both form and content would be common to all men, uniting them universally in both thought and action, theory and practice.

For Kant, however, all these concepts – perfect community, the kingdom of God on earth, knowledge of things in themselves, the holy will, the unconditioned – are suprasensible ideas which man can never realize here on earth through his will and his action. Because he *must* strive towards them, towards the only real spiritual values, without ever being able to attain them, man's existence is tragic. And Kant sees only two possible grounds for hope that this tragic situation might be overcome: *rational faith* and the still insufficient hope for the future of the human community, *history*.

With this vision of man, Kant had laid the foundations for an entirely new conception of the world. Before him, almost all the really important philosophical systems (with the sole great exception of Spinozism) reduced to two fundamental types. The ancient Greek philosophers and most of those who had lived since the end of the middle ages saw the individual as an autonomous and independent being who, as such, could attain the absolute, or at least the highest conceivable human values. The community, the whole, was for them only a *secondary reality*, the result of the mutual influence of autonomous individuals. The Christian philosophies of the middle ages saw the individual as an imperfect being belonging to a larger whole, and the empirical human community as an imperfect reflection of the kingdom of God. But the perfect whole, the kingdom of God, was for them something real and existent, although transcendent. Faith for them was *knowledge*, a certainty and a consolation, not as for Kant *hope* and a reason for action.

Kant opened the way to a new philosophy which unites the Christian idea of the limitation of man with the immanence of the ancients and the philosophers of the seventeenth and eighteenth centuries in considering the intelligible world, the totality, as a human task, as the object of the authentic destiny of man and the product of human action. Whilst the classical philosophers, starting out from the individual, had been centrally concerned with *epistemology* (rationalist or empiricist) and *ethics* (Stoic or Epicurean), and Christian thinkers, starting out from God, had made *theology* the basis of their systems, Kant for the first time created the possibility of a philosophy based on the idea of the *community* and the *human person*, that is to say, on the *philosophy of history*. It is in this direction that philosophical thought has continued to develop in the works of the three most important thinkers since Kant, in the works of Hegel, Marx and Georg Lukács.

Kant's philosophy was, however, immediately followed in Germany by two systems which, in spite of their undeniable importance, seem to me nevertheless to represent a step backwards from Kant's position, and which indeed Kant recognized as such. These were the systems of Fichte and Schelling, two philosophers whose thought took quite different directions from that of Kant.

Kant's philosophy was much more a beginning than an end, and thus only thinkers who have understood and perceived it as such have been able to appreciate its true philosophical importance. This has been achieved by starting from the most important question left by Kant's philosophy to its successors: *Is the tragedy of human existence really insurmountable? Is there no way for empirical man to achieve the unconditioned, the highest good?*

The principal philosophers of German idealism, Fichte, Schelling and Hegel, as well as its 'materialist heir', Marxism, have been concerned to give a positive answer to this question.

It is impossible here in this conclusion to analyse the factors which explain why the German bourgeoisie of the early nineteenth century could in the long run accept neither the individualist activism of the young Fichte nor the reactionary philosophy of Schelling (a philosophy which presented itself as a conscious reaction against the French Revolution), or why this bourgeoisie which lived in the hope of a progress which it could not itself bring about found its ideological expression in that mixture of a progressive and revolutionary world-view with a reactionary apology for the Prussian state which constituted the Hegelian system. If, however, we ask what is still living and important for us in the thought of Hegel, its importance seems to me to lie in having overcome the rigid separation between philosophy and empirical anthropology which still dominated the thought of Kant. Hegel consciously made the philosophy of history the decisive element in his system, and thus also incorporated in it the positive empirical sciences of sociology and history.

An even more important step on this road was taken in the work of Karl Marx. Marx was the first of the great thinkers of post-Kantian Germany to spend a large part of his life abroad, in Paris and London, and he was thus able to free himself from the limitations resulting from the specific historical conditions of the Germany of his time. Only with Marx does the union of philosophy with empirical sociology prepared by Hegel take on a truly scientific character.[1]

---

1. It would be wrong, however, to follow certain 'Marxists' in taking every one of Marx's pronouncements as a sacred and immutable truth. As with Kant and Hegel, there are in the works of Marx both a great number of living ideas which retain all their validity, and others conditioned by his historical circumstances which are today obsolete. It is the task of the philosopher and

After Marx, towards the end of the nineteenth century, a perceptible diminution in understanding and in the need felt for a coherent philosophical vision of man and of the universe took place not only in Germany but throughout the whole of European intellectual life. With the sole exception of Nietzsche, official philosophical thought was dominated by 'neo-Kantian' and 'neo-Hegelian' professors to whom can also be added many of those 'Marxists' concerned with philosophy and the history of ideas. It was then that innumerable commentators studied almost every line written by Kant and Hegel and interpreted them in every possible or imaginable way – a labour whose results are so paltry that it is difficult to decide which is the sadder, the incomprehension with which the works of most of the great German poets and thinkers were received by their contemporaries, or the conscious or unconscious impudence with which the *epigoni* trivialized, falsified and 'interpreted' them after their deaths.[2]

Later, after the First World War, under the influence of the profound social, economic and cultural crisis of Europe, there developed the various forms of the philosophy of feeling, of intuition, of anguish and of despair, typified by the works of Henri Bergson, Martin Heidegger and Jean-Paul Sartre. This is not the place for an analysis of the causes or the consequences of their rise and of their success. (These causes and consequences are today in any case apparent.) What seems to me important, however, is that even before the war there had arisen in France a reaction

the historian to distinguish the former from the latter, and it is this which constitutes the only acceptable form of 'orthodoxy'.

2. The way in which the history of German thought and literature has been written up to now would provide all the materials for a tragi-comedy. In the considerable number of works which I have read on this subject, no more than four or five times have I felt that the author was really introducing me to the essence of the philosophy under consideration. The exceptions were: Franz Mehring's *Lessing-Legende*, the work of a German socialist which far outstrips all the others, and then, if only in passing; Georg Lukács's *History and Class-consciousness*, the work of a Hungarian; Edmond Vermeil's *L'Allemagne*, the work of a Frenchman; and the countless scattered observations in the works of the Austrian journalist, Karl Kraus, against whom the official press organized a veritable conspiracy of silence. It is no coincidence that the 'serious' literature on the subject almost completely ignores all these works.

against this psychosis of anguish and despair, a movement which found its most powerful expression in personalism, as developed around the journal *Esprit*. This had certainly not become a conscious philosophical world-view or a fully developed system. Its most important analyses were to be encountered in conversation with young people who in most cases had not yet published anything. Everything was in the course of development when war broke out. It is today impossible to evaluate philosophical developments over recent years, since the most important contributions may well not have been published.

After the philosophical silence of Georg Lukács which has already lasted for more than twenty years, personalism seems to me to have been the most important philosophical occurrence during the years immediately before the war. Of course, this French personalism sprang from traditions quite foreign to German humanism, and was scarcely aware of its affinity with it. It is thus all the more significant that it arrived spontaneously at the same questions, and indeed usually at similar answers.

This is also the justification of the present work. I have not the slightest desire to echo the oft-repeated slogan 'Back to Kant'. On the contrary, any going back seems to me a betrayal of the thought of a philosopher who made the future and not the past the centre of his system and who constantly repeated that he wished to teach his students not *a philosophy* but *how to think philosophically*. Our attention should be directed not towards the past, seeking to go 'back to Kant', but forwards towards a better human community; only then shall we be able to see the figure of Immanuel Kant in his true light, to see his living and real significance for the present and for the future. He will appear to us then as one of those great thinkers who took the first difficult steps through the wood and opened the way on which we still proceed. When we see things in this light and focus our attention on the future of the human community, then beside the immense figure of Immanuel Kant many a philosophical celebrity of recent years will fade into insignificance. For nothing deserves the name of philosophy which is not aimed at the liberation of man and the realization of a true community.

If I have succeeded in awakening in some few readers the conviction that all those who struggle today in the various countries of Europe for their national liberation and for freedom and the rights of man in general are the heirs not only of their own national traditions and of the traditions of the French Revolution but also of the ideals and hopes of German humanism, that the heroic resistance movements in France and so many other European countries are engaged in the struggle for the only genuine form of European cooperation, for the cooperation of the spirit, of freedom and of European humanism, and that *the realization of this humanism is also the most essential and urgent problem of philosophy*, then my work will have fulfilled its purpose.

Index

Radical Thinkers

Maurice Godelier
The Mental and the Material

Lucien Goldmann
Immanuel Kant

André Gorz
Critique of Economic Reason

Fredric Jameson
Brecht and Method
The Cultural Turn
Late Marxism

Ernesto Laclau
Contingency, Hegemony,
* Universality*
Emancipation(s)
Politics and Ideology in
* Marxist Theory*

Henri Lefebvre
Introduction to Modernity

Georg Lukács
Lenin

Herbert Marcuse
A Study on Authority

Franco Moretti
Signs Taken for Wonders

Chantal Mouffe
The Democratic Paradox
The Return of the Political

Antonio Negri
The Political Descartes

Peter Osborne
The Politics of Time

Jacques Rancière
On the Shores of Politics

Gillian Rose
Hegel Contra Sociology

Jacqueline Rose
Sexuality in the Field of Vision

Kristin Ross
The Emergence of Social Space

Jean-Paul Sartre
Between Existentialism and
* Marxism*
War Diaries

Edward W. Soja
Postmodern Geographies

Sebastiano Tempanaro
Freudian Slip

Göran Therborn
What Does the Ruling Class
* Do When It Rules?*

Paul Virilio
The Information Bomb
Open Sky
Strategy of Deception
War and Cinema

Immanuel Wallerstein
Race, Nation, Class

Raymond Williams
Culture and Materialism
Politics of Modernism

Slavoj Žižek
Contingency, Hegemony,
* Universality*
For They Know Not What
* They Do*
The Indivisible Remainder
The Metastases of Enjoyment

Alenka Zupančič
Ethics of the Real